BACKSTAGE WITHOUT A PASS

Backstage WITHOUT A PASS

PAUL GREGG

My life in music, football & theatre –
by the man who brought
The Lion King to the UK.

Includes five chapters
on Everton F.C.

First published in 2024 by
Paul Gregg, in partnership with Whitefox Publishing

www.wearewhitefox.com

Copyright © Paul Gregg, 2024

ISBN 9781915635723
Also available as an eBook
ISBN 9781915635730

Paul Gregg asserts the moral right to be
identified as the author of this work.

All rights reserved. No part of this publication may be reproduced, stored in a retrieval system or transmitted in any form or by any means, electronic, mechanical, photocopying, recording or otherwise, without prior written permission of the author.

While every effort has been made to trace the owners of copyright material reproduced herein, the author would like to apologise for any omissions and will be pleased to incorporate missing acknowledgements in any future editions.

Photographs and illustrations in this book
© Paul Gregg, © Yoshiko Gregg, © Darko Vrcan / Alamy Stock Photo, © Chon Kit Leong / Alamy Stock Photo, © PA Images / Alamy Stock Photo, © Trinity Mirror / Mirrorpix / Alamy Stock Photo, © Variety

Designed and typeset by Couper Street Type Co.
Cover design by Hybert Design
Cover photo by Oleg Micheyev
Project management by Whitefox
Printed and bound by CPI Group (UK) Ltd, Croydon CR0 4YY

For my princess Yoshiko San.
With much appreciation for everything
new in our new lives together.

Contents

Introduction   1

1. The Ultimate Prize   3
2. Early Memories   13
3. A Tearful Farewell   25
4. A Bolt of Lightning   41
5. From Sunday Night Fever to *It's a Knockout*   55
6. Apollo . . . We Have Lift-Off!   71
7. A Theatre in Every City   87
8. Camelot, a Crisis . . . and a Royal Wee   105
9. Planes, Trains . . . and Michael Jackson   123
10. Variety is the Spice of Life   141
11. Into the Lyceum   159
12. The Balloon Bursts   179
13. 'Welcome to Everton'   195
14. A Stadium Fit for Kings   211
15. A Disaster for Everton   231
16. From Wayne Rooney . . . to a Russian Oligarch   253
17. Goodbye, Everton   273
18. Sweetness and Sorrow   287
19. A Family at War . . . and a New Beginning   299
20. Japan, India and Enlightenment   315

Epilogue: And Finally   335

Acknowledgements   343
Endnotes   345
Index   349

Introduction

At the age of fifty-eight, I sold the entertainment company that I had spent half a lifetime building up from nothing. The sum that it changed hands for at the time was the equivalent of over £350 million in today's money. It was the culmination of an amazing journey: from growing up in a council house to founding what became the UK's largest privately owned leisure group. Along the way I was privileged to meet many wonderful people including showbiz performers, fellow entrepreneurs and even royalty.

In particular, I would like to thank my former colleagues David Rogers, Steve Lavelle and Sam Shrouder (who sadly has now passed away), without whom the Apollo Leisure Group would not have been a success. Since selling the company, I've remained active in business – among other ventures, I bought and later sold a substantial chunk of Everton Football Club. I've also found lasting love with my third (and final) wife, Yoshiko, with whom I've been blessed to spend time travelling in Japan, India and the Far East.

My name is Paul Gregg. So please sit back, relax and enjoy while I attempt to entertain you with my story . . .

PG

The Ultimate Prize

The Lyceum Theatre is an imposing sight. If you take a stroll from Trafalgar Square up to the top of the Strand and veer to the left, it's one of those majestic old buildings that epitomises the magic of London's West End. The theatre's spectacular facade with its neoclassical pillars was constructed in the first half of the nineteenth century, but if you look closely above the portico entrance to the right you'll also see a tablet engraved with the year 1996. With that date now set in stone, the story behind it seems like a fitting place for me to begin this book.

It was a wet Tuesday in the autumn of 1993 and I was walking through theatreland, having just finished a business meeting nearby. As I glanced up at the grey sky, my eye caught something interesting: a 'For Sale' sign, perched near the top of the Lyceum. I should point out here that the building was looking decidedly worse for wear at this time: its doors were boarded up and its lights had been dark for a decade. Having survived a plan to demolish it in 1939 to make way for a road, it had been converted into a dance hall after the war before closing down for good in the 1980s. By now it appeared to be derelict, and anybody with an ounce of common sense could see it would cost a fortune to restore to its former grandeur.

But I wasn't worried about that, not for a moment. I've been passionate about live entertainment ever since I was a small boy growing up on council estates in Scarborough and Hull in the north of England. For me, a chance to own the Lyceum was an opportunity too exciting to miss.

I heaved a mobile phone the size of a house brick out of my jacket pocket (this was the '90s, remember) and out of curiosity I called the number on the sign.

'Hello – I'm contacting you about the Lyceum. Is it for sale?' I enquired.

'That's what it says on the sign, doesn't it?' replied the guy on the other end of the call. I didn't mind his abrupt response; in fact, I welcome it when somebody is willing to get straight down to business.

'I'd like to buy it, I think,' I said, equally to the point.

'How much do you have in mind?' he asked.

'Well, it seems to me like a million quid,' I replied.

'That sounds like enough. Come and see me,' said the guy.

This might sound like a novel way of kicking off a major business deal, but that was how it started on that first call. We exchanged details and arranged to meet on the following Monday. Of course, I also told him a bit about myself and my privately owned company, which I'd been quietly building with colleagues ever since we acquired our first entertainment venue in Manchester. By now we were a successful theatre group in our own right, although our original background in light entertainment meant that we remained slightly outside of the theatrical establishment. Despite this, my work had brought me into regular contact with some of the biggest stars in the world. They included wonderful international performers such as Dean Martin, John Denver and Liza Minnelli, as well as British household names like Cliff Richard and Shirley Bassey. I also enjoyed a close business relationship with Barry Clayman, one of the UK's top showbiz promoters (who later received an OBE for services to entertainment and charity). Barry was a colourful character who looked after top artistes like Tom Jones, Barbra Streisand, Neil Diamond and even Michael Jackson. I was confident that I had a good instinct for how to fill a venue, even one as grand as the Lyceum, so I was feeling pleased with myself as I travelled home to Oxford after making the phone call.

Unfortunately, not everybody agreed with me. When I told my wife Nita about it over dinner that night, her response was characteristically colourful. In fact, she went absolutely berserk.

'Dear God! You'll never fucking stop! How many more theatres do you want to own?' she wailed.

To be fair, our company – Apollo Leisure Group – had already acquired rather a lot of venues. They included some of the biggest theatres in London, as well as numerous others in cities such as Manchester, Oxford, Edinburgh, Bristol, Coventry, Dublin and Llandudno, along with assorted bingo halls, cinemas and even a brewery at one point. However, there were good reasons for building up a nationwide network, and I was eager to add the Lyceum to our portfolio.

'Well, actually, this particular theatre is quite prestigious,' I replied. 'It has a wonderful history, and restoring it to its former glory would be a terrific project for us.'

'You're fucking mental,' was Nita's succinct assessment. We

then had a huge row about my determination to buy yet another theatrical establishment.

That evening I called our finance director, David Rogers.

'We are buying the Lyceum next week, David,' I said chirpily.

Of course, I got much the same reaction from him as I had from my wife. David remains a very dear friend of many years' standing, but he never tires of reminding me about how I once nearly brought the company to its knees by paying the actor Richard Harris approximately £40,000 a week (a gargantuan sum at the time) to appear in a stage production of *Camelot*. With regard to the Lyceum, the thing everybody feared the most was that it would become a huge money pit. The purchase price for the lease was one thing (a million pounds was still a considerable sum back then), but the building itself would also require many millions more to restore it to its original opulence. Hence the next name on my list of people to call: our property director, Steve Lavelle.

'Can you get yourself down to London next week and have a look around the Lyceum while David and I are there?' I asked him. 'I need to know what it would cost to put it back in order.'

Steve indicated that with a building of that age, his first concern would be the state of the roof. If it needed to be replaced, and especially if the building turned out to be damp inside, then the costs involved would be truly astronomical.

Even so, in my opinion the Lyceum was a perfect project for us to undertake. Ever since childhood I've loved the feeling of being part of a live audience. There's nothing that quite matches the excitement and buzz of people enjoying a show or a sporting spectacle in great numbers. For me, the Lyceum represented the ultimate prize: not only did it have a wonderful history, but it was also a cultural landmark. The theatre's earliest origins predate its 1834 stone facade, which was designed by the English architect Samuel Beazley. Prior to that there had been an earlier building, constructed in the mid eighteenth-century, which had hosted circuses and operatic events as well as the first ever waxworks exhibition in London by Madame Tussaud. In 1879 Charles Dickens Jr wrote glowingly about Beazley's building, stating:

> It is one of the prettiest houses in London, and, while large enough to enable the poetical drama, even in the case of the heaviest Shakespearean play, to be effectively mounted, is not too large for the requirements of a modern audience. It may be noticed that evening dress is more commonly in vogue in the stalls and dress-circle here than at other theatres, but there is no absolute rule.'[1]

Who could argue with that?

The location of the Lyceum is simply perfect: just a few minutes' walk from Covent Garden tube station in the bustling theatre district. It has room enough to entertain a seated audience of over two thousand people in great comfort. But I had another reason for wanting to acquire such a prestigious theatre. I knew that the Royal Opera would soon be looking for a new home for a period of several years while the Royal Opera House in Covent Garden was refurbished. Where better to go than the Lyceum, so nearby that patrons could continue to dine in the same restaurants before a show?

So, despite my colleagues' understandable concerns about financial matters, I was very much looking forward to meeting the gentleman with whom I'd spoken on the phone. When Monday arrived, David and I travelled up to London together from Oxford on the early train. Meanwhile, Steve travelled down separately from Preston and went straight to the Lyceum to start checking over the building. This would be the first time any of us had an opportunity to inspect the interior. When we stepped inside and peered into the shadows, we were greeted by a musty smell and the sight of a floor knee-deep in rubbish. The Lyceum had been left to rot, despite the fact that it was designated as a Grade II★ listed building of national importance. To be perfectly frank, it was a mess.

However, I'd been expecting that to be the case: we knew what we were getting into. In fact, if you looked beyond its battered fixtures, you could sense that the building had once been a magnificent theatrical establishment. It was steeped in history. As we explored we found lots of period features, including elements of decor dating back to the previous century, albeit in a dreadful state. I was pleasantly surprised to find that the building had access to a power supply, so it was possible to switch on the lights. Steve's appraisal of the roof was also tentatively positive.

'It's in a bit of a state but the structure itself is sound,' he told me. 'There's some damp that will need addressing. But when they built this place all those years ago, they knew what they were doing.'

Slightly more sobering was his estimate of what it would cost to renovate the building, based on our previous experiences at other theatres.

'I think we're looking at a budget in the region of nine million pounds,' he said.

Ouch! That was an eye-watering sum in the mid-1990s, way in excess of anything we'd spent on refurbishing other theatres (and we had done plenty). Given the state of the work required, I felt that £750,000 was a fairer asking price for the building's lease, rather than £1 million.

It was time to renegotiate with the gentleman I had previously spoken to on the telephone. He turned out to be a very interesting character. I learned that he was a former executive of the property corporation Brent Walker, founded by George Walker (brother of the famous boxer Billy Walker). The man on the phone was now working for the bankruptcy administrator in order to handle the sale of the building, as Brent Walker had collapsed.

David and I were ushered into an office to be greeted by our host, who was in his early fifties and wearing an expensive suit. We exchanged pleasantries before getting down to business.

'I'd still like to buy the theatre, but having looked it over, I think the price that we are at is actually £750,000,' I explained.

However, the man was having none of it.

'No you're not,' he replied. 'The price you're at is one million, if you want to buy it. It's a million or no deal. If you don't want to buy it for that, then it's not for sale.'

I'd like to think that I've been involved in enough business negotiations over the years to be able to tell when somebody is bluffing. I could sense this guy was serious.

'OK – one million it is, then,' I said, holding out my hand.

After a brief pause, the man reached out too and we shook hands. His name was Tim Quinlan, and this was the start of a friendship between us that would last for many years. Tim always insisted on meeting in the morning (afternoons were for more important matters, such as a visit to a nice restaurant). He would entertain me with stories about all the colourful goings-on in the boxing fraternity. Apparently, it wasn't unheard of for a person to occasionally arrive at a business negotiation with a rifle hidden down their trousers. No wonder he wasn't fazed by my attempt to renegotiate!

I was delighted with the outcome of the meeting – even at a price of £1 million – but I had failed to anticipate the fierce opposition we were about to face. When word began to spread, the theatrical establishment reacted as if we were a bunch of upstarts who'd been caught backstage without a pass. People were horrified that a company with a background in light entertainment had succeeded in taking over the Lyceum. Not only that, but the renovation costs soon rocketed way beyond our original estimates.

So in summary, my wife thought we were crazy, the theatrical industry thought we were crazy, and even our own bankers thought we were crazy. At various times over the next three years the project would stretch us to the very limit, but against all the odds we achieved what everybody thought would be impossible. On 31 October 1996, His Royal Highness The Prince of Wales attended the newly restored Lyceum Theatre. The first production we hosted was *Jesus Christ Superstar*, the hit musical by Andrew Lloyd Webber (now Baron Lloyd Webber) with lyrics by Sir Tim Rice.

That night was the crowning glory of twenty years of hard work. Our achievement at the Lyceum was also a prime example of how I became successful in the first place, which was by opportunity rather than by grand design. I didn't set out with an intricate master plan, but I believe that if you take every opportunity that comes your way, you'll end up where you want to be. Following the grand reopening, I began working to bring the hit musical *The Lion King* to the Lyceum, where it has continued to run for over twenty-two years. Looking back, that was the high point of my time at the Apollo Leisure Group, which I eventually sold, against my better judgement, for about £160 million – much of which I subsequently lost!

Later on in this book, I'll tell you about the boardroom war I got dragged into at Everton Football Club. But before I do that, I want to rewind the clock – back to when I was a small boy growing up on a council estate . . .

Early Memories

My fascination with light entertainment and theatre goes all the way back to my early childhood. As a small boy my favourite toy was a miniature stage. I can remember one particular Christmas Eve when I was aged about five or six. I was very excited, having perhaps sensed that I was due to receive something special the following day from Santa Claus. I awoke during the night at around three a.m. and I could see that a large oblong package had been placed at the foot of my bed.

Creeping out from under the covers, I switched on a light to discover a toy theatre that my father had made with his own hands, complete with a wooden stage. It had rows of footlights on the front and an opening at the back so that you could reach inside and perform a miniature show with puppets. The box measured three feet wide by about two feet deep. It was a beautiful creation. As I stared at it in wonder, I heard my father's voice calling from the room next door.

'Switch off that bloody light and get back to sleep!' he boomed.

With hindsight, the theatre was an interesting choice of gift by my father. I was completely thrilled by it and one of my favourite pastimes became entertaining members of the family with 'Punch and Judy' shows and theatrical performances. I wonder now if it helped to inspire me to go into the theatre industry in later life.

I should point out here that my relationship with my father, Kenneth, got off to an unusual start due to the fact that we didn't meet for the first time until I was nearly five years old. I was born in the city of York in the year 1941, while my father was away fighting in the Second World War. He served as a corporal in the infantry with the Alexandra, Princess of Wales's Own Yorkshire Regiment, known as the Green Howards. He saw action in North Africa in the Western Desert before being captured by German forces in the summer of 1942 during the Fall of Tobruk, when General Rommel's Afrika Korps overran the region. Then he was handed over to the Italians and spent most of the next three years as a prisoner of war.

His experiences as a POW must have impacted upon him a great deal, but like many men of that generation, he preferred not to speak about them. He must have gone through unimaginable suffering, so it's perhaps understandable that he simply wanted to forget about it and return to a normal life. I only have a very hazy recollection of meeting him for the first time when I was a small boy. One of my cousins later recalled being in our house that day and seeing me run inside to tell my mother that there was a man in the garden. That man was my father.

After he returned home, the war was hardly the type of subject you'd expect to discuss with a child. I learned that he had apparently once rescued a wounded colleague, but I knew very little else. It was only many years later that I discovered details of his service record. His regiment, the 5th Battalion Green Howards, was part of a division tasked with protecting what was

EARLY MEMORIES

known as the Gazala Line. With their ammunition expended and no support on the way, the battalion was overwhelmed and hundreds of men were captured. They were forced to unload German bombs from freighters before being passed into the custody of the Italian armed forces. The prisoners were trucked off to Tripoli in stifling heat and put aboard a ship to Naples, then sent north to Rome. My father's record shows that he was interned at an Italian prison camp, No. 78 near Sulmona, an industrial town about a hundred miles east of the capital. Prisoners there were housed in brick huts and lived on a meagre diet of watery soup.

My father might have spent the rest of the war at Camp 78, were it not for another dramatic twist of fate the following year. In the late summer of 1943, with the Allied armies advancing, American forces began to bomb the town nearby. On the 8th of September the POWs awoke to find that most of their guards had deserted during the night and the Germans were intending to take control. During the confusion a large group of inmates escaped from the camp, and it's likely that my father was one of them. A well-armed contingent of Germans then arrived and put a price on the head of every fugitive. Some of the escapees survived in the hills for months but the majority, including my father, were recaptured. I don't know how long he was on the run from the Germans, but what's certain is that he was later sent to the infamous Stalag IV-B POW camp at Mühlberg on the River Elbe. It was one of the largest prisoner of war camps in Germany. Tens of thousands of men were kept there in atrocious conditions and around 3,000 inmates perished due to sickness during the course of the war. The British prisoners famously attempted to keep their spirits up by producing a single copy of an underground newspaper, called *Flywheel*, which recorded many of their hardships. On 23 April 1945, the Red Army liberated the POW camp – but it wasn't until the 1st of August that the War Office in Britain formally confirmed that my father was alive and free.

Of course, as a small child I remained blissfully ignorant of his ordeal. Nor was it something we ever discussed in later life. 'War is a terrible thing, son. I hope you never have to endure it,' was how my father would typically brush off any questions I might ask about his past.

While he was away in the army, York became a target for German bombing raids. Thankfully my mother and I were able to spend most of the war at a guesthouse owned by my grandmother in Scarborough on the Yorkshire coast, along with members of my father's family. Scarborough was considerably safer than York but we would occasionally move back and forth between the two areas. I started life surrounded almost entirely by women. There was Auntie Marjorie, my mother's favourite sister, as well as my father's sister, Auntie Gertrude. Then there was Nanny Gregg, who was also from my father's side of the family. Nanny Gregg was very much the matriarch of the group. She owned the boarding house where we spent most of our time living during the war. I don't know if the constant company of so many strong women influenced the way I saw the world, but for as long as I can remember, I've always been comfortable around women.

My mum, Joan, was a gentle lady whom I loved very much. She was very young, having been only nineteen when she gave birth to me. My earliest memories of her are of somebody who was always happy and enjoyed life. She was good fun to be with and she cared a great deal for me. She did well to keep her spirits up, as she'd been through a tragic childhood. Her own mum had passed away after a short illness when my mother was aged eight, and her father had died in ill health when she was seventeen or eighteen.

The boarding house where we lived was a little oasis of tranquillity at number 135 Columbus Ravine, in quite a fashionable part of town. Scarborough was an upmarket resort during the fifties, with fantastic amenities. Wealthy people from all over the North would come to spend time there, browsing in the posh boutiques and department stores. The place to go for fashion and luxury was a retailer called Marshall & Snelgrove, part of a prestigious London-based chain that located its flagship stores in affluent areas.

Nanny Gregg's boarding house was perfectly located for enjoying the town's many attractions. It was a five-minute walk north to Peasholm Park, famous for its Oriental-style gardens and magnificent boating lake, which would host mock naval battles. We were also within walking distance of a huge open-air swimming lido, which we would visit two or three times a week if the weather was fine. And then, of course, there was the beach. As a boy I would go for long, balmy walks down the marine parade with my mother and we'd often end up at a corner cafe that served the most wonderful waffles, which were decorated with cream, jam or honey. Near the lido was a magnificent open-air theatre that would host amateur operatic performances twice a week, plus a weekly comedy show in which hapless local teams competed against each other in ridiculous tasks (in much the same way that later became famous on the TV show *It's a Knockout*). The theatre was a much-loved destination and it could sell out 6,000 seats a night, attracting 18,000 patrons during the space of a week at the height of summer.

Nanny Gregg, whose husband had passed away some years earlier, was quite strict about the type of guests she would accept at the boarding house in order to ensure it remained respectable. We would often be joined by relatives of hers who came to stay with us from other parts of the country, such as Birmingham or the Black Country. The house had about eight or nine guest rooms as well as a communal lounge and dining area. Nanny Gregg was in her sixties and always wore old-fashioned spectacles. She would serve breakfast in the morning and high tea in the afternoon, which normally consisted of slices of ham and a tomato salad. She did her baking in an ancient range cooker in the kitchen, with a coal fire in the middle and ovens to either side. The range had to be polished regularly to keep it shiny black, which required a lot of effort. The house was generally fresh and bright; the only exception was a dark room on the ground floor that was rented out to an elderly woman. The old lady lived with the curtains always drawn and she cooked on a one-ring gas cooker, making the air smell strongly of cabbage. For me as a child, that room always seemed gloomy and scary.

Auntie Marjorie was a wonderful character. She drank tea all day, every day, and she lived to be 104 years old. She was a feisty woman until the end, still capable of giving the gardener a rollocking when she was 103. But she also had a kind heart and was always happy to make a sacrifice to help my mother.

My favourite, though, was Gertrude – Auntie Gertie, as I called her. She was charming but was regarded as the black sheep of the family. There were dark rumours that Gertrude had once had a bad experience when she'd been discovered in a pub and Nanny Gregg had dragged her outside to give her a huge dressing down. I could imagine Nanny telling her sternly: 'You will *not* frequent public houses! You are expressly forbidden to go drinking alone in public.'

Gertrude was also a secret gambler. Nanny Gregg, who was very strait-laced and proper in her approach to life, would have been mortified if she had known the full extent of this habit. Gertie was addicted to the 'Spot the Ball' and crossword competitions that appeared in Sunday newspapers such as *The People* and the *News of the World*. You could pay to enter Spot the Ball in the hope of winning a large sum of money if you could correctly mark a letter 'X' on the spot where a missing football was deemed to be in a photograph. Auntie Gertie would sometimes fill in over a hundred competition forms a week. Each entry would only cost a few pennies, but she went about it with such enthusiasm that it often became a drain on her finances. Occasionally this meant that the boarding-house guests would have to go without their afternoon tea. However, to her great delight, Gertie did sometimes enjoy the odd payout, resulting in much mirth. On one memorable occasion she caused huge excitement by rushing in to announce to the family that she had won £1,000 – a massive sum of money at the time, equivalent to several years' wages.

'I've won! I've won!' she declared, dancing a little jig of joy. 'Quick! Quick! Get ready to go out – I'm going to buy us all fur coats to celebrate!'

She then insisted on taking Nanny Gregg and my mother on a shopping expedition to Marshall & Snelgrove, where the manager was ordered to fetch a selection of the finest mink coats. These were duly purchased at full price and the three ladies later proudly posed for a family photograph in all their finery, sitting on a bench amid the landscaped gardens of Peasholm Park.

Altogether, they were a formidable group of ladies who looked after one another and shared many happy times. One of their favourite pastimes was going to psychic evenings at local hotels and church halls, which were always well attended by members of the community. Nanny Gregg and Auntie Gertie had a firm belief in the afterlife and were of the opinion that messages could be passed back and forth from 'the other side' by mediums and spiritualists. My mother would sometimes accompany them.

On one such occasion, the three of them were in the audience at a packed psychic evening held in a Methodist church. A spiritualist gentleman was in full flow on stage in the gloomy hall when Nanny Gregg and Auntie Gertie were aghast to discover that my mother appeared to have fallen into a deep trance. Convinced that she had been mesmerised by their psychic host, they began frantically shaking her in an attempt to rouse her from her catatonic state. Having disrupted the proceedings by causing a minor scene, they were relieved to find that my mother had simply become bored by the show and dozed off to sleep!

Auntie Gertie could be very generous with me, particularly when it came to trips to the cinema, and I enjoyed being spoiled by her. On one occasion, her benevolent bribery helped me overcome a fear of going to the dentist.

'I don't want to have my tooth out – it will hurt too much,' I complained.

'Come on, Paul, you know it's for the best. If you're a good boy, I will take you to the theatre afterwards,' she promised.

She was as good as her word. After we visited the dentist together she took me to see a film at the Futurist Theatre, an enormous venue on the seafront. Part of my reward included a Mars bar and plenty of candyfloss, which might not exactly have worked wonders for my remaining teeth.

Auntie Gertie never got married or had children of her own; I suppose that, as her young nephew, I was the next best thing. Unfortunately, her gambling eventually got the better of her. She began working at a fashionable boutique located on Scarborough's busy West Street – but when it was discovered that there was a shortfall in the takings, she was asked to leave. On another occasion the local constabulary became involved following reports that people's handbags were being 'borrowed' by a mystery culprit, who would then discard the item with a note inside thanking the owner for 'donating' its contents. And finally, many years later – after I was fully grown – the boarding house that we had all shared went bankrupt, and it emerged that Gertie had blown all the money on gambling rather than paying the mortgage. In my early childhood, however, all of that was still to come and for the time being, we were happily unaware of the full extent of her sins.

★

When my father came home from the war, his presence added a new dimension to our lives. My mother had previously worked in a cake shop, which is where the two of them had met before the outbreak of war. She had fallen pregnant shortly before he was called up to fight. I don't remember having any conversations as a small child with family members about my dad while he was away. Apparently news had reached him that he now had a son back home in England, but even so, I think it was a bit of a shock to him when he arrived home and found me there. It was a bit of a shock to me, too, when he suddenly turned up in the garden.

I imagine that my mother would have said, 'Pay attention, Paul – I would like to introduce you to a very important person. This is your father.'

Although I have very little memory of our first meeting, I do recall that I wasn't sure what to make of this strange man who'd suddenly entered our cosy existence. However, I could see that my mother and Nanny Gregg welcomed him with love and warmth, and things eventually settled down. Despite our mutual surprise at meeting for the first time, he and I eventually managed to bond reasonably well. He was an intelligent man with good technical skills and he landed a job as a refrigeration engineer with a company called Prestcold, owned by the Pressed Steel Company. They were a good employer and my father seemed to enjoy his new role. The Pressed Steel Company also owned a huge car body manufacturing plant in Oxford that later merged with the British Motor Corporation (which acquired Jaguar and eventually became part of the British Leyland car conglomerate).

EARLY MEMORIES

My father was an interesting man. He had a strong work ethic and he very much believed that it was his responsibility to provide for the family. In those days, the man of the house was expected to be the sole breadwinner, so work was his main focus in life. He enjoyed talking about his job, and I would often listen as he told me stories about his working day. He was clearly proud to be employed by such a prestigious company and it seemed to give him a great deal of affirmation in life.

My father's career must have got off to a good start, because within a year or two he won promotion and my parents were able to move out of Nanny Gregg's guesthouse into their own council house in Scarborough. Our home was newly built, so it was comfortable and modern, on a nice estate in Eastfield towards the south of the main town. All of the residents on the estate took great pride in their homes and there seemed to be very little crime compared to today.

One of the many wonderful things about growing up in Scarborough was that it probably had the best fish and chips in the whole country. A takeaway van used to rock up onto the estate once or twice a week and there was also a fantastic fish and chip shop in Dean Road that sold its own fishcakes. They were made from layers of fish and slices of potato, topped with little pieces of crispy batter. I used to go to Boy Scouts not far from there and it was always a great treat to enjoy fish and chips after the meeting. Looking back, I think this was one of the happiest periods of my parents' life together – unfortunately, though, there were tougher times ahead.

A Tearful Farewell

The relationship between my mother and father continued to blossom now that the war was behind them, and the next few years saw the arrival of my siblings. My sister, Christine, was born when I was eleven years old. This was followed by the birth of my brother, David. My father very much enjoyed being a doting dad to my sister and brother when they were toddlers; it's a shame that the war prevented him and me from having the same close experience. But he was a good father to me despite our late start together and I respected him a great deal.

Not long after Christine and David were born my father was promoted again, this time to a new position in the city of Hull, where we moved into another council house. It was on a corner plot, which meant it was slightly bigger than a terraced house. My mother adored our new home just as much as our old house in Scarborough, so she was happy about the arrangement.

Hull seemed like a magical place. Not only were there countless cinemas, but the city felt exotic and exciting with its extensive docks and its rich connection with seafaring. Hull has long been known as Yorkshire's 'Maritime City' and there was always plenty for us to see and do. I attended school there, but I'm afraid I wasn't particularly good at mathematics or English. In fact, not to put too fine a point on it, I was rubbish! I like to think this was probably because I was always more interested in the fun side of life, such as a trip to the movies.

My parents' marriage might have seemed idyllic from the outside but, as in most relationships, there was occasionally tension between them. I remember coming home after school one afternoon and finding my mother in floods of tears. She had been expecting our regular weekly delivery of groceries from the local shop, but it had failed to arrive – because, as it turned out, my dad had neglected to pay the bill. She was upset because there was very little food in the house, and it hurt me bitterly to see her crying like that. There were no supermarkets in those days, so we relied on the delivery for staples like eggs, bacon and flour. It turned out that Dad hadn't paid the bill for several weeks. I know now that he enjoyed betting on the horses; so, looking back, I wonder if gambling was something that affected my father as well as his sister Gertrude. Perhaps it was a family trait. If so, there might even be an element of it in me; at least, I've often been known to take a calculated risk in business for the promise of a decent return! Despite that incident – and whatever the full story of my father's finances in those days – he had a steady income and we remained relatively comfortable.

My teenage years were spent rocking the night away at the Astoria cinema in Hull, which in addition to showing films would host rock 'n' roll concerts on a Sunday evening. The 1950s and '60s were a time when artistes were experimenting with new types of music and there were some fantastic local bands to go and see. There would usually be an old black-and-white film on the same bill (which would be as ancient as the hills), but it was the live performances that I loved. The Astoria could seat a thousand people in the stalls with a further five hundred on a vast balcony. The ceiling of the auditorium formed a beautiful saucer-shaped dome with concealed lighting that would slowly dim before a performance. When a band was in full swing, the audience would dance in their seats and spill out into the aisles. It would be packed solid with people having a great time.

I would have been in good company at the Astoria because it was owned by Jack Prendergast, father of the legendary composer John Barry, who went on to write musical scores for the James Bond films along with other classic movies like *Zulu* and *The Ipcress File*. Many years later, I shared a Japanese meal with John in New York while we discussed a business proposition to create a stage musical based on the Bond movies; but I must confess that I never bumped into him or his father at the Astoria (I was probably too busy bopping in an aisle).

The other magnificent venue that I regularly attended in Hull was the ABC cinema. In fact, Hull seemed to be blessed with great cinemas. At one point it had over fifty picture houses and was referred to as 'Cinema City'. There was plenty of entertainment to choose from, including midweek events. I used to hang out with a friend called Brian, and sometimes his sister would also come along for the night. Brian, who worked as an interior designer and decorator, became a close family friend and we enjoyed many wild nights out. The bands that performed at the ABC were often a notch up from those who appeared elsewhere. I was even privileged to see the mighty Beatles play there in the early sixties, when they were as hot as mustard. Most bands had relatively basic sound equipment in those days, but The Beatles were using the latest Vox amplifiers and sounded truly amazing. I watched in awe as they performed great numbers like 'Twist and Shout', 'A Hard Day's Night' and 'Long Tall Sally'. The audience was just madly in love with them and it was a crazy time, with girls screaming and waving their arms.

Other great musicians who performed at various venues in Hull during the fifties and sixties included Buddy Holly, The Rolling Stones and Jimi Hendrix. There was also a plethora of local talent including the legendary guitarist Mick Ronson, who played on David Bowie's album *The Rise and Fall of Ziggy Stardust and the Spiders from Mars*. Mick was born in the city and joined several local bands including a group called The Crestas, who performed regularly at venues such as the Halfway House and the Ferryboat Hotel. Other famous sons of Hull included the singer and radio presenter Ronnie Hilton and the top-selling tenor David Whitfield, who toured in the stage version of *Opportunity Knocks* with Hughie Green and was the first artiste to have a number one hit in both the UK and America. When people refer to the Swinging Sixties today they typically talk about London and the influence of Carnaby Street, but we also enjoyed a thriving music and fashion scene in cities in the North. In fact, London to us was a distant place that only seemed to exist on black-and-white newsreels.

I grew up during a time of great transformation for Britain and it was a wonderful period to live through. It was as if the country was finally ready to sweep away the austerity of the Second World War and start having some fun. Culturally, a new approach to life was beginning to emerge. People wanted to enjoy themselves and even the way that we dressed was starting to change, with fashion becoming more relaxed and daring. This was despite the fact that the old guard still very much considered itself to be in charge of the nation – hence extreme contrasts in style were starting to emerge in society. The type of person you would usually find running things would be a gentleman in a pinstriped suit who prided himself on conducting matters in a 'proper manner'. His mantra would be that things needed to be done in a certain way, because 'that's the way we've always done it'. The old guard valued propriety above all else, but in truth they were often lacking in flair and vision. Meanwhile, the rest of us were just intent on having a great time!

Even though I had a strong interest in cinema and live music, it didn't cross my mind at this point that I might make a career in the entertainment industry. Instead, because I knew that Hull had an excellent nautical college (the equivalent of high school), that was where I set my sights. Nautical college was a potential fast track into a career in the Royal Navy or a well-paid job with a merchant shipping line. My vision for the future was that I would go to sea, and I discussed the matter with my father.

'If you're keen on it, then I think it's a good idea, son,' he said.

Both he and my mother were very supportive. I think they had ambitions that I would become the captain of a big cruise liner like the *QE2*, or something like that! So, with the decision made, I applied to Hull Nautical College and was accepted.

The instructors were very good and they treated us well. We learned about all aspects of seamanship. I made plenty of new friends and on a Saturday we would all go boating together in the docks, which was always good fun. I also soon realised that there were a number of advantages to be gained from the fact that we wore a nautical uniform, complete with a sailor's cap. This had the effect of making us look much older than we actually were, because people assumed we were enlisted in the forces. It made it easy for us to gain entry to the latest 'X' films (an X being the equivalent of a Certificate 18 film at a cinema today). When we were not gatecrashing cinemas, we would sneak off during the day to a snooker club located above a branch of Burton's menswear shop near the college. We would sometimes hide in there for hours on end!

I was still dreaming of a career at sea when life took an unexpected and unwelcome turn: my mother, who was by now in her late thirties, became pregnant again. This no doubt came as a shock to my parents, since she was at the upper limit of what was then considered the safe age range for a woman to bear a child. Things are obviously very different today but at that time, if a woman fell pregnant at close to the age of forty or beyond, it could often lead to complications. So although there was much genuine excitement at home about the prospect of a new baby, beneath it there was also a sense of foreboding.

Unfortunately, the pregnancy did have a catastrophic effect on my mother's health. In those days doctors preferred to let a pregnancy go to full term even if there were serious complications. Tragically, the baby was stillborn and as a consequence my mother suffered renal poisoning. Her kidneys were badly damaged and she was left in very poor health.

It was a bitter blow to our family. My mother, somebody who had always been ready to face the world with a smile, was now a shadow of her former self. Of course, we all attempted put a brave face on things.

'I hate to see you like this, Mum – but don't worry. I know the doctors will make you better,' I told her.

However, deep down, I feared for her. The two of us were very close. She would kiss me goodbye in the mornings before I went off to college and she was always there for me at the end of the day for a motherly chat. I felt that I could confide in her about anything that was troubling me. In many ways she was my rock.

By the time I graduated from nautical college, her health had deteriorated quite badly. The expectation was that I would now go off to sea, so I began looking for a job; but in the circumstances I was reluctant to leave my family.

Before long, I was offered a position as a midshipman with a company called Ellerman Lines. They had been a major operator of cargo and passenger vessels all over the world since the late nineteenth century and were still going strong, despite having suffered heavy losses to German U-boats during the war. In other circumstances they might have been the ideal employer for a young man starting a nautical career – but my mother was going through such a tough time that it didn't feel right for me to take the job.

'Please don't give up anything for me,' she urged. 'It's a wonderful opportunity, and you must do whatever is best for you.'

However, my mind was made up. I informed Ellerman Lines that I would not, after all, be able to accept their offer of employment.

My memories of my mother from this stage onwards are mainly of her being seriously ill. This was very foreign to her because she had previously been so bubbly, laughing and full of life. She was taken into hospital in Hull several times and her condition became progressively worse.

With cruel timing, my father's employer then transferred him to Sheffield. This proved to be a total disaster. My mother now faced the wrench of moving seventy miles away at the worst possible time. To add insult to injury, our new accommodation was a soulless flat above the Prestcold offices – far from ideal, given the state of her health. She had lost her beautiful council house in Hull and was now stuck in a third-floor apartment in a commercial building, which must have felt like a huge kick in the teeth. Brian, my decorator friend, kindly tried to help by brightening up the apartment to make it as comfy as possible, but it made little difference.

★

With a life at sea no longer on the horizon, I began looking for employment elsewhere. My father kindly helped me to get a job in the maintenance department at Prestcold, but while I was grateful, I wasn't sure it was right for me. I learned that there was a vacancy for a trainee at the local Odeon cinema in Sheffield. The prospect of working in a cinema appealed to me given my love of going to the movies, so I decided to apply. I was invited for an interview and things were going reasonably well until the manager decided to test my maths skills.

'Can you please tell me the correct figure for five per cent of one hundred pounds?' he asked.

I froze.

'I'm sorry, but I haven't got a clue,' I stuttered.

I then struggled to come up with any further answer, despite the fact that it was such a basic question. This might strike you as surprising for somebody who would later run a business with a multi-million-pound turnover, but I had always struggled with maths, and being put on the spot made things even worse. The manager was far from impressed. Needless to say, I didn't get the job.

Undeterred, my next port of call for a vacancy was the local ABC cinema. The ABC was a cut above the Odeon, far grander in many ways. It was located in Angel Street, near the centre of Sheffield, and it was the most modern cinema of its day – newly opened and equipped with the latest stereophonic sound system. It also had a sixty-foot-wide screen, one of the largest in the UK at that time. There was a plush concourse at the entrance and the main auditorium could seat more than 1,300 people in the lap of luxury. An imposing awning sat low on the building's facade and would light up at night to display the details of films, dominating the street.

This time I was determined not to make any mistakes at the interview. Thankfully, I was on good form. The managers seemed impressed by my love of movies and I suspect my nautical training also reassured them that I would be a disciplined employee (I obviously didn't mention sneaking off to play snooker while I was at college). I was delighted to be offered a position as trainee manager for the princely sum of £12.50 a week!

I loved my new role. The golden age of cinema was in full swing, with spectacular movies like *Dr Zhivago* and *Ryan's*

Daughter, *West Side Story* and *The Guns of Navarone* dominating the box office. There were also screenings of *Ben-Hur* starring Charlton Heston, which had been released a couple of years earlier. The famous chariot race was amazing to behold on the huge screen, made all the more effective by a terrific sound system. This was the future of entertainment!

It was while I was working at the ABC that a good-looking girl caught my eye. She was a sales assistant at the cinema and she had a beautiful smile, which was one of the first things I noticed about her. Her name was Jetta and we got on very well together. She was impressively organised in the way that she went about her job – and very petite and attractive too! I was a young man who'd not long turned twenty and I'd dated the odd girl in the past, but nothing serious. I started to look forward to chatting with Jetta during quiet moments at work, and I got the impression that she enjoyed speaking to me too. Eventually I plucked up the courage to ask her out.

'Would you like to come for an evening out with me? We could go somewhere nice on your night off,' I suggested.

I was delighted when she accepted, but only on the condition we go somewhere interesting. Believe it or not, I think we opted to see a film together, although I can't recall exactly which one. It must have seemed a bit like a busman's holiday but it worked out fine, because there was plenty of time to chat before and after the film. I discovered that Jetta came from a large family, with whom she lived in the nearby town of Chesterfield. She had several brothers and sisters and her father was a miner who used to go down the pits to evaluate new coal seams.

Jetta and I got to know each other well and we enjoyed one

another's company. However, although she was initially bubbly and bright, I soon sensed that deep down she was a troubled person. There were times when the mask slipped and I could see that she was haunted by an inner sadness. It feels wrong to go into too much detail here about her situation, especially after so many years; but she confided in me that she'd previously had some experiences that had affected her mental health. I felt a great deal of sympathy for her and I thought that perhaps, if we were to settle down together, I could make her happy.

With hindsight, I can see that the idea of getting married to someone I hardly knew was foolish. When I told my mother I was thinking of proposing to Jetta, she was aghast. 'You're far too young to get married,' she told me in no uncertain terms – perhaps speaking from experience. 'Besides, you need to be sure about what you would be taking on. Are you ready for that level of commitment?'

'I'm as committed as I'll ever be,' I said.

Undeterred by Mum's objections, I went ahead and proposed to Jetta and she accepted. We were married at a church in Chesterfield and then we moved into rented accommodation in Sheffield.

Looking back, I think we both realised fairly early in the marriage that we were going to face a tough time together. Jetta was a beautiful person and she could be very kind, but she was a troubled soul and we just weren't right for each other at that stage in our lives. Of course, there were some happy times – but we were storing up problems for the future.

★

My mother's health continued to deteriorate as time passed, and she eventually became so weak and poorly that she was mostly confined to bed in the apartment. She was placed under the care of the Jessop Hospital for Women in Sheffield, where she was regularly admitted for treatment. In fairness, the hospital did a great job: the doctors and nurses were devoted to their duties and the wards were clean and tidy. Mum did seem to improve slightly whenever she spent time recuperating there. However, as soon as the doctors pronounced her well enough to be discharged, she would come home and quickly begin to deteriorate again. She became caught in an endless cycle of hospital stays interspersed with occasional periods at home. An additional problem, as we all knew, was that the apartment in Sheffield was the last place on earth she wanted to be following these spells in hospital. Auntie Marjorie then came up with a suggestion that we hoped might make things easier for everybody.

'I want your mother and your brother and sister to come and live with me,' she told me. 'I can help to look after the children.'

It was a kind gesture and it seemed to make good sense, but there were some obvious drawbacks. Auntie Marjorie's house was in Malton in the North Riding of Yorkshire, which is a long journey from where my father and I would remain in Sheffield; so it meant splitting up the family. And her house was small, so there wasn't a great deal of room to accommodate Mum, Christine and David. However, Marjorie felt strongly that it would be better for everyone if my siblings went to Malton, so we decided to give it a go.

While my mother was away I did my best to go and see her whenever I could, but it was difficult because the journey took

EARLY MEMORIES

two and a half hours by road in those days. In the end, it all proved to be too much for everybody. Mum was just too ill; Marjorie couldn't cope with the demands of caring for her as well as two young children. Reluctantly, my mother returned to Sheffield, which was a real shame. I'm not knocking my aunt, though – she did her level best and she loved my mother dearly.

My father was very concerned throughout all of this but felt he was doing the responsible thing by continuing to work in Sheffield, because he needed to earn money for the sake of the family. People's relationships with their bosses were far more formal in those days than they tend to be today. Although my father got along well with his employers, it was still a world in which you could be dismissed instantly if you upset your boss. If that were to happen, the chances of any financial redress would be very remote – and jobs that paid well were hard to come by. To be fair to my father, he had a pretty tough time of his own. He was juggling the difficult situation at home with the responsibility of running a demanding maintenance section at work, which sometimes required him to be called upon in an emergency. He did his best to look after my mother, my brother and my sister after everybody returned to Sheffield, but it wasn't much of a life.

Things reached crisis point in the spring of 1964. My mother had been in and out of hospital again for several months during a difficult winter, with no sign of improvement. Eventually, the staff at the Jessop sat down with my parents to talk about what the future was likely to hold.

'We believe that we have done everything we can for you here for the time being, and we think you will be more comfortable if we transfer you to the infirmary at Hillsborough,' said the doctor.

It was a polite way of delivering the worst possible news. We all tried to stay positive, but deep down inside both my father and I now feared the worst.

The hospital where they sent my mother was a depressing place, formerly the site of a Victorian workhouse; it was an ugly stone building that seemed to have retained an atmosphere of misery. My mother was given a bed in the corner of a dingy room in a part of the infirmary where everything looked dilapidated. Visiting hours were strictly controlled – usually limited to just one hour in the evening, except at weekends, when it was possible to go in the afternoon. My father and I made sure Mum was never alone during visiting times, going along whenever we could. There was a rule that only two visitors at a time were allowed at a patient's bedside. On the occasions when my father brought along Christine and David, he would take them in to see her one at a time while I waited outside in a car with the other sibling.

Ironically, I think my mother's illness brought my father and me closer because it was a shared experience that led to us spending a lot of time together. We both had busy jobs, but thankfully our respective employers were understanding of the position we were in. It was never a problem getting away from work in time to visit. I'd often accompany him back to his apartment above the office after going to the hospital. We would sit chatting together and try to lift our spirits by tuning into some of the crazy comedy shows that were popular on the radio in those days. It was good to enjoy the odd moment of laughter as a way of relieving the pressure. Sometimes, if we could arrange for somebody to stay in with Christine and David, my father and I would go to a nearby pub for a quiet game of snooker.

Unfortunately, things went downhill very quickly once my mother was at the infirmary. Within the space of about a month, it reached the point where she was barely conscious at visiting time and her appearance began to change. I can vividly remember going to see her one evening and noticing that her tongue was very dry and small – it had shrunk drastically because she could no longer take liquids in the normal manner. My father used to drip water into her mouth at the bedside. We knew that the inevitable was going to happen sooner or later, but it still came as shock when the doctors told us to expect the worst.

'We're afraid it is only a matter of time now,' they told us.

My memories of her in those last two or three days before she died are terribly sad. She now had difficulty breathing and she could no longer communicate, but I could sense that she knew we were there. Her breathing would relax a little and become slightly calmer while we were at her bedside.

Finally, the doctors informed us one evening that she was very close to the end. I kissed her on the forehead and told her that I loved her, but she could no longer hear me. My father then asked for a few moments alone with her, so I went off to stretch my legs.

She passed away peacefully while I was outside the hospital.

All I can remember thinking at the time, repeating over and over again in my head, was: *Why has my mother died?* She was only forty-two years old. I found it hard to understand why some people were able to live such long lives when my mother's had been cut so short. It seemed terribly unfair. Even now, over half a century later, it's still hard to find the words to express how it affected me. I was numb. I also felt for Christine and David, who were aged around eleven and twelve. It was a rotten time for them to lose their mother.

She was buried at Woodlands cemetery in Scarborough, not far from her beloved former council house. We made sure that there were plenty of her favourite flowers, which were mimosas and sweet peas, at her funeral. It was a tearful farewell during which I thought about all the love and kindness she'd shown me over the years, including all those special memories of walks on the beach followed by waffles at the corner cafe.

One of my greatest regrets is that she never got the opportunity to share in some of the experiences I later enjoyed in the entertainment industry. My mother would have loved seeing the likes of Dean Martin and Shirley Bassey, and maybe she would even have met some of them if we'd gone out for dinner after a show.

She was my best friend.

A Bolt of Lightning

They say that grief can affect people in a variety of ways. I think my method of coping with the loss of my mother was to absorb myself in work. My role at the ABC became my main focus in life, possibly to the further detriment of my marriage. My relationship with Jetta continued to be a bittersweet experience. We were starting to drift apart when, ironically, we were blessed with the arrival of a child. We hoped that the birth of our son, Anthony, who was born shortly before my mother's death, would help us to make a go of things. For a while it looked as if that might be the case and our second son, Robert, was born a year later. But in truth, the gulf between Jetta and me was growing all the time, and a great deal of pain lay ahead.

Jetta and the boys would often go to stay for long periods with her mother in Chesterfield, while I remained in Sheffield. I think Jetta felt more comfortable surrounded by her own family, which was understandable given the circumstances. Meanwhile, I followed my own father's example and threw myself into my work. There was plenty to concentrate on. The manager at the ABC in Sheffield was an eccentric character called Reg Helley, who loved dressing up in a formal outfit whenever he was 'front of house'. He would put on tails and black tie and pace up and down outside the cinema in all his splendour, smoking a big cigar and welcoming the patrons.

'Good evening, ladies and gentlemen! Form an orderly queue here, please. Have your cash ready, we still have a few seats available.'

The rest of our management staff would wear black tie if we were out front and we were instructed to always be on our best behaviour. The punters loved it. In those days going to the cinema was regarded as a proper night out and we did whatever we could to boost the pomp of the occasion. Reg was the number one promotional genius when it came to filling a cinema and he adopted a 'hard work, hard play' attitude. In quieter moments during the daytime he would go to a nearby pub, the Hen & Chickens, which had a reputation for being very upmarket. He would enjoy his beer during a nice lunch with the local clientele. During the evening, after the main film had started to play, Reg would send a doorman back to the pub with an empty container known as 'The Baby' – it was a type of large orange squash holder that was popular in cinemas at the time. It would be filled with beer and brought back to the office in order to provide Reg with further refreshment!

There were approximately twenty other cinemas in Sheffield, but our biggest rival was the Gaumont, a former theatre that was now a flagship cinema within the Rank Organisation. The Gaumont was in Barker's Pool, a ten-minute walk away from us, and was regarded as the enemy, although our rivalry usually remained good-natured. Reg would relish any opportunity to go into battle. The manager of the Gaumont was an equally colourful character called Harry, whom Reg regarded as a bit of a miseryguts. We also competed with the Odeon in Sheffield, where I had a friend called Jim Whittell who was deputy manager.

There was constant competition between the cinemas over which of us could dream up the best promotions. This included trying to secure favourable articles in the local press about various PR stunts that we attempted to pull off. The major film studios had huge promotional budgets, which they would share with their respective cinema partners if we could build a strong case for assistance. The financial arrangement was that we would 'rent' a newly released movie from a distributor for a share of the box-office takings. In return we would negotiate a contribution towards advertising and other costs incurred at a local level, before subsequently sharing the proceeds of any ticket sales.

The manner in which the global movie distributors aligned with individual cinema groups created an interesting scenario. At ABC in Sheffield we had agreements with MGM Studios (Metro-Goldwyn-Mayer), Warner Brothers, and Columbia Pictures. This meant that we were first in the queue for blockbusters such as *Dr Zhivago* (MGM), *My Fair Lady* (Warner Brothers) and *Dr Strangelove* (Columbia). The Rank Organisation was meanwhile aligned with 20th Century Fox, Walt Disney and United Artists. Our rivals therefore had access to an equally impressive array of movies, including *The Sound of Music* (Fox) and all of the James Bond films (which were distributed by United Artists).

In order to negotiate the maximum amount of promotional support, we would submit a marketing release plan. In the case of MGM, the studio actively encouraged this process by running a competition known as the Lion Awards (a reference to the famous lion that starred in the Metro-Goldwyn-Mayer logo at the start of a film). We would go to great lengths in the pursuit of 'winning a Lion'. This included organising regional premieres that would be attended by local dignitaries and members of the press. We also arranged window displays with local retailers that featured movie posters and other promotional material. There was plenty of scope for mischief. What we said we would do and what we actually did would sometimes be very different. For example, we would occasionally employ unorthodox tactics such as placing posters in strategically valuable locations without permission. These might miraculously appear inside a branch of a local retailer such as Boots, where a quick photo would be taken of it on the sales floor. The snap could then be used as evidence of our marketing prowess if we were hoping to win a Lion Award. I suppose it was an early forerunner of what today would be called guerrilla marketing!

We would always face our toughest challenge at the ABC if the Gaumont was about to screen a new Bond film. Reg and I would frantically study the schedules to find something that was equally appealing to a mass audience. This would require a major attraction, such as *Blue Hawaii* starring Elvis Presley, who as the King of Rock 'n' Roll was one of the few icons with enough firepower to go up against Agent 007.

'I don't want those bastards at the Gaumont to get one over on us,' Reg would bark. 'We need to get organised and throw everything we've got behind Elvis!'

The Odeon would specialise in showing what we referred to in the trade as 'roadshow movies'. These were monster-sized hits like *The Sound of Music* that they would screen for several months in a row, with special screenings at various times of the day. Reg would never miss an opportunity to wreak his revenge if we'd been beaten to the punch. Sometimes our tit-for-tat battles would become farcical and we did some wonderfully stupid things. On one such occasion we managed to secure a promotional budget for a black comedy called *Nothing But the Best* starring the actor Alan Bates (who later famously wrestled naked with Oliver Reed in *Women In Love*). There was a bedroom scene on the poster for *Nothing But the Best* and a tooth-powder brand had agreed to provide some sponsorship, which was probably linked to a product placement arrangement in the movie. Reg hit upon the crazy idea of organising a procession through the city led by a four-poster bed on wheels in order to publicise the film – and he knew exactly where to begin the fun.

'We're going to start the procession slap bang in front of the Gaumont! That should wind up the bastards,' he announced with glee. 'We're going to properly rub their noses in it.'

He then set about organising the procession with all the fervour of a general commanding a military campaign. A marching band was booked to accompany the mobile bed as the procession snaked its way from Barker's Pool in the city centre to the ABC in Angel Street. Of course, the local press were tipped off in advance and were in position, much to the annoyance of our rivals.

We also managed to steal the Gaumont's thunder when they booked Cliff Richard and the Shadows to perform live. We couldn't believe our luck when Cliff and the band turned up at the ABC the same afternoon to watch a matinee movie. Reg ordered a scramble to try to get a photo of them on site, but they left too quickly. However, it didn't stop us from boasting to anybody who would listen that even though Cliff performed at the Gaumont, the ABC was his cinema of personal choice.

During my time with ABC I would occasionally work at other cinemas within the group, including at Scunthorpe. In contrast to Reg, the manager there was fixated on discipline and gave me strict instructions on my first day about how he liked everything to be done. This included a warning about the potential dangers of spending time in the stock room with his young secretary! I also spent a brief period at the ABC in Wakefield, which hosted concert nights as well as showing films. While I was there, I stayed in a small B & B where the elderly landlady wore a hairnet that made her look just like Ena Sharples from *Coronation Street*. She insisted on cooking me an enormous breakfast every morning consisting of mountains of eggs and beans, which I struggled to eat.

My manager in Wakefield, whose name was Fallas Simpson, was determined to win a Lion Award, but unlike in Sheffield (where we had won several) he had been unsuccessful. However, the release of *Dr Strangelove* presented us with an opportunity to try again. It was decided that we would publicise the nuclear theme of the film by building a fallout shelter in the car park.

In those days the film companies had marketing teams who were always looking for a novel idea, so the project was quickly approved. The public were then invited to take a tour of our 'bunker'. In order to ensure maximum authenticity it was stocked with all the foods you would need to survive, which had been supplied courtesy of Heinz. There were shelves full of baked beans, cans of soup and tinned puddings with custard. It was like an Aladdin's cave crammed with tinned food. There was so much of it that certain members of staff occasionally took some home. Fallas himself was said to be partial to the odd can of spaghetti hoops, which he usually ate while watching the latest movie in the cinema after the food had been warmed up for him by the ice-cream lady. We had all assumed that Heinz wouldn't want the goods back, so it came as a shock when the supplier asked for it all to be returned. By then, we'd scoffed the lot!

'I'm afraid it won't be possible to return the goods. The patrons must have helped themselves to everything from the display,' fibbed Fallas.

Amid all the fun and chaos, I learned some important lessons during my time at ABC. I saw the potential value that daring marketing and promotions could bring to a business and I was keen to learn more. I was also starting to develop an instinct for what would make the public enjoy an evening out. It wasn't just a great movie (although that was obviously the first and foremost attraction). It was the whole experience, including the surroundings and facilities. At the ABC back in Sheffield the kiosk and pay box were at ground level, with stairs that led up to a concourse area where you could order food. It had large windows looking out onto Angel Street, so you could sit back and enjoy the view from the cinema while watching the bustle of the city outside. A good proportion of our income came from the sale of snacks, popcorn and ice creams, which all added to the bottom line. These things weren't just 'add-ons', they were an integral part of the business. The seating in the auditorium was designed to ensure that everybody had a great view, and the toilet facilities were immaculately clean. I learned that all of these things, along with Reg's innate showmanship and charm, contributed to the fact that we had people queuing around the block. Our motto seemed to be, 'If you make it comfortable, they will come.'

I was also beginning to notice other important things about the economics of the entertainment industry. Cinema tickets in those days were sold on the door. There were no advance bookings, unless it was a special roadshow screening. This meant that we had to wait until a movie was actually screened before we received any cash – and in those days, it was physical cash. This worked fine, but later on, when I became interested in the theatre industry, I found that things were completely different. In theatre, the emphasis is on advance bookings, which means you receive a large chunk of your income up front. The result is that at any one time you hopefully have a lot of cash sat in the bank – which, as I would discover in the future, opens up a whole world of possibilities. This wasn't something I consciously thought about while I was working for ABC, but it would come to seem very significant later on.

★

It was my growing interest in marketing and promotions that probably explains the next stage in the development of my career. I heard about a vacancy at the head office of an independent cinema group who were doing some very interesting things at the time. Star Cinemas weren't quite on the same level as the ABC Group or Rank, but they were certainly going places. A pair of colourful entrepreneurs, the Eckarts, ran the company. They tended to acquire buildings in smaller towns that they could pick up cheaply and then develop according to their own needs. Interestingly, they had started to move into bingo, which was developing a huge following during the sixties and seventies. People would flock to the larger operators such as Mecca Leisure in order to play for large cash sums.

Star Cinemas would typically buy up a derelict cinema or theatre and then convert the stalls into a bingo hall. Meanwhile, the circle would be divided into two smaller auditoriums, each of which would have a cinema screen. So the owners of Star were, in effect, among the first people in the country to develop the concept of what later become known as the multiplex. Today we're used to going along to entertainment complexes with multiple facilities, but before this point it had been very rare.

The vacancy I had spotted at Star Cinemas was in the marketing department at their head office in Leeds, where I figured there would be plenty of opportunities for promotion. Although I'd had a great time at ABC, the company had recently reorganised and I'd found myself back in Sheffield after my spell in Wakefield. It felt like it was time for a change, and the chance of moving on to work for a progressive group like Star was an appealing opportunity. Reg, my old boss, was magnanimous about my decision to leave.

'Good luck, Paul. Make sure you give the bastards hell,' he told me with typical bluntness, shaking my hand warmly.

My new bosses, the Eckarts, were brothers called Derek and Rodney – Derek being the elder. They were astute operators and certainly had more acumen than their modern namesakes, Del Boy and Rodney from *Only Fools and Horses*. One of the cinemas they owned was on the Wicker, a colourful street in Sheffield. It had a reputation for showing triple-X-rated movies and risqué French films featuring a lot of naked writhing. A sizeable chunk of their income also appeared to come from slot machines placed in their bingo halls. The brothers drove around in Jaguar cars which apparently had built-in safes hidden in the boot so that they could ferry around cash takings, something that later got them into hot water with the authorities.

I was staying in a rented flat in a picturesque part of Leeds called Gledhow Valley. I had very little contact with the Eckarts but I would see them when they came into the office; they were an impressive pair, immaculately dressed and very focused. My role was to oversee all of the advertising and marketing for their cinema division alongside a man called Edgar Craven, formerly the editor of the *Yorkshire Evening Post*. Edgar was a gentleman and I learned a great deal from him. Once again, part of my duties involved negotiating to secure a sizeable chunk of the funds that the film rental companies set aside to contribute towards local marketing costs.

I spent a good couple of years at Star Cinemas, but eventually it became clear that the opportunities for promotion were not as great as I'd hoped – mainly because the people above me in the organisation were unlikely to retire in the near future. So when a vacancy arose at Mecca Leisure, it caught my eye. I hadn't been involved in the bingo division at Star, but even so I could see that as a game it was growing in popularity. Compared with Star, the Mecca Group was a huge corporation with an empire that included not just bingo but nightclubs, hotels and theme parks. Mecca ballrooms hosted the BBC TV show *Come Dancing* (the forerunner to *Strictly Come Dancing*) – Eric Morley, founder of the Miss World competition, was head of dancing at Mecca and he had invented the original format of that programme in 1954. Mecca was certainly a company that was on the map. I applied for a job as trainee manager in their bingo division in Leeds, where a new Mecca hall was set to open on the site of the old Capitol cinema in the north-west suburb of Meanwood.

I think it's fair to say that we had our share of teething problems at the new location. The opening itself went according to plan in terms of the logistics and organisation of the building; problems arose, however, owing to Mecca's choice of bingo caller, a former bandleader from Yorkshire whom they'd persuaded to come out of retirement. The caller in any professional bingo operation is a key figure. Serious bingo players like to concentrate on hearing the numbers being called clearly and concisely. The patrons might be playing for small sums per line locally, but at this time there were also national games in which the prizes could be life-changing amounts running into many thousands of pounds. It soon became obvious that our caller lacked the necessary experience to do the job (which made two of us). I must confess that I didn't take to bingo in quite the same way that I'd enjoyed working in the cinema sector.

★

It was while I was working at Mecca Leisure that my marriage to Jetta suffered a terminal blow. We had been struggling in our relationship for some time when Jetta unexpectedly fell pregnant again, but sadly there were severe complications. She gave birth to a baby girl, whom we called Wendy, but our new daughter suffered from a congenital spinal anomaly. Tragically, she died the following day. In the pain and darkness that followed, our marriage fell apart; I think the emotional trauma was simply too great for it to survive. Soon afterwards, Jetta went to live back in Chesterfield with her family, accompanied by our sons, Anthony and Robert. It was a period of immense suffering, one from which she never quite recovered.

It would be wrong of me to pretend here that my own behaviour was faultless throughout this difficult time. As Jetta and I became more distant, we began to lead separate lives, and while we were apart I met the lady who would eventually become my second wife. Her name was Nita (short for Anita) and she worked in the catering department at the bingo hall in Leeds.

It was towards Nita that my attention increasingly turned. I felt comfortable in her company and looked forward to chatting to her whenever I saw her in work. She had a bubbly personality, but she was also very headstrong and I got the impression that she always aimed to be number one at anything she did. I think I was attracted by her confident approach to life (as well as her long legs and short skirts).

Nita's parents lived in Derbyshire, where her father, who was originally from Ireland, was employed as a manual worker for a large chemical company. Like me, Nita was married with two

A BOLT OF LIGHTNING

children; her husband was a trombone player called Jerry and they had a son and daughter, Debbie and David. It was hardly an ideal situation, but nonetheless we began to date in secret. The attraction between us was more than just physical. It would transpire that our relationship would stand the test of time, because we eventually married and stayed together for nearly forty years. I think we both knew from early on that we would spend our future together.

It wasn't long before Nita and I started to plan a new life. I was aware that there was a vacancy for an entertainments manager with Pressed Steel Fisher (part of the group that employed my father) in Oxford, which seemed like an ideal place to escape. I applied for the job and was accepted. It was a messy sequence of events – and one that I am not proud of today – but I was convinced it wouldn't be right to tell Jetta, now that we were no longer together. We had very little contact in the months that followed after I moved to Oxford and she eventually learned about my relationship with Anita from a third party.

Then came the final bolt of lightning. I received a phone call a few months later to inform me that Jetta had died at home from an overdose of pills. It was later reported in the press that she had previously made several suicide attempts, including two before she met me.

Anthony and Robert were still very young and were traumatised by what had happened. They continued to live afterwards mainly with Jetta's family, apart from short spells when they stayed with Anita and me. We briefly attempted to live as one blended family, with Robert and Anthony along with Nita's own children, when we later moved to Southport; but the arrangement was a disaster. Anita and the boys simply could not bond with one another and it came to the point of social services being involved. In the end, for everybody's benefit it was decided – in conjunction with social services – that it would be best to let Anthony and Robert have a fresh start in their lives without us.

Today, I often think about whether I could have done more to convince Nita to make a go of things with my own sons. Hindsight is a wonderful thing and perhaps we should have handled many aspects of the situation in a different way. It would be many years before I saw Anthony or Robert again. The experience taught me that life can sometimes be painful in ways that you never intended or imagined.

Sometimes we must learn to live with our regrets.

From Sunday Night Fever to *It's a Knockout*

It was while I was working in Oxford and Southport that I began to build up a network of contacts that would later enable me to connect with the crème de la crème of showbiz. My job at Pressed Steel Fisher was a perfect opportunity for somebody like me who was learning the ropes in the entertainment industry.

My new employer manufactured car bodies at a huge vehicle plant located off the main ring road to the east of Oxford. Pressed Steel Fisher was a supplier to prestige marques like Rolls-Royce and Jaguar, so the company had plenty of cash that it was willing to invest in order to keep its workforce happy. There was another vast car facility next door, operated by British Leyland (which owned Morris Motors). Leyland was also doing very well, famously assembling the iconic Mini cars. By the early 1970s, more than 20,000 people worked across the two sites. Of course, all those employees created a big demand for entertainment – and I was the man tasked with delivering it. The company had demolished its old social club and reconstructed it in a larger building within a new sports and leisure complex that would serve workers from both of the plants.

The change of scene appealed to me after my experiences in Leeds. In addition to my own problems, things had turned acrimonious between Nita and her husband Jerry, perhaps not surprisingly given the circumstances. On one occasion when Nita and I met for a secret tryst together in my flat in Leeds, we were interrupted by somebody hammering on the door.

'Come out, Nita! We know you're in there,' screamed an angry male voice.

I peered out of the window and spotted Jerry down below in the darkness, accompanied by three of his burly mates. Jerry was a good musician – and ironically, later in life we became good friends – but I was pretty certain that he hadn't come round in the middle of the night to discuss playing the trombone. I didn't fancy my chances given the numbers involved, so we made a hasty exit through a rear window.

By the time we relocated to Oxford, Nita and I were very much in for the long haul and we rented a place together. Her young children, David and Debbie, initially stayed behind with other family but they came to join us once we'd had a chance to settle in. The house was very basic. It was freezing cold and had metal window frames that leaked moisture, but we did our best to decorate it. The local bus service was also awful, but it was either that or a half-hour walk. Thankfully, I was able to borrow a company car at weekends to get me to the social club during its busiest times.

Nita was also determined to make a financial contribution to our new life together. She applied for a catering position at a

Bernie Inn nearby and when she came back from the interview she was bounding with enthusiasm.

'I've got the job and we're going to make a fortune!' she beamed.

'Oh yes, how's that going to happen?' I replied, somewhat sceptical.

'I'm going to sell coffee,' she said.

Anita explained that she had negotiated a deal with the pub landlord, whereby she would work behind the bar and in return she would keep the proceeds from any hot beverages. It was a clever but wonderfully simple arrangement. It summed up one of the things I admired about Anita: her positivity and willingness to seize an opportunity. In that sense, I think we were kindred spirits.

★

I was surprised to discover that the newly built sports and social club at Pressed Steel Fisher wasn't particularly well equipped to host live entertainment. There was an excellent bar area and kitchen, but the main room was a big cavern with no stage or raised seating. One thing it did possess, however, was a huge amount of open space, which meant that it had great potential. The company had invested a huge amount of money in the complex and a committee was appointed to oversee the finances of the club. The committee members were drawn from various sections of the plant: the paint shop, the body shop, the production lines. The one thing everybody agreed upon was that they were keen to start hosting cabaret evenings on a Saturday.

The idea was to put together a package including a sit-down meal followed by dancing and a live act, all for one affordable ticket price.

My task as the entertainments manager was to provide great value for the workers, while also being creative with the entertainment. I reported to the club secretary, who was very traditional in his approach. He was keen to ensure that everything was voted upon 'in the proper manner'. There was also a senior accountant on the committee, plus a deputy finance guy and several other individuals. Nobody among them had any creative experience of running cabaret evenings, but then I was hardly an expert myself. However, thanks to learning from old masters like my former boss Reg in Sheffield, I had a knack for creating a sense of occasion. I felt that what we needed in Oxford was a grand opening – a headline act that would capture people's attention. If I'd learned one thing at ABC, it was that if you had a big name on the bill it would bring in the punters – and I had a specific act in mind.

I was aware of a humorous rock group called The Barron Knights, who had previously supported the likes of The Rolling Stones and The Beatles. They had gone on to become a huge phenomenon in their own right by developing a unique style of show that parodied popular bands. They would take a well-known song and change the lyrics around to make it humorous. They'd had a string of hit singles including one that reached number three in the charts; and this was back in the days when if you got to number three, you'd hit the big time! They were an ideal choice for cabaret because they were funny and entertaining, as well as actually being decent musicians in their own right. Even now, at the time of writing, they continue to perform occasionally – so if you ever get the chance to see them, I can recommend them.

Of course, talent always comes with a hefty price tag. I looked up The Barron Knights' agent, Colin Hogg (with whom I would later form a great relationship). He indicated that we would need to budget for a sum in the region of £1,500. That sounds like a snip compared to today's prices, but when you included expenses, it was the early-1970s' equivalent of around £25,000 today. That was a hefty sum for the social club committee to get their heads around, so it was necessary to put the matter to a vote.

At our next meeting, the club secretary announced: 'Paul would like to propose that we book The Barron Knights for the grand reopening of the social club.'

There was a stir in the room. The members were impressed by the prospect of landing a famous act, but they were understandably nervous about the cost. We could seat five hundred paying guests in the social club, but it would be a challenge to keep the ticket price down. Nonetheless, I was determined to argue the case.

'If we book The Barron Knights, we will sell out. It will be a great evening and word will go around,' I said. 'There are twenty thousand employees based here, so even if we make a small loss, we'll soon recoup it at subsequent events due to the halo effect.'

To be fair to the committee, they wanted to make a big splash just as much as I did. There was a show of hands and they voted to approve. My next task was to ensure that the atmosphere in the club was as warm and welcoming as possible. We devised a seating plan and experimented by placing miniature candle-holders and decorations on every table. It wasn't perfect, but I hoped that whatever we lacked in style, we would make up for with the quality of the entertainment.

When the big night finally came around it was a huge success. The Barron Knights performed with their usual mixture of craziness and exuberance, which had the audience whooping and cheering for more. It was a great start and just as we'd hoped, Saturday nights soon became a big draw at the club. The committee gave me plenty of freedom to experiment by booking different types of act. We also arranged theme nights on special dates such as Valentine's Day, Easter and New Year's Eve.

Before long, things were going so well that we also branched out into holding live music on Sunday nights. In contrast to our cabaret nights on a Saturday, there was no seating so the audience stayed on their feet, meaning that we could accommodate well over a thousand people. We planned to book the best up-and-coming bands that were on the verge of making it big, but still affordable. This benefited the club because we could sometimes hire bands for as little as £50 or £75 a night, which they accepted because it gave them good exposure. It also meant that I began to build up a network of contacts in the music business, which would prove to be very useful in my next job.

The club was always packed solid during our music nights. It was as if our own version of Sunday night fever descended upon the car plant: people would be queuing outside in order to make the most of the weekend! In fact, the Sunday night events eventually became so successful that they attracted the attention of the local constabulary.

'I'm afraid we've been contacted by the police,' explained the club secretary. 'They say they've received a number of complaints about the noise on a Sunday evening.'

That sounded crazy to me, as the nearest houses were a considerable distance away. But there was more to come.

'The police have also reminded us that our licence stipulates that we are a members-only establishment. However, on a Sunday evening we've apparently been selling tickets to every Tom, Dick and Harry who wants one!'

That aspect was certainly true. Thankfully, we had a good relationship with the police, and they agreed that if we quietly dropped live music on Sundays there would be no further action.

★

My relationship with Nita continued to grow ever closer while we were in Oxford. With our experiences in Leeds behind us, we began to plan for a settled future and the subject of marriage inevitably came up. I didn't exactly get down on one knee to propose or anything like that – it was more a mutual meeting of minds. It felt like the right thing to do, so we chose to get married in a quiet ceremony at a register office in Sheffield (where my father still lived), accompanied by just a couple of witnesses. Afterwards we went for tea together at John Lewis, which may not sound very romantic, but in fact we greatly enjoyed our wedding day!

I continued to enjoy life at the social club, but once again the opportunity arose for an interesting change of scene. I heard through the grapevine that the borough council up in

Southport was looking for a manager for a seaside venue called the Floral Hall. It was an appealing prospect, given my early love of seaside towns. The hall – a traditional civic building, set within beautiful landscaped gardens – could accommodate an audience of around a thousand standing or about four hundred seated. The prospect of working for a local authority seemed like a step up from running the social club. Nita and I discussed the matter and she agreed it would be a welcome chance to find somewhere better to live than our leaky old rented house in Oxford. We were delighted to discover that the job came with accommodation, which would mean we could save for a deposit on a house of our own.

My boss in Southport was a man called Harold Barber, who was chairman of the committee that oversaw the town's attractions on behalf of the borough council (which later became part of Sefton Council on Merseyside). He was a pleasant gentleman and very supportive. I soon discovered that he had an avid interest in live jazz, which was music to my ears. The Floral Hall (which is still there today) hosted lots of different types of event at the time, including formal dinners and dances, flower shows and exhibitions – but there was potential to expand its volume of concerts. I got back in touch with the showbiz agent Colin Hogg, who in addition to The Barron Knights also looked after a whole roster of musical talent, to explore possibilities. It was through Colin that I was introduced to a Merseyside band called The Spinners (no connection to the US group of the same name). They were a great bunch of guys and it was the start of a friendship that would later see me become involved in promoting the band.

Meanwhile, I also got to know an agent called Harold Davidson, who was part of a tour management company called MAM in London. Harold handled all the great jazz acts of the day including James Last and his orchestra, as well as A-list mainstream artistes such as Frank Sinatra, Perry Como and Liza Minnelli. MAM was one of the top tour promoters in the UK, with a formidable team that also included Barry Clayman (another significant contact later on in my career). I began to regularly book jazz acts at the Floral Hall, including the percussionist and bandleader Lionel Hampton, trumpeter Maynard Ferguson and the jazz drummer Buddy Rich. These were names you would normally only expect to find at major venues like the Liverpool Empire, but when we brought them to Southport they proved to be just as popular. This brought in a steady flow of cash, and within the space of around eighteen months the Floral Hall went from making an annual deficit of around £17,000 to turning a small profit of around £3,000. We discovered that if we hosted high-profile acts, people would travel to the town and would often stay overnight. This provided a welcome boost to the local hotels and restaurants, which greatly satisfied my chairman and his colleagues on the council. It also gave me an idea.

'You know, if we had a bigger venue we could give the Liverpool Empire a serious run for its money and expand the conference market,' I said to my council colleague, Harold.

'Do you really think so?' he replied.

'I'm certain – and the whole town would benefit,' I said.

This set in motion an interesting chain of events. Harold soon began to think along the same lines and we began to develop the idea further. We eventually drew up a formal proposal to build a brand new venue next door to the Floral Hall, using part of the gardens to accommodate the new building. The plans were designed in such a way that the space could be used as a full-time theatre, cinema or conference centre. Amazingly, the scheme was approved almost as soon as we submitted it. I think the council leadership had witnessed the economic benefits that had been provided by the Floral Hall and they were keen for more. The building took just six and a half months to complete and it was constructed from stone and brick, with a spacious indoor foyer and capacity for seating 1,650 patrons. The cost to the borough was £264,000, although today you would need to spend £10 million or more. It was an amazing achievement in such a short space of time. I doubt there is a local authority in the UK today that would be capable of moving so quickly!

The next challenge we faced was to organise a grand opening, and it needed to be something spectacular that would send out a message that Southport was open for business. Once again, I felt that only a household name would create the right sort of buzz. In 1973, they didn't come much bigger than Morecambe and Wise, whose long-running BBC TV show and Christmas specials attracted audiences in excess of 20 million. We made enquiries but, not surprisingly, they were unavailable.

I broadened our search and arranged to go and see a number of tour promoters in London. Among them was a young agent called Robert Paterson. He had previously worked for the stage impresario Victor Hochhauser, who had brought the Bolshoi Ballet to the UK. Robert was a sharp dresser in his early thirties and his career was on an upward trajectory. He formed his own company representing an impressive array of stars, including the likes of Nana Mouskouri, Tina Turner, Shirley Bassey, Bing Crosby and Neil Diamond.

I caught an early train from Liverpool down to Euston Station to meet Robert in his office in Wigmore Street. After exchanging pleasantries, we got straight down to business and I told him about our ambitious plans to put Southport and its new theatre on the map.

'We need a major artiste for the grand opening,' I explained.

'How major?' he asked.

'It needs to be somebody really special, a top-quality headline act.'

'Well, how about Marlene Dietrich?'

At first I thought he might be joking, but I could sense from his demeanour that Robert was being serious. There was no doubt that Dietrich had exactly the right appeal. Not only was she a Hollywood legend, but she'd also become a renowned cabaret artiste, famously performing in Las Vegas in a 'nude dress' of beads and sheer chiffon. However, Marlene hadn't performed for some time, having fallen into ill health. Would she really want to come to Southport – and if so, what would it take to persuade her?

'Well . . . she would only consider coming if you also booked Burt Bacharach to do the musical arrangement,' Robert said. 'And of course they would need a full orchestra.'

With a legendary musician like Burt Bacharach also on the bill, I feared that the cost would be enormous. But then, I'd been pleading with my chairman Harold to think big – and if we could pull this off, it would be *very* big. Dietrich would bring that special type of star quality and glamour that we needed if we were going to take on the Liverpool Empire and pull in other major acts. If Southport Theatre was good enough for Marlene Dietrich, it was good enough for anybody. Looking back, I suspect that Robert was already on the lookout for an opportunity for Dietrich to make a comeback performance in the UK, but to be fair to him he was as good as his word and he made it happen. Robert was an interesting man. He was born in the UK but had spent a large part of his childhood in South Africa, which probably gave him the ability to see things from an international perspective. He suffered from terrible asthma as a child and never seemed to be in particularly good health, but he was a wonderful promoter and we eventually did a lot of business together.

The cost of booking Marlene Dietrich was indeed huge, running into tens of thousands of pounds, but it was worth every penny for the hype alone. There was no point in spending the equivalent of millions on a new theatre if you were then going to skimp on the acts! We produced some very classy marketing, including a poster featuring a black-and-white line sketch of Dietrich looking very much like a Hollywood sex symbol. Her name appeared below the sketch in large red lettering, as did the name of the theatre.

The gala opening of Southport Theatre was heldon Wednesday 23 May, 1973. You could sense the excitement as the lights dimmed in the packed auditorium. Marlene made a grand entrance by sexily wrapping her leg around a curtain and swinging on the drapes! She looked stunning and the show was magnificent. She had a magnetism that was very alluring, although afterwards she was quite formal when we were introduced and she didn't chat a great deal. She seemed much older in person than on stage, although still very glamorous at the age of seventy-two!

The local press were enthralled by the success of the event and afterwards it proved to be a watershed for the town. It became a regular occurrence for household names to appear at Southport Theatre. I learned that if we ensured the artistes and their promoters were treated well when they came to the theatre, it would pay dividends: not only would they be willing to come back again, but word would go around and others would follow. Our facilities and dressing rooms were modern and comfortable, which worked in our favour. All of this enabled us to achieve a position whereby promoters would proactively call us if they were planning a tour, rather than us having to chase them for bookings.

Over the next few years we enjoyed hosting shows by most of the big British stage acts of the time, as well as a large number of international performers such as Johnny Mathis, Perry Como, Ella Fitzgerald and Shirley MacLaine. The list just seemed to grow and grow and continued to also include top American jazz stars of the day like Henry James, Count Bill Basie and Jack Jones (who was dating the actress Susan George). James Last also continued to appear every year and would stay for supper afterwards with his entourage of thirty people. We were always happy to cater for artists after a performance, which helped to further boost our reputation for being good hosts. Our policy of booking a broad range of different acts meant that we occasionally encountered some very eccentric characters. On one occasion when we hosted The Three Degrees, the singers arrived with a heavily built American gentleman who demanded the balance of their fee in cash. It was a hefty sum of money and I explained that due to it being a weekend, the banks were closed, so a cheque would need to suffice.

'It's gotta be cash. No cash, no concert,' he growled.

Somehow I got the impression that he might have a gun in his jacket pocket, although I may have been mistaken. In any event, one way or another it was clear he had me over a barrel. I began frantically ringing around my contacts in the local business community, attempting to borrow a five-figure sum in ready cash, and eventually I was able to pull the money together. I handed it over with a small scowl – but was careful not to complain too much, owing to my theory about the gun!

The excitement that the new theatre created in Southport worked greatly in my favour and I was promoted to the position of Director of Publicity and Attractions. One of my favourite artistes was Cliff Richard, who would also join us for something to eat after a show. I had a wry smile at my memory of previously trying to chase him around the Sheffield ABC for a photograph. I built up a good relationship with Cliff's tour manager Eddie Jarrett and his roadman, Ron King. Cliff was a true professional who would arrive in the afternoon for a soundcheck before retiring to his dressing room. Our kitchen manager, a lady in her late fifties called Nellie, always used to make a fuss of him. Nellie had a cubbyhole of an office in the Floral Hall next door, where she would sit complaining about the head chef (who she was convinced was in the habit of serving over-generous portions to certain dinner guests). However, when it came to looking after Cliff she would spare no trouble. Nellie would serve him her 'special coffee', which she would enhance the flavour of by adding a hint of salt. Cliff loved it so much that Nellie would make up a bag of it for him to take home after a show.

All this activity had a tremendous impact on Southport's economy. By the Easter bank holiday of the year after Dietrich appeared, the whole town was fully booked. Every hotel, guesthouse and restaurant was packed, along with all of the various entertainment venues. Easter Sunday coincided with the town hosting a regional heat of the BBC TV show *It's a Knockout*. We worked around the clock to make a success of this, even helping to build a mock galleon ship in the town's open-air swimming pool to host the competition. In my new role as Director of Publicity and Attractions, I spent a small fortune promoting the event. We placed prominent adverts across the regional press, not just in the North West in Liverpool and Manchester, but as far south as the Midlands and Birmingham. We were blessed with balmy sunshine on the first day and there were so many tourists flocking into town that for a while the roads were gridlocked.

The live entertainment that we regularly offered also included well-known comedy acts like Ken Dodd, Cannon and Ball, Les Dawson, and Little and Large – all of whom were destined for television stardom. We even managed, finally, to achieve the Holy Grail of booking Eric Morecambe and Ernie Wise. As a professional act, they were able to switch on the magic the moment they walked onto the stage. The public simply adored them. Behind the scenes, Eric and Ernie were very business-like in their approach. They insisted on separate dressing rooms and their agent demanded a 95 per cent share of the box-office takings. As we'd previously discovered with Dietrich, it was worth every penny for the halo effect that it created. I was learning fast that if you spend big on talent, you're eventually likely to recoup it one way or another. With Morecambe and Wise, it wasn't about making money for the venue – it was about making us the attraction! By maintaining such a busy calendar, we were able to transform Southport from a seasonal destination into one that was popular all year round.

Apollo... We Have Lift-Off!

Life seemed pretty rosy and it wasn't long before Nita and I were able to think about buying a home of our own. Our accommodation in Southport was initially a small house that had once been a 'fireman's cottage'. It was cosy and convenient, just a short walk from the Floral Hall – and it was also rent-free courtesy of the council, so we had been able to save for a deposit. Nita no longer had to work, as she had when we were back in Oxford, so she could concentrate on being a mum to her children, Debbie and David. For my own part, I always accepted both Debbie and David into our lives. The fact that they were Jerry's children made no difference to me in any way at all, and both grew up to be an important part of my life.

Once we were confident we could afford to pay a mortgage, we began to look for a property in a beautiful part of the town. One of Nita's favourite hobbies was interior design and decorating, so she took to house hunting with great enthusiasm. When we viewed one particular property together near Lord Street in the town centre, she fell instantly in love with it. It was a beautiful semi-detached Edwardian house in Melling Road, with its own driveway and plenty of room inside for the children.

'I love it,' said Nita, thrilled. 'Let's buy it!'

I agreed that it was perfect. Ironically, we later discovered that the chairman of the council lived in the house next door, so we were in good company. We just about had enough money in our account with Barclays to pay for the deposit, which was in the region of £500. Everything seemed fine – until I made my first big mistake with money. I had a bright idea to make our deposit go further, but it turned out to be a disaster. The council booked a lot of jazz concerts with big bands and an orchestra, which always did well. I thought that if big bands were successful in Southport, why not elsewhere? I believed I had the expertise to make it work, so Nita and I used the deposit money to privately fund a concert promotion of our own. I reasoned that there was nothing in my contract of employment with the council to prevent me from having outside interests, so we booked an American jazz act with an orchestra and we hired Sheffield City Hall. The venue had over two thousand seats and we hoped to earn several hundred pounds in a single evening.

Unfortunately, we were wrong. The ticket sales were dreadful but we were contractually obliged to go ahead with the show. It resulted in us losing our house deposit, plus more on top. Counting out the balance of the fees to the band that night was a miserable task. It was a wake-up call that being a promoter is not easy – there is always a degree of risk involved.

Nita didn't mince her words over my lack of financial acumen. 'It may have been a creative idea, but it's put our house at risk,' she told me.

To be fair, she had a point.

With the deposit gone, we visited Barclays to ask for a loan to cover the balance, but they were not helpful. We had to think again about where we could find the money. Thankfully, when we went to see the manager of the local Midland Bank he agreed to take on our account and lend us the deposit. This was the start of a long relationship with the Midland (which is now part of HSBC).

The house in Melling Road was much bigger than the council house we had left behind. It had a large kitchen, dining room and lounge on the ground floor, bedrooms on the first and second floors, and gardens to the front and back. It became a very special home to us and we were lucky enough to share some wonderful times there together.

I felt I had learned a good lesson over the loss-making concert in Sheffield, so I persuaded Nita to give it another go – although I was far more cautious this time around. We started to book popular acts like James Last or Jack Jones, and we managed to make some extra money to complement my salary at the council. It was around this time that my relationship with The Spinners – the Merseyside group I'd met through Colin Hogg – also became a source of extra income. By now Colin and I had become good friends, and he approached me with a business proposition.

'Would you be willing to manage all of The Spinners' tour dates in the north of England?' he asked.

I knew the group were a fine bunch of lads and I got on well with all of them, including their frontman, Tony Davis. They had a huge following and they would go to most cities twice a year and sell out all their dates. Colin wanted somebody to help look after the administration side of things while they were on the road. The idea was that I would take care of them in the

North while he and his colleagues managed the Midlands and the South. The work involved booking concert dates, organising the marketing and then going along to the venues when they performed. In return, I would earn something like a couple of thousand pounds a year. It seemed like a harmless venture and I knew the extra money would be most welcome, so I agreed, although I didn't tell my bosses.

The Spinners' dates that I managed included performances at Newcastle City Hall and other venues further south down to Hull, plus Sheffield City Hall. In the North West there were dates in Preston, Blackpool and Bolton. Working with the group gave me a great insight into life on the road and what was expected backstage. It also allowed me to meet other venue managers, see what they were doing and discover who was working where. All of this was good information that helped me in my day job, because it meant I had my finger on the pulse across the whole of the North. I used to earn about a hundred pounds a night, minus travel expenses. I would generally make my way home late the same evening, in order to be with the family in the morning and get into the office on time. Eventually I formed a company called Kim Promotions (Kim being Nita's middle name) and arranged for my books to be handled by an accountant called Lionel Becker, who was with a company called Beever and Struthers (with whom I was to enjoy a long association). As anticipated, my fees from working with The Spinners initially averaged about two thousand pounds a year, rising to three thousand or more when the group were at their peak.

All in all it was a happy time, and Nita and I remained very much in love. She was feisty and unafraid to speak her mind

– hence her refreshingly frank use of colourful language on occasion, which I actually grew to find quite endearing. In early 1975, she told me that she had some important news to share.

'I'm pregnant,' she said.

'That's fantastic news,' I replied.

Our son, Simon, was born at hospital that summer in Southport and Nita returned home very quickly after he arrived. Simon was a lovely baby, always happy, and when he started to grow he enjoyed playing with musical toys, which was very amusing to watch. Nita was very much a full-time mum at this point. She no longer had much involvement in our business dealings (although that would change later on), but she regularly accompanied me to concerts and events. She liked all the old jazz artistes that were popular at the time and she also enjoyed comedy acts like Cannon and Ball. We became friendly with Syd Little and Eddie Large (a.k.a. Little and Large), whom we would occasionally join for dinner. All in all, Nita and I felt very settled. Our financial situation had improved when I was promoted to Director of Publicity and Attractions. I imagined that I would probably continue to work at the council for a number of years, but I was due a rude awakening.

*

I received an unexpected phone call from the head of the council's legal department in the summer of 1976. That was the year of a heatwave that many people now look back on with fond memories; the skies were blue and every day the temperatures were in the eighties and nineties (on the Fahrenheit scale

– nobody used Celsius back then). However, despite the warm weather the attitude of the lawyer was distinctly cool.

'We need to see you in private,' he said. 'Something has been brought to our attention which requires an immediate explanation.'

I assumed we'd had a legal letter or a dispute relating to council business, but when I met with the legal team I learned that it was an issue relating to me personally.

'We understand that you have entered into a commercial relationship with a musical combo called The Spinners,' said the lawyer. 'If that's correct, it is a clear conflict of interest with your professional duties at the council.'

There was no point in denying it; besides, I'd been doing it discreetly for a number of years, and it had never impacted upon my work at the council. I hoped it wouldn't be too much of a problem.

'I am afraid it *is* a problem,' insisted the lawyer. 'The council takes a very dim view of the situation.'

I tried to argue my case, but with hindsight I can see why my bosses may have got the wrong idea. When I first joined the council, I'd been employed at a salary grade that allowed me to have secondary interests, but now that I was in a more senior role they felt it was inappropriate for me to be organising concerts in other parts of the country. I wondered if they also felt that I'd become a bit too big for my boots. One or two people locally had commented that some of the events I'd arranged in Southport weren't to their taste (we occasionally showed X-rated films like *Confessions of a Window Cleaner*, which were considered very racy at the time but were essentially just sexy comedies). Of course, we also hosted a large number of cultural events, including opera and ballet. However, I must admit that I could be fairly dismissive of any criticism of our light entertainment policy.

'If we had two dancing bears playing dustbin lids and we made money, that's OK because people must want to see it,' I told a journalist on one occasion.

Despite my protestations, my bosses were not backing down over my work for The Spinners. Eventually it was mutually agreed that I would resign, despite the fact that they accepted there had been no actual abuse of my position. In fact, the council lawyer later paid me a guarded compliment about the entrepreneurial nature of my extracurricular activities: 'I can envisage you one day driving along the seafront in a Bentley,' he told me on the day that we parted company.

It had been a wonderful few years, but my time at the council was over.

★

As the old adage goes, when one door closes, another one opens, and that turned out to be true for me. Shortly after leaving the council I received a phone call from my old acquaintance Barry Clayman, by now one of the country's most successful music promoters. He had formed MAM (which stood for Management, Agency and Music) back in the sixties, after linking up with the manager of an obscure young singer called Tom Jones. Tom's first release was 'It's Not Unusual', which of course went to number one, and Barry never looked back.

MAM had recently floated its shares in order to become a public company off the back of the success of Tom, Engelbert Humperdinck, and Gilbert O'Sullivan. Barry also represented artists such as Neil Diamond, Charles Aznavour, Shirley MacLaine and The Moody Blues. He and I had worked together on various concerts at the council and we had a good rapport – he was one of life's gentlemen, and a shrewd businessman. Like me, he had apparently been poor at maths at school, but he never had any trouble instantly working out the terms of a deal in his head. He once joked that he had a little calculator hidden inside his brain. My work had also briefly brought me into contact with Barry's brother, Arnold, who was chairman of a company that owned that several hotels including the Prince of Wales Hotel in Southport.

Following my unceremonious exit from the council, I was pleased to hear from Barry as I assumed it was a good omen, which turned out to be correct. He was well aware of my achievements in Southport. Like many seaside towns, it had previously always been quiet outside of the summer season, but now it had been transformed into a year-round destination. Barry respected this and he had a proposal for me to consider.

'Would you like to work with my brother at the Prince of Wales Group?' he suggested. 'We have a new venture that may be of interest to you.'

It was the start of a long association that would see Barry and his wife Linda become good friends with Nita and me. Barry and Arnold had decided that they would like to form a subsidiary of the hotel group that would go into concert promotion. They thought I would be the ideal person to run this new division, which was called Prince Theatres and Prince Concert Promotions. The plan was that we would promote music events at hotels and other venues around the country. I had the relevant experience, so I readily accepted. We agreed that I could keep my relationship with The Spinners as a separate concern, so it was an attractive deal. I would be based at the Royal Hotel in Southport – which is where I first met my future colleague David Rogers, who looked after the accounts for hotel group.

It wasn't long before I settled into my new role and we organised several concerts locally, mainly jazz bands and the like. It was a relatively modest start but I wasn't too concerned; I knew business would grow. I was pleased to be able to advance book my old friend Cliff Richard for some future dates tied in to packages at our Southport hotels.

In fact, things took off far more quickly that I had originally anticipated after a boost came from an unexpected direction. It happened a few months after I'd started, when Barry was promoting the American folk singer John Denver, who'd experienced a string of hits with songs like 'Take Me Home, Country Roads'. Barry had organised a forthcoming performance by Denver in Manchester at the Apollo Cinema, which was owned by the EMI group. The venue was a movie house that could seat over 2,600 with room for 3,500 standing, but it had seen better days. The place was rarely full so as a result the first twenty or so rows of seats had been removed, which Barry was not aware of at the time. The audience was therefore seated a considerable distance away from the main stage. Tickets to see John Denver was nonetheless sold out in advance and there was a great deal of anticipation ahead of the big night. I was at home on the evening in question as I had no direct involvement, but the next day I spoke to Barry.

'How was John Denver?' I asked.

'It was a great opening night, barring the fact there was no audience! It's caused an almighty row,' replied Barry.

He explained that because of the way the lighting and the stage had been configured, when John Denver came out to perform he was unable to either see or hear the audience. They were seated too far away in the darkness of the auditorium. If you watch old footage on YouTube of Denver at other concerts, you'll see that he was typically at his best when he was stood close to the audience with his guitar so that he could develop a rapport with the fans. Unsurprisingly, he was very unhappy with the situation in Manchester and after coming off stage he went absolutely potty, blaming everyone including Barry. Denver's manager then also went berserk at Barry. As a promoter, you never want a big star to be unhappy, so after receiving an earful Barry in turn got on the phone and went potty at Lord Delfont, head of EMI's leisure division. Lord Delfont reacted by deciding to wash his hands of the venue altogether, telling Barry that if he could do a better job of running the place, he was welcome to try!

In summary, everybody had gone potty.

'What exactly did Lord Delfont say?' I asked Barry.

'He told me to "keep the bloody place!" He said they run cinemas, not music venues, so he's suggested that they'll do us a soft deal on the building and we can take it off their hands. It could be quite interesting, don't you think?'

I agreed with Barry that it was a great opportunity. Lord

Delfont must have been in a rush to get rid of the venue, because we completed the deal within the next few weeks. Barry and I initially agreed that we would incorporate the Manchester Apollo into the Prince of Wales Group. However, the existing company already had plenty to concentrate on within the hotel sector, so I suggested we form a new entity called Apollo Theatres Ltd. The founders were myself, Barry and his colleague Colin Berlin, along with Lionel Becker, the accountant who looked after my relationship with The Spinners. This new arrangement would turn out to be a turning point in my life and a wonderful opportunity for me personally.

★

We kept the name 'Apollo' on the front of the building in Manchester. The venue has a beautiful art deco facade that was constructed in 1938 by the celebrated British architect Peter Cummings, whose family had escaped persecution in Russia when he was a boy. The Apollo remains on the same site today in an area of Manchester called Ardwick Green, about a mile to the south-east of the city centre. According to my granddaughter, Sarah, it's still one of the best places in the county for live music, so I like to think that we helped to breathe life back into it. Nearby is a beautiful park containing a cenotaph dedicated to the fallen troops of the Eighth Ardwicks, a Territorial Army unit that belonged to the Manchester Regiment. The Apollo building is arguably an important part of the city's cultural heritage, although it was in desperate need of some TLC when we took it over.

Our first priority was to sort out the backstage areas, including all of the dressing rooms. I'd learned at Southport how important quality dressing rooms are in ensuring a live venue is commercially viable. If you provide your star performers with a superb dressing room, it will pay dividends. The next challenge was to build a crew room with TV, snooker table and an arcade-style amusement machine. Showbiz logic dictates that if the crew is happy, we can all be happy. We completed our upgrade with a huge green room and a well-equipped kitchen for catering to artistes and VIP visitors. You might think this doesn't exactly sound like rocket science, but you would be amazed at how many venues neglect this essential part of the business. We then turned our attention to the main auditorium, which we decorated in a sparkly shade of pink. Two new bars were also added in order to ensure customers could stay well refreshed (which would also help to boost revenue). All we needed now were some major acts to agree to play at the upgraded Apollo. The bank had helped with a loan for the refurbishments, but our priority was to get money flowing in through the box office as soon as possible in order to make the venture a success.

'We need to host around a hundred and fifty nights of entertainment each year if we're going to make a profit,' Lionel informed me after he'd assessed the finances.

Attracting so many acts was going to be a challenge for a venue that had recently been in decline as a cinema. But I'd proved in Southport that it was possible to quickly build a reputation as a destination for great entertainment, and with the help of Barry and Colin, we were able to start booking acts almost immediately. In addition to MAM we also worked with virtually every major promoter in the country to actively chase any act we thought would sell in Manchester. This was at the beginning of the heyday of punk rock and during our first year we were very successful in attracting bands like The Clash, The Stranglers and The Boomtown Rats. The American star Iggy Pop, who had a similarly edgy reputation, was also among those to perform at the Manchester Apollo during its early days under our ownership. Iggy played twice within the space of a year. On the first occasion the great David Bowie joined him on stage on keyboards, so from the very beginning we were able to attract big names. We were careful to also appeal to mainstream audiences by booking popular acts like Greg Allman and Cher, Jethro Tull, Status Quo and Procol Harum.

The fact that we could make life as comfortable as possible for performers no doubt played a significant part in this early success. The other factor working in our favour was the size of the venue. This was before the advent of stadium gigs and so, from our perspective, high-capacity theatres or cinema auditoriums were the number one choice for major live shows. I'm happy to say that we traded at a small profit in our first year, and the venue has made money ever since. Today it remains a first-choice venue for artistes playing in Manchester.

Many of the acts we booked would sell out very quickly in advance, which meant we had a regular flow of funds streaming into the business. There was obviously no internet at that time, so people would buy hard tickets in paper format, which generally saw them queuing at the box office before handing over their cash – very few people used debit or credit cards. There's an old saying in business that 'cash is king', and this proved to be very true. Of course, we still had to deduct our costs and pay tax on any profits, but it made life much, much easier to be paid by customers upfront. I quickly realised that the best way to grow our business would be to use the benefit of advance box-office takings. It was like have a large interest-free credit facility to draw upon whenever it was needed – something that most companies can only dream about. In fact, throughout the period of expansion we undertook during subsequent years, the management of advance tickets for cash was always our main priority.

I wasn't able to go to every show or event that we hosted, but I probably attended on about half the dates we booked. The best live performance by far that I ever had the privilege of watching was the rock group Queen, who played at the Manchester Apollo in November of 1979. The band's crew built an amazing lighting rig that was in an upright position at the front of the stage at the start of the show, so that you couldn't actually see the band. Initially, all that was visible to the audience was a huge wall of light that burst to life at the beginning of the performance. The rig then pivoted back and raised itself upwards to reveal the band. The sensory impact of the light show – and the accompanying wall of noise – was simply stunning. The first number the band performed was 'Let Me Entertain You' – and wow, did they do that! Freddie Mercury was fantastic; how could he possibly be anything else? His energy on stage was electric. He began the show adorned in a leather bomber jacket complete with a red silk tie, and his trademark leather peaked cap. He then proceeded to shed individual items of clothing during the show, until he was down to his leather pants. The

APOLLO... WE HAVE LIFT-OFF!

showbiz photographer Denis O'Regan, who was on duty that night, later described Freddie as 'the Shirley Bassey of rock' and said the performance was like a cross between a fashion show and a striptease. The band closed the show with a triumphant encore consisting of five numbers, including 'Crazy Little Thing Called Love', 'Sheer Heart Attack', 'We Will Rock You', and 'We Are the Champions', before (finally) a rendition of 'God Save the Queen'.

I felt a huge sense of contentment that night. Every major venue in the county had been desperate for a chance to book Queen, yet we'd landed the gig, beating formidable opposition from other venues in the North West. When you go along to an event like that which you've played a big part in bringing to the stage, it's a fantastic feeling. As I watched the audience enjoying the show and having a great time, I thought that things couldn't get much better than that; but there was more to come.

In fact, much, much more to come – the Apollo Group had only just lifted off!

A Theatre in Every City

The cash just kept on flowing after we acquired the Apollo in Manchester, enabling us to grow at a phenomenal rate. Emboldened by our early success, we started to take on other venues whenever the opportunity arose.

Ironically, at the same time that we were getting ready to spread our wings in the summer of 1977, the rest of the commercial theatre industry was going through a crisis of confidence. The advent of punk had ruffled feathers in the world of entertainment and bands like The Sex Pistols were shaking up the old order. In theatrical circles, the actors' union Equity issued a stark warning to the government that seven historic theatres in five different cities were in danger of closing unless they could be bailed out by their local authority or the Arts Council. These venues were described as 'touring theatres'. They had been built during a bygone age, before television, but crucially they had capacities of 1,500 to 2,000 or more. This meant they were among a relatively small number of venues capable of hosting touring productions for the likes of the Royal Ballet or English National Opera. Everybody agreed that it would be a tragedy if such grand old theatres were to be sold off to property developers. However, neither the Arts Council nor the local councils had enough cash to mount a rescue – whereas we now had a plentiful supply of funds, thanks to our success with live music.

The Arts Council was already providing touring theatre groups with subsidies of £1.1 million a year and the government was loath to increase its level of support. This led to a fierce debate in the press. *The Times* in London published a leader column describing the theatres in question as 'imposing, expensive to run and difficult to fill'. However, the paper concluded that it was nonetheless vital that they should be protected for future generations – after all, nobody was ever likely to build another 2,000-seat theatre with an orchestra pit in a city centre, hence the importance of preserving those already in existence. The list of venues under threat included the New Theatre in Oxford and the Bristol Hippodrome, as well as theatres in Birmingham and Liverpool and two additional sites in Manchester.

There were a number of theatre chains operating at this time, two of which in particular were facing financial difficulties. Between them, these two chains owned the seven venues that Equity was concerned about. One of the groups was a traditional provincial theatre company called Howard & Wyndham, whose sites included the New Theatre Oxford, the Opera House in Manchester, and the Royal Court, Liverpool. The other company was Stoll Moss, whose portfolio included the Bristol Hippodrome, the Birmingham Hippodrome, the Empire in Liverpool, and the Palace Theatre in Manchester. Eventually, the Arts Council stepped in to promise temporary funding in order ease the situation, but it was really just a sticking plaster. What the industry really needed was a way to make these buildings commercially viable. At the Apollo Group, we had the perfect recipe – and within the space of a decade we managed to save five of the seven theatres that were under threat, plus more besides. Most of them remain open for business and are still profitable to this day.

This wasn't something we necessarily set out to do at the beginning. We initially just wanted to make money and have fun, but when the cards fell our way we were happy to play our hand to the full. The owners of many of the theatres complained that they found it difficult to attract big names because leading acts preferred to appear on television or in the West End. In my opinion, that was not really true. We'd proved in Southport and Manchester that if you provided the right environment, most well-known performers were more than willing to appear at large provincial theatres.

Our first acquisition after the Apollo in Manchester was the New Theatre in Oxford. There had been a theatre on the site, in George Street in the city, since 1836, although it had been rebuilt several times over the years. The current building dates from 1933 and was designed by the Milburn brothers, William and Thomas, from Sunderland. Their previous work included designing the famous Dominion Theatre on Tottenham Court Road in London (another grand old building that we would eventually acquire). The New Theatre in Oxford had been well cared for by its owners, but they were struggling to fill it on a regular basis. The auditorium had a modern art deco interior and approximately 1,700 seats, with a large dress circle and an upper circle. I knew from my previous time living in Oxford that the theatre was highly regarded.

'The building itself doesn't require a great deal of refurbishment, it's been well cared for over the years,' I said to Nita, when we discussed our latest project. 'What it actually needs is "product" – it's crying out for some decent shows.'

The managing director of Howard & Wyndham said that he was minded to sell, and they asked for £85,000 for the lease. That was not an insignificant sum at the time, but my fellow director Lionel and I examined the projected box-office takings, which included the pantomime *Jack and the Beanstalk*. We worked out that with a decent panto run and some additional investment from Lionel, we could afford the deal.

However, Barry and Colin were not sure about the project. They expressed their reservations and indicated that, rather than get involved, they would prefer to sell us their Apollo shares. After much discussion, Lionel and I agreed to buy them out. It cost us in the region of £25,000 and it meant that the two of us would now be running the company together. I had 80 per cent of the company and Lionel (who later based himself in the Isle of Man) had the remaining 20 per cent. It was an amicable arrangement for all concerned. Barry and Colin were great believers that a pound today is worth more than the promise of future riches. Besides, they had a thriving business of their own to concentrate upon. We agreed that we would continue to partner with MAM for bookings, and that relationship served all of us well for another twenty years.

At around the same time that we were negotiating to take over in Oxford, we also received an approach from the owners of the Glasgow Apollo. This was a venue that had recently become famous for staging rock bands, but it had originally been built in 1927 as a cinema called Green's Playhouse. Unlike in Oxford, the building was in a dreadful condition. When I flew up to Scotland to take a look I was surprised to find that it still had the original carpet from decades earlier, embroidered with the words 'Green is Good'. The place was musty and past its prime, but it did have room for over 3,000 seats. The owners were called Unicorn Leisure and were due to relocate to the US, so we were able to acquire the building for a relatively small sum. We weren't sure about its long-term viability, but we decided to run it as a sister venue to the Manchester Apollo.

Once again, we found that musical acts continued to love a venue of that size. When it was completely full the atmosphere in Glasgow was excellent. I remember attending some great concerts there by international acts such as ABBA – that was an amazing show. The comedian Billy Connolly performed a sell-out season. Elton John also played there, as did Rod Stewart the following year, along with all the major music acts of the time. When people were standing up to dance during these huge concerts I swear you could actually see the balcony bouncing, although perhaps that was my imagination!

★

Soon after we took over the New Theatre, Nita and I decided that the time was right for us to move back down to Oxford. We found a house in Iffley village on the outskirts of the city but it needed redecoration, so until it was ready we lived at the Randolph Hotel. Debbie and David went to stay with Jerry temporarily while Simon, who was now a toddler, accompanied us to the hotel. Sometimes he would sneak out of the room and sit on the stairs in his pyjamas, watching people check in and out down at reception.

It felt like we were embarking on an exciting new adventure. Nita didn't seem to mind the domestic upheaval in the least. I set up a new HQ for the Apollo Group in the New Theatre's office – it was a tiny space that I shared with the theatre manager, but there was enough room for the time being.

One mistake I made early on was to announce that I intended to rename the venue as the Apollo Theatre Oxford. I soon discovered that the local population far preferred the old name, and there was no end of negativity about the decision on the letters page of the local newspaper. Eventually we were forced to change it back to its original name, by which it continues to be known today. That experience taught me that a community could become very emotionally attached to its local theatre – a valuable lesson.

Now that we were running three different venues of our own in Manchester, Glasgow and Oxford, I felt I needed some help. I approached David Rogers, the accountant with whom I'd worked at the Prince of Wales Group, and asked him if he would join us as finance director. At first, David wasn't convinced we were big enough for somebody with his skills.

'I think you'll find we are big enough, David,' I told him. 'We're building up something special and we'll need a great accountant.'

Eventually I managed to persuade him. It was a big decision for David, but once his mind was made up he threw himself wholeheartedly into it and moved down to Oxford with his family. We also needed somebody reliable up in Glasgow, so I approached my old colleague Fallas Simpson from the ABC cinema days in Wakefield and asked if he would like to go to Scotland for me. After taking some time to think it over he said it would be a pleasure, although I'm not sure that when he arrived in Glasgow he still felt the same way. The crowds there were big and they liked to drink, which could sometimes make things a bit of a challenge; besides which, we needed to put on about 120 concerts a year to make money. However, with David Rogers's arrival life improved for everyone. He managed the company's cash flow and was careful to monitor advance ticket sales, a role he would carry out brilliantly for the next twenty-five years. With perseverance, we were able to cement the Apollo Glasgow's reputation as the number one venue for live music in Scotland.

Nita and I sold up in Southport and arranged a mortgage to buy the house in Iffley village. It had four modestly sized bedrooms and a swimming pool in the garden. This nearly led to a tragedy one afternoon, which I learned about in a phone call from Nita while I was at the office.

'Paul, I need you to come home,' she sobbed. 'It's Simon. He nearly drowned!'

Apparently, Nita had been pottering about in the garden while Simon was playing on a little plastic buggy, on which he liked to zoom around. While her back was briefly turned, he'd plunged into the pool. Thankfully Nita was able to pull him out of the water in time, but it gave us both a nasty shock.

We only lived at the house in Iffley for a relatively short time, because we were soon able to buy a nicer home – albeit with the help of a huge mortgage. We had found a magnificent house set in three acres of land in Boars Hill, one of the best parts of Oxford. I think it's fair to say it was our dream home, but at the time I was concerned that we would be overstretching ourselves.

Mindful of Lionel's financial background, I asked him for his point of view. 'I'm worried that we can't afford it,' I confided.

'You may think that you'll struggle, but you'll never regret buying something bigger than you can afford,' he said.

This turned out to be wise advice, because Nita and I never regretted arranging the bigger mortgage. The house was delightful. Not only were there beautiful gardens, but there was plenty of room to create a small suite of offices from which we could run the Apollo Group. I think this was the period of my life when I began to find my wings as an entrepreneur; I was my own boss, and I must admit that I loved every moment. It gave me the freedom and the confidence to diversify.

One of my associates at the theatre in Oxford was a guy called Terry Allerton, who was very keen on horse racing. He lived with a friend of his called Philip. They asked if we would back them in opening a bookmaker's shop. We went through the numbers and it seemed like a good idea, so we invested some start-up funding and the business grew to include to six shops. However, I think Terry felt that he and his partner were doing all the work, so we agreed a deal that allowed them to buy us out. We made a small return on our investment and it was an interesting experience, but entertainment and leisure were our main focus. Our efforts included opening a nightclub called Downtown Manhattan in the basement below the foyer of the New Theatre. It became quite successful and was a popular haunt for local revellers. We also added another venue to our portfolio when the lease for Coventry Theatre, owned by EMI, became available and once again, we were in a position to negotiate a good deal. It was a reasonably sized venue with room for over two thousand seats, but it was past its heyday. We rebranded it as the Apollo Coventry but it struggled somewhat as a consequence of its close proximity to the Birmingham Hippodrome, which was a more attractive venue.

One advantage of owning several venues in different parts of the country was that it put us in a strong position when trying to attract acts. It meant that promoters could potentially book a number of dates on a tour with a single phone call to us, which made life easier for everybody. Our vision was to one day have a big theatre in a major city in every region, so that we could host a national tour for any given artiste or show.

With all this activity going on I felt that we needed another pair of hands operationally, so I approached Sam Shrouder, an entertainments officer for the borough council in Blackburn. Sam was a fun character with a scruffy mop of long hair, enormous glasses and a broad, infectious grin. He had made his name by booking acts such as Andy Williams, Suzi Quatro, and The Three Degrees. Sam loved the showbiz lifestyle and was not afraid to try new things – he had famously once booked The Sex Pistols to play in Rochdale. When I approached him, he initially turned me down, but after I explained what we were attempting to do as a company he agreed to come on board as operations manager. He was brilliant backstage; managers and promoters loved him. He was the perfect complement to David Rogers and myself.

Sam joined the small group of staff working at our office suite in Boars Hill. The place had a jovial atmosphere, and Nita loved to drop by during the day to catch up on all the latest gossip from the office girls. Our two pet Labradors, one blonde and the other dark, also had the run of the building – they were beautiful, friendly creatures, but for some reason they always became agitated when Sam arrived in his car. They would rush up to the vehicle barking and yelping, forcing him to run the gauntlet across the gravel drive each morning. Much to the amusement of the office girls, he would burst into the room with his hair dishevelled after fending off the dogs with his briefcase. Sam was in love with a beautiful girl from Blackburn called Freda, whom he later married in the grounds of Boars Hill. It was a wonderful afternoon and they became an important part of the Apollo family.

By that point the staff in the office numbered six, as well as Sam and myself. At the end of a busy day we'd often break off for a drink – Nita would issue the signal for this in her own inimitable style by bursting in with a bottle of wine and blowing a whistle.

'It's time for wine!' she would yell.

★

If we were truly to achieve our goal of a theatre in every city, sooner or later we would need a strong presence in London, so I began to look around the capital for opportunities. I was aware that the New Victoria Theatre in the West End had been dark for nearly five years. Various people, including the distinguished producer and promoter Danny O'Donovan, had tried to make it work as a venue without long-term success. We felt that we should take a fresh look at it as a site for concerts and other attractions, so I approached the theatre's owners to see if they would be interested in leasing it to us, which they agreed to do in the spring of 1980.

The New Victoria is an impressive building with an unusual design featuring two identical facades and separate entrances on Vauxhall Bridge Road and Wilton Road. The theatre is sandwiched between these two busy roads, but rather than an obvious front and rear it has a foyer on either side. We found that this created a bit of a logistical problem – you couldn't greet the public at a single entrance, and two sets of door staff were required – but that was a minor consideration compared to everything positive the building had to offer. It was a magnificent structure that had been designed for the Gaumont-British cinema chain in 1929 by the English architects William Edward Trent and Ernest Wamsley Lewis; the main auditorium was originally conceived of as a 'mermaid's palace'. The building had been granted Grade II listed status in 1972.

Despite having been closed for five years the building was relatively well preserved when we took over, although it still required significant refurbishment. The location was perfect. It was the only venue of its kind within that immediate locale of the West End, and it was next to a major rail junction, making it easy to reach from anywhere in the county. Crucially, it was also the largest theatre of its kind in the West End – it could seat approximately 2,800 people, consisting of nearly 1,800 in the stalls and 1,000 in the circle.

My first task after negotiating the lease was to test the water with some of the producers we worked with and find out whether any of their high-profile artistes would be available to play at the newly reopened theatre (which we christened the Apollo Victoria). I went to see my old contact Eddie Jarrett, who still looked after Cliff Richard. Eddie and I shared a tradition: every year we would spend a day together drinking the latest batch of Beaujolais nouveau when it arrived from France, so we were on good terms. I suggested that Cliff would be the ideal act for our grand opening. Eddie provisionally agreed, and off the back of that we also booked dates with Liza Minnelli (for three weeks) and John Denver (for seven nights) – however, Cliff's office later got in touch to rework the plan. They were feeling nervous about him being the theatre's inaugural attraction; I think they felt that a newly reopened venue might experience teething problems, so they preferred to let another artiste perform first with Cliff appearing a few weeks later. Our working relationship with Cliff is a good example of how well it worked for us to be able to book multiple dates with the same artiste at different venues. During that same month, he also appeared twice at the New Theatre Oxford as well as performing at Apollo venues in Manchester, Glasgow and Coventry.

Things fell into place for our opening night at the Apollo Victoria when Barry received a phone call from Oscar Cohen, an American agent who had recently added the singer Shirley Bassey to his roster of stars. He indicated to Barry that Shirley would be available, but there was a snag that needed to be overcome. Shirley was currently under contract to Robert Paterson – the agent through whom I'd booked Marlene Dietrich for

Southport Theatre. This meant that any dates with Shirley in the UK could only be booked through Robert.

'Well, then, let's do that,' I suggested.

'It's not that simple,' replied Barry. 'Shirley and Robert have fallen out and she's refusing to have anything to do with him.'

Oscar had indicated that if we were somehow able to resolve matters with Robert, Shirley would be thrilled to open the theatre and would play for seven nights. We agreed that the only way forward was to meet with Robert and try to come to some type of arrangement. We invited him to come to the MAM office in Conduit Street in London, where Barry explained our position, but Robert was having none of it.

'Dearest, she's simply not playing here,' he insisted. 'If she can't work for me, she can't work for anybody in the UK. I have a watertight contract, so you can tell your friend Oscar to go and screw himself, in a very American way!'

This was not an ideal start to our meeting. Barry and I spent the next two hours pleading our case, and Robert was friendly but immovable. In the end, we agreed to pay him a hefty sum to rip up his contract with Shirley. I seem to recall that the figure was in the region of £75,000 – but don't quote me on that!

It turned out to be a wise investment, because when we put the tickets on sale they went like hot cakes. As a result, Barry was able to plan a whole tour for Shirley, and we would end up doing all future UK tours of hers for the next seventeen years. She is a delight to work with, but at that time she had a reputation for being a bit of a perfectionist, so everybody backstage was slightly nervous during the dress rehearsals three days before our opening night. When Shirley arrived, she remarked that there was a smell of paint in the theatre – hardly surprising, given that we'd just had the dressing rooms fully refurbished. I knew from past experience that this type of distraction could sometimes become a major issue. A former general manager at the Dorchester Hotel in Park Lane once told me that every time Barbra Streisand was due to stay, he would always keep two suites vacant; this was so that if she complained, he could offer her an alternative. On one occasion, he apparently kept a bride and groom waiting in the foyer for Barbra to make a choice!

Thankfully, despite her comment about the smell of paint, Shirley was wonderful throughout. She was dating an Australian gentleman and seemed blissfully happy in his company; she made it clear that she was pleased to be working with us, and she made the opening of the theatre very special. We celebrated afterwards at the White Elephant Club in Curzon Street, one of the best places to go in Mayfair after ten o'clock at night.

A few weeks later it was Cliff Richard's turn to play at the Apollo Victoria and, like Shirley, he was very complimentary about the venue. In fact, he returned a few years later to perform for six weeks as part of his Silver Tour celebrating twenty-five years in showbiz. I'd heard that Cliff was partial to playing the video game *Pac-Man*, so we welcomed him by placing the latest machine in his dressing room. We gave it to him as a thank-you gift at the end of the season.

It wasn't long before we were in a position to host our first full-scale theatrical production at the Apollo Victoria. This came about when I was contacted by a gentleman called Ross Taylor, a flamboyant theatre producer who had enjoyed great accolade as the creative genius behind a recent stage run of *The*

King and I at the London Palladium, starring Yul Brynner. The success of the show in London resulted in Ross becoming very popular with the people in America who controlled the rights to stage musicals by Rodgers and Hammerstein, including *The Sound of Music*. I was intrigued when I received a call from Ross inviting me for 'a secret conversation' over lunch at Cecconi's in Savile Row.

If ever there was someone who revelled in being described as a showbiz luvvie, it was Ross – and I mean that as a compliment. He was born in Stockport before the war and worked as a dancer and choreographer before becoming a producer. He was as camp as they come and liked to call himself 'the first working-class impresario'. He arrived for our lunch in his usual dandy attire: a cashmere V-neck jumper, a crisp buttoned-up collar and a spotted silk tie.

'The people in America are being frightfully nice,' he told me. 'They were delighted with what I did with *The King and I*. My next production is going to be *The Sound of Music*, and I would like it to be at the Apollo Victoria Theatre.'

This was an exciting prospect. If we could agree a deal with Ross it would transform the image of the Apollo Victoria, establishing it as a home for large-scale musicals. Everybody had assumed his next production would be at the Palladium, but apparently he had fallen out with Louis Benjamin, managing director of Stoll Moss (the Palladium's owners). I bore Louis no ill will, but in this instance his loss would be my gain.

Ross, however, was a terrible fusspot, and it took a further three months to negotiate the deal, which eventually included us providing him with an office at the theatre. In return, he agreed to share his thoughts on marketing and on which stars we should hire. The next few months were spent casting; Ross suggested Petula Clark as a headliner, in the lead role of Maria. He insisted on conducting dress rehearsals in secret, although I was allowed the odd sneaky peek. And when it came to the all-important posters and flyers, I must admit that he was a bit of a nightmare. We had a top advertising agency, Dewynters, lined up to blitz posters across the capital, but Ross kept on making endless changes to the design.

'No, it's not right, darling! Can we just adjust the width of this line a little bit here, and add a little bit of shading there.'

In the end, I begged him to get on with it: 'Will you just approve the thing, so that we can release the posters and get some money in the bank!'

Ross relented and, after what felt like a hundred amendments, the poster layout was finally agreed. We went on sale and achieved heavy box-office receipts. By the time we opened, we had over £2.5 million in advance sales. The opening night went well and press reviews were good; Ross was happy, we were happy, and the Rodgers and Hammerstein estate was thrilled. Most importantly of all, the audience was happy. The *Guinness Book of Theatre* later stated that the show had achieved the highest ever audience for a single week of any British musical production at the time, achieving 101 per cent of our seating capacity. I'm not quite sure how that extra 1 per cent above capacity was accounted for; somebody must have squeezed in two dozen temporary stools to add to the theatre's 2,600 permanent seats!

Among those attending on the opening night was the real Baroness Maria von Trapp, who afterwards told Ross: 'If I never see *The Sound of Music* again, this is the way I want to remember it – and I want to remember Petula's performance as the greatest performance of Maria.'

We had a big hit on our hands and the show ran for nearly two years. It was the last show that Ross produced, as he retired afterwards, which was a shame for the industry. Although he could be difficult, he was a shy person at heart with good marketing skills and a strong sense of what kind of show would appeal to the public. He moved to Australia, where he enjoyed a long and happy retirement before passing away in 2017.

As for the Apollo Leisure Group, thanks to Ross, our reputation as a theatre operator was vastly enhanced. For a time, it seemed as if nothing that we touched could go wrong – but I was about to learn another rude lesson.

Camelot, a Crisis . . . and a Royal Wee

The recognition we received for restoring the Apollo Victoria was extremely flattering. The ultimate accolade came in the form of a glowing article in *The Stage*, the newspaper of note for the theatrical world. 'They probably haven't realised it yet themselves,' stated the publication. 'But Apollo Leisure have been responsible for creating an entirely new profession. Theatre Doctors. They take ailing theatres, refurbish them, prescribe a far-sighted marketing policy and set them on their feet again.'[2]

That article appeared soon after tickets went on sale for *The Sound of Music* and it included a discussion about the fact that prices were pegged at £7.50 for the first six months, with some priced as low as £2.50. This was unquestionably good value and it left many people wondering how we were able to afford to put on such an extravagant musical at that price.

'According to the Apollo's Managing Director, Paul Gregg, it's because Apollo think big,' stated the article. 'They pay big prices. They present big stars. The stars fill a big theatre – the biggest in the West End, and full houses slash overheads and facilitate cheaper ticket scales.'

I was describing the same recipe I'd used at other venues in the past. However, with hindsight, I think what I said may have ruffled a few feathers in the theatrical establishment, some of whom considered my approach to be brash. Later on, we encountered some opposition when we tried to take over other venues, and on occasions we were referred to as 'the Oxford mob'.

Nevertheless, we were able to acquire the leases to two more London theatres: the Cambridge Theatre in Covent Garden, and the Phoenix in Charing Cross Road. As word of our success spread, I received a number of interesting approaches. One of them was from the producers of the stage musical *Camelot*, starring Richard Harris, which was playing to large audiences in the USA. Harris, a huge star, was enormously popular in the lead role as King Arthur. He had been nominated for an Oscar for the 1967 film adaptation, which had grossed over $33 million (more than double what it had cost to make), and the Broadway revival was now pulling in $500,000 dollars a week at the box office.

The producers invited me to see the show in New York along with Nita, as their guests. I was very excited about the trip – Nita less so. She took a keen interest in our business and in the office gossip, but international travel would mean being away from Simon, who was still very young. However, she agreed to come along, and we flew to the States together. My fatal mistake was insisting we see the show on the same day we arrived in America, with no accounting for jet lag. By nine p.m. I was asleep in the middle of the performance – with my head on the shoulder of the chap next to me, or so I was told afterwards!

CAMELOT, A CRISIS... AND A ROYAL WEE

'What's the point of coming all this way if you're going to fall asleep during the show you want to book?' Nita chastised me afterwards.

'Never mind that all that – what did you think of it?' I asked.

Nita's view was that it was a good production for an American audience, but that some of the cultural references might not translate very well to London. However, I remained convinced that *Camelot* had the makings of a success in the UK. The musical was the creation of the celebrated composers Lerner and Loewe, who also wrote *My Fair Lady*. Their version of *Camelot* had enjoyed a run at the Theatre Royal in Drury Lane during the '60s, which as far as I knew had been a reasonable success. In my opinion, Richard Harris possessed the necessary charisma and star quality to bring the show back to the West End. Besides, we could do our own bespoke production, tweaking it for the benefit of a London audience.

Fresh from my experience of working with Ross Taylor on *The Sound of Music*, I felt that I might even have the talent to become a producer myself. I'd already had a brief excursion down that road by producing an African American musical called *One Mo' Time*; I'd been warned that so-called 'black shows' would not do well in the West End (which I considered to be insulting), but in fact the production was a critical success that eventually recouped most of its costs.

In light of that experience, I was convinced that I knew best and that *Camelot* would be a winner. The finances would be a potential challenge, but I had never let that put me off the past. When negotiations began, I learned that Richard Harris was demanding £40,000 a week to appear in London. This was a staggering sum at the time – equivalent to more than £115,000 a week today. I queried the figure with Harris's agents, who insisted it was non-negotiable: 'Richard says that is what he's making in the USA, so why would he come to London for any less?'

Harris had his point of view. Besides, I'd already told the press that we were the people who paid 'big money for big stars'. Looking back, I should have questioned the figures more closely; perhaps I was beginning to believe our own hype. David Rogers expressed his reservations, but I did my best to reassure him that advance ticket sales would be more than enough to cover the cost of casting Harris.

'I hope you're right,' replied David, with his customary caution.

On that basis, I went ahead and signed the deal for *Camelot* to open in November of that year at the Apollo Victoria. We appointed a talented young American, Peter Schneider, to manage the production; he had originally come to the UK as general manager for *One Mo' Time*. The well-known actress Fiona Fullerton was cast as Guinevere, with Robert Meadmore, who'd previously appeared in stage musicals including *My Fair Lady*, in the role of Lancelot.

As the clock ticked towards the grand opening, I knew that all eyes in the industry would now be questioning our judgement and our production skills. I made enquiries about the possibility of organising a charity premiere, which I felt would be a fitting way to launch the show. Among the organisations that expressed an interest in taking part was a charity called the St Joseph's Hospice Extension Appeal, whose patron was

CAMELOT, A CRISIS... AND A ROYAL WEE

HRH Princess Margaret. A gala premiere that was attended by the Queen's sister would truly be an honour for us to host, so I was pleased when Kensington Palace confirmed that Princess Margaret would be delighted to attend. We arranged a number of preview shows prior to the gala, which all sold out. Our first week's advance take at the box office was in the region of £135,000, a record for the West End at that time.

We received a visit from Special Branch ahead of the grand opening so that the necessary security checks could be made in order to ensure that Princess Margaret was well protected. The IRA was very active in London at that time and the police were taking no chances. I was told that I must greet Her Royal Highness at the front of the theatre and then escort her to her seat.

As the big day approached, we did our best to make sure everything was perfect. During our refurbishment of the building, we had gone to great lengths to ensure that any modern facilities we installed were in harmony with the original decor. The theatre looked magnificent and it was a big moment for me when the Princess arrived. She looked beautiful and as I escorted her to her seat I made polite conversation, explaining a bit about the theatre and its history. The Princess listened with apparent interest but then, just as we reached the Royal seating area, she made a remark that shocked me a little.

'I cannot stand this show,' she said – or words to that effect.

I don't think she meant it with any malice. I assumed that she'd seen a previous production somewhere else and was simply making an observation, but even so, I felt a twinge of unease and wondered if it was a bad omen. However, as soon as the show got under way, I put it to the back of my mind. Richard Harris was on brilliant form and the quality of the production was excellent; at least, so I thought.

When the show officially opened to the public later that week, the audience certainly seemed to love it. The applause and cheering at the end of the show was rapturous. Harris did a number of ecstatic curtain calls, much to the delight of the auditorium. Then, after his final bow on the opening night as the curtains closed for the final time, he made one last grand gesture. Poking his head round the drapes, he planted a couple of empty milk bottles on the stage.

The message was simple: *'I'm here to stay!'*

The crowd loved it and they whooped and cheered, but I was conscious of that same sense of unease I'd experienced during Princess Margaret's visit a few days earlier. During the after-show party, everybody seemed to be in agreement that the night had been a huge success. My colleague Sam Shrouder was in his element, doing what he did best, mixing and being the life and soul of the party. Afterwards, he recalled people lavishing praise upon us, saying things like, *'Darling, you must be thrilled – it will run forever!'* or *'Sweetheart, you have a smash hit on your hands.'* The consensus was that our show was excellent. I did my best to relax, but at the back of my mind I kept thinking about Princess Margaret and those milk bottles. And when the newspaper reviews were published, I discovered that we had a problem.

A rather big problem.

★

CAMELOT, A CRISIS... AND A ROYAL WEE

Critics hated the show. Far from being a smash hit, as far as the gentlemen of the press were concerned our production of *Camelot* was a turkey. *The Times* described it as a 'lugubrious revival' featuring 'gloomy backcloths' and 'dilapidated interiors'; it managed some mild praise for Richard Harris, but was otherwise scathing. 'Robert Meadmore and Fiona Fullerton get all the life they can from the youthful vanities of Lancelot and Guinevere, before subsiding into lifeless patterns of perfection. The production is not particularly well moved, but in a show that gives small scope for this there is no point in complaining,' added the reviewer (who actually seemed to be complaining a great deal).[3]

Unfortunately, it wasn't just one bad review. They were all in a similar vein and the effect on our box-office takings was disastrous. Prior to the opening, we'd been banking advance sales of around £20,000 a day, but this halved almost overnight. Worse still, the takings continued to decline over the coming weeks. For the first time in my career, I was faced with the very real prospect of being caught up in a financial disaster. It was far more serious than the time in Southport when I'd lost our deposit money on the concert at Sheffield City Hall. This time, the survival of the entire Apollo Group was under threat. We had budgeted for *Camelot* to run at a profit for at least a year, and almost overnight we'd found ourselves losing substantial sums of money every week.

'How serious is it?' I asked David Rogers when we met to assess our position.

'About as serious as it can get,' he answered. 'I'm afraid we'll need to meet with our bankers as soon as possible in order to negotiate some breathing space.'

Not long afterwards David, Sam and I sat down with a representative of our bank, who went through the figures and told us in no uncertain terms that the situation was very grave. I don't remember his exact words, but according to Sam's recollection, the banker told us: 'Gentlemen, you are fucked.' By this point we could see that nothing was going to save the show and that it would need to close very quickly. Even then, our problems would not be resolved, because we had nothing lined up to replace it at the Apollo Victoria. In the end, *Camelot* finally limped to a close in early February, barely ten weeks after it had launched amid a huge Royal fanfare.

It was a desperate time, and I experienced plenty of sleepless nights in the weeks that followed. One thing we could do was try to call in as many favours as possible. Barry Clayman threw us a lifeline by giving us the opportunity to book *Fiddler on the Roof* for late June, with the Israeli actor Chaim Topol in the lead role. But we still needed to fill a four-month stretch before that, during which time it would be costing us £10,000 a week to keep the venue empty. Combined with the vast production expenses we'd incurred on *Camelot*, our overall losses amounted to £750,000. To put that figure in context, it was nearly ten times the amount we'd paid for the New Theatre in Oxford.

Thankfully, advance sales for *Fiddler on the Roof* were reasonably healthy, giving us enough cash flow to limp along. We were also introduced to Robert Sangster, the Vernon football pools magnate and millionaire racehorse owner, whom my colleague Lionel Becker knew via his connections in the Isle of Man. Robert agreed to become chairman of the company, a role that Lionel had filled until now. Lionel became vice-chairman, and

CAMELOT, A CRISIS... AND A ROYAL WEE

meanwhile a representative of Robert's called Ken Paul joined the board. Robert brought a great deal of business connections to the company, which helped to open doors.

It was largely thanks to our contacts in the entertainment industry that we were able to pull through the crisis caused by *Camelot*. The dancer Wayne Sleep was on the road at the time with his own hit show, *Dash*, which was selling out everywhere. Wayne was a class act who'd trained at the Royal Ballet School, so I thought that if he could be persuaded to come to London, he could fill the gap until it was time for *Fiddler* to open. I met Wayne's manager at a bookshop he owned in Covent Garden and persuaded him to play Wayne at the Apollo Victoria for several weeks. This covered the rent, significantly easing our finances.

Slowly, as the year progressed, we were able to get back on our feet. I had learned a salutary lesson: sometimes it's when you are flying highest that you're most likely to have your wings clipped. I also learned that the best way to produce a show is through a single committed individual, rather than a group of people or someone who (like me at that time) has many plates to spin. A good producer is somebody who, like Ross Taylor, is prepared to devote absolutely every minute of his time to a show until it's in the best possible shape to succeed at the box office. Similarly, the best producer in the UK today is Cameron Mackintosh, whose focus on any given project is total with no distractions. In contrast, we may have done a decent job with *Camelot* but in truth, it just wasn't good enough.

★

One artiste whom we had the pleasure of working with that year while we were getting back on our feet was the singer Dean Martin. He was known as the King of Cool and will always be remembered with great fondness as one of the Las Vegas 'Rat Pack', alongside Frank Sinatra and Sammy Davis Jr. We were lucky enough to book Dean for four nights at the Apollo Victoria in early June, ahead of the opening of *Fiddler on the Roof*. His performances that week were hailed as some of his finest. One of the shows was recorded for a TV special that you can still find on YouTube today. If you have a spare moment, it's worth looking up. It was filmed in the same week that Dean received a Lifetime Achievement Award from the Royal Variety Club of Great Britain. His understated style and relaxed demeanour on stage made him a delight to watch. Many people have speculated over the years about whether or not he used to get drunk before a show, because he would sometimes slur his words while cracking gags. I don't think that was the case. He was far too professional, and besides, his timing was always so perfect. His gags were risqué but harmless. One joke was about his mother-in-law, whom he described as 'the most remarkable little old lady. She's eighty-six years old and she don't need glasses . . . she drinks right out of a bottle!'

We laid on all the creature comforts for Dean in his dressing room, which even featured a Jacuzzi that we had installed while refurbishing the theatre. However, one thing that I found interesting was that he never actually used the room. He would arrive by chauffer-driven car in his dress suit, looking flawless. He would then stand in the wings and watch the warm-up act, before eventually bounding on stage. At the end of the show he

CAMELOT, A CRISIS... AND A ROYAL WEE

would stay for a few moments, shaking hands with members of the audience and accepting flowers at the front of the stage. He would then get straight into his car and go back to his hotel for a quiet dinner. Throughout all of this he was quite charming and at the end of the week he took time to personally thank all of the musicians and stagehands, giving each of them a generous cash tip.

I think Dean must have enjoyed his time at the Apollo Victoria, because Nita and I were later invited to see a new show that he was headlining in Las Vegas and we went to dinner with him afterwards. Nita was rarely star-struck and, as usual, she was somewhat loath to travel.

'I don't know why you need to go all the way to Las Vegas to see a show that you've already seen in Victoria,' she complained. This was in marked contrast to how she spoke about the trip afterwards, when she delighted in telling everybody about her new friend Dean Martin!

Our long association with Cliff Richard also proved very valuable. The singer's Silver Tour was due to go on the road around this point, and we were able to book him to appear at the Apollo Victoria for six weeks in November. Tickets went on sale in late spring and were sold out within seven days. This presented us with a somewhat unusual (but very welcome) problem. Orders were coming in so fast that it was a challenge to process them all. Everything was still done manually in those days, so people would send in cheques by post and then receive their paper tickets by return. Normally, one or two of the girls in the office at Boars Hill would process the orders, but Cliff's tour created such a rush that everybody had to join a mini production line in the office – even Nita and the children. There were bags of post stacked up at one side of the office, bulging with envelopes from customers. The contents of each bag would be transferred onto a giant desk so that we could sort through it all. Working around the clock, we managed to manually process nearly 90,000 tickets in the space of a couple of weeks. The seats were priced at £8 to £10 each, which added up to advance takings equivalent to £2.5 million in today's money. A full theatre would also mean additional revenue from the sale of refreshments, plus we would receive our customary 25 per cent cut from the sale of souvenir programmes. It wasn't lost on me that just a few months earlier we had been struggling to keep the business afloat, whereas now we were surrounded by enormous piles of cheques in the office!

★

In the spring of that year I received an approach from Brian Brolly, entertainment entrepreneur and MD of Andrew Lloyd Webber's Really Useful Theatre Company. Brian was an interesting person: he had previously been MD of Paul McCartney's music company, MPL, and was a bit of genius when it came to picking winners. He had talent-spotted Andrew and his songwriter partner, Tim Rice, a few years earlier and introduced them to the showbiz impresario Robert Stigwood, who managed the Bee Gees and Andy Gibb. It was Stigwood who helped to make Andrew's musicals *Evita* and *Jesus Christ Superstar* into hits.

When Brian called, it was to invite me to the workshop production of a new musical Andrew was planning. I was eager

CAMELOT, A CRISIS... AND A ROYAL WEE

to attend, but the date was inconvenient as it was on the morning of a football cup final at Wembley, to which a friend had invited me.

'I think you'll find it will be worth coming to the workshop,' promised Brian.

Andrew had recently enjoyed a huge hit with *Cats* and everybody was keen to know what his next masterpiece would be. In reality, there was no way I could miss such an opportunity. I decided to go along in the morning, hoping I'd still make it to that afternoon's match as well.

The workshop was in a dusty church hall just behind Leicester Square. When I arrived I spotted lots of ramps, a bit like you might see in a skateboard park. There was a young company of dancers on roller skates whizzing around the space, performing all sorts of tricks. After a while, things settled down and the dancers took up their positions in order to begin their routine. I then sat open-mouthed through the first ever performance of what was to become *Starlight Express*.

I was blown away. I had never seen anything quite like it – it was bursting with energy and thrilling to watch. Brian was passionate about *Starlight*; I think he believed in it even more strongly than Andrew! His vision was to see the skaters performing among the audience, with ramps that went around the auditorium and up into the circle. The idea was that you could sit and watch as they zoomed past you in your seat. Not only that, but Brian had also decided that the ideal venue for the show would be the Apollo Victoria.

I loved the workshop – so much so that I ended up missing the first half of the football match. I couldn't stop telling people what I had seen and how fantastic I thought it was. Brian had no difficulty in persuading me that we should do a deal for the show to open the following spring. I told David Rogers that this time around, I was very sure we were looking at a hit. The only downside was that it was going to take an unusually long time to get the production into the theatre, and structural changes to the auditorium would be required. Brian asked if we would help by offering them a rent-free period at the theatre while they made the necessary adaptations. I took the view that if we got it right, the show would run for many years; so I agreed, although this presented David Rogers with a cash-flow challenge that needed careful management.

Starlight Express was launched the following year and sure enough, it became Andrew Lloyd Webber's latest blockbuster musical. Advance bookings were very good, grossing over £1 million during the first three weeks. The box office eventually took nearly £7 million in advance sales, which was another record at the time.

By the time we were ready to open, the auditorium had been transformed into a wonderland that looked a bit like a giant magical version of a children's train set. Its construction required the removal of several hundred seats to make room for the huge set, which spilled out on ramps into the auditorium. Tracks were installed at the back and front of the stalls and also at the front of the balcony. Cameras were also added so that everybody could have a clear view of every part of the track. The show famously told the story of a small boy who falls asleep while playing with his toy trains, which then come alive and compete with one another in a championship.

CAMELOT, A CRISIS... AND A ROYAL WEE

The opening of the show was a notable event in the theatrical world and a Royal Gala Performance was scheduled for 22 March 1984. The arrangements were made through Andrew Lloyd Webber's office and this time around, it was to be attended by Her Majesty Queen Elizabeth II. My role as the owner of the building would once again be to greet the royal party at the front of the theatre. There would be a line-up of people in the main foyer so that everybody could be presented to Her Majesty, including Andrew and his partner, Sarah Brightman. The gala would be an especially busy day for Andrew and Sarah, as they were also planning to get married that morning, which would mean that they could be introduced to the Queen as husband and wife. The instructions that we were all given were fairly relaxed. I've learned over the years that these occasions are often not as formal as people perceive them to be, although obviously the security is very tight. We were told that the correct way to address the Queen was 'Your Majesty' rather than 'Your Highness' (which is for lesser royals). It is fine to shake the Queen's hand and make polite conversation, but hugging is out of the question.

When the big day arrived I must confess I was slightly nervous, just as you might expect anybody to be before meeting the Queen. I was very aware that it was a special occasion and I wanted everything to be perfect, especially given the fact that I was welcoming Her Majesty to the building. Nita was equally excited and had a fun time choosing her outfit. She settled upon a black silk trouser suit complemented by a pearl necklace and earrings. We agreed that I would travel to the theatre alone earlier in the day to ensure everything was running smoothly, while Nita got ready at home before being driven to London to join me.

Everything went to plan for most of the day, but as the clock ticked towards the moment when Her Majesty was due to arrive, I became increasingly concerned that there was no sign of Nita.

Where the hell is she? I wondered. I knew she was with our driver, who would normally allow plenty of time for the journey, but it was starting to look as if she would be late. Andrew and Sarah, having got married earlier in the day, were already lining up in the foyer along with other people from the production. There were only minutes to go before the Queen arrived, so I went outside onto the red carpet.

Her Majesty arrived in perfect time at the Vauxhall Bridge Road entrance, accompanied by the Duke of Edinburgh. I greeted the royal party as planned. Then, as I escorted the Queen inside, I spotted Nita from the corner of my eye. She seemed to pop up from nowhere, dashing into the line-up to stand beside Andrew just as he and Sarah were presented to the Queen. The official photographer from the Press Association stepped forward and as the flash went off, Nita was positioned between the Queen and Andrew Lloyd Webber. We hadn't planned it that way, but it was a wonderful photograph – possibly the greatest ever example of what is today known as photobombing. Nita looked superb that night and she had a big, bright smile in the picture, which was widely used the next day by many newspapers.

Thankfully, Nita's late arrival was the only hitch that occurred that day. The show was magnificent, the party afterwards was wonderful, and this time the reviews were excellent. More importantly, *Starlight Express* went on to run at the Victoria Apollo Theatre for the next eighteen years.

As for why Nita arrived so late, there was an unusual anecdote behind her indiscretion. She told me that she had arrived with seconds to spare at the theatre's second entrance in Wilton Road, on the opposite side to the Queen's arrival, and had just managed to dash through the foyer in time. Her car had been caught in heavy traffic on the way up from Oxford and by the time it reached the outskirts of London, she'd had an overwhelming urge to use the loo. Just as the driver was about to pull onto the Westway dual carriageway, Nita realised she could wait no longer.

'Pull over! Pull over!' she ordered.

There was a row of private houses next to the road. Nita marched straight up to the nearest front door and knocked on it, explaining to the bemused homeowner: 'I am very sorry to trouble you, but I am on the way to meet the Queen and I need to use the bathroom.'

In any other country in the world, the occupant of the house would probably have slammed the door when confronted by this glamorous stranger demanding to use the toilet. Thankfully, in true British spirit, the homeowner immediately grasped the gravity of the situation and ushered Nita inside.

Nita and I may have had our differences over the years, but stories like that always made me remember why I'd married her!

Planes, Trains... and Michael Jackson

It was a warm day in the early autumn of 1987 and Nita and I were travelling to Japan to see the launch of Michael Jackson's *Bad* tour at Tokyo's Korakuen Stadium. This was Jackson's first solo tour, and at that time he was the hottest star in the world. The global fanfare and feverish hype that surrounded him was off the scale.

According to the press, Jackson didn't travel lightly. His entourage included nearly 150 people and twenty-two truckloads of equipment, all of which was being flown to Tokyo on a chartered jumbo jet. Jackson had arranged for his chimpanzee, Bubbles, to fly on a separate plane and there were hundreds of fans waiting just to catch a glimpse of the cuddly ape. When Jackson himself arrived at the airport in Tokyo, the crowd was too big to count. Everywhere the star went, he was mobbed: the King of Pop had come to town.

Thankfully, Nita and I travelled away from the bustle, in the quiet first-class cabin of a British Caledonian airliner. I'd like to be able to say that we were enjoying the hospitality, but we were seated apart from one another in the last two single seats of the cabin. We were travelling with Barry and his wife Linda, who were sitting together a few rows away. This irritated Nita, as it was only because I knew the airline's marketing manager that the four of us had been upgraded from club class.

'Why did you let Barry and Linda have the best seats?' Nita asked.

'Don't worry, perhaps they'll offer to swap with us for the later part of the flight,' I replied hopefully.

The plane took off with us sandwiched between other passengers, all of whom refused to move in order to let us sit together. Nita was greatly upset by the time we landed in Tokyo twelve hours later, as there was no opportunity to swap.

'I hope you enjoyed the flight and that you feel nice and refreshed,' she said to Barry and Linda, through clenched teeth.

I was too excited about what lay ahead to be cross with Barry. The reason we were travelling together was that he had secured a deal to promote the British leg of the *Bad* tour through his new company, BCC (Barry Clayman Concerts). The Apollo Group was a silent partner in this business. It had been three years since the opening of *Starlight Express* and the group had continued to expand. In the meantime, the Chrysalis Group had bought Barry's original company, MAM. This enabled him to join the board of Chrysalis alongside Sir George Martin, but Barry missed the freedom of having his own company, so he asked if Apollo would be willing to form a partnership to help fund his new venture. I agreed, of course, because together we were a formidable force.

Every promoter in Britain had been desperate to represent Jackson for the European tour, but Barry was the one to land the big prize. He'd spent three weeks in LA negotiating the deal, which was 'on and off' right up until the last moment when he signed a provisional agreement.

When we arrived in Tokyo we checked into a beautiful hotel and, in the interests of keeping the peace, I made sure Nita and I had the best room. We were travelling privately rather than with anybody from the Jackson camp, as we were mainly there to observe. It was important for us to see Michael perform on stage in order to plan our leg of the tour, which was scheduled for the following year.

On that first night in Tokyo, Jackson gave one of the best live performances I've ever seen. The stage was kitted out with hundreds of lights, lasers and amplifiers, plus two giant video screens on which the action was projected. There was an electric atmosphere in the large stadium. Fifty thousand people were seated in rows, the vast majority of whom seemed to be young women, all with similar bobbed haircuts. The audience erupted when Jackson came on stage kicking off two fantastic hours with a performance of 'Wanna Be Startin' Somethin''. This was when he was in his prime, and little was known about the troubles that would beleaguer him later in life.

We stayed in Tokyo to watch the show for a second night, which was equally impressive. Next on our itinerary was a short stay in Kyoto before we travelled onwards by train to Osaka, where Jackson was scheduled to appear at a civic function.

On arrival at Kyoto station, we discovered that the platform was thirty steps above the main entrance – and we had six heavy cases between us. Barry had a bad back and could not carry anything. I wasn't going to volunteer to lug all the cases down the stairs by myself, but luckily a porter arrived with a flatbed platform on wheels. Despite the language barrier, it was pretty clear that he was offering to take our cases to the taxi rank. I wondered if we were waving goodbye to the luggage for good, but when we reached the taxi queue we found the porter waiting patiently for us. We boarded a cab with our cases and made our way to the hotel.

Upon checking in we found that all the rooms were prefabricated, with the bathroom built into an alcove and a very small bedroom. I was nominated to complain – with the result that we checked out again within the hour! We were directed to another hotel and the porters from both establishments met midway to take care of the bags. The good news was that we now had excellent rooms with proper bathrooms, which made Nita and Linda very happy.

That evening we were recommended a Japanese beef restaurant, which was managed by some American expats. It was traditional in style, but with the added twist of having an art gallery on site. We enjoyed the best possible steak and sat all evening drinking some wonderful *sake*, only to discover that we had spent nearly £700 – a very large sum at the time for a dinner for four! I rounded off the night by buying a painting by an American artist, much to the delight of Nita and Linda.

The following day we continued our train journey to Osaka, where the local mayor was due to present Michael Jackson with a key to Osaka Castle. In true showbiz style, Jackson insisted on taking Bubbles along for the occasion. While we were in town, we visited another highly rated Japanese restaurant; it was very upmarket and the menu had no English translation. I was nominated to order, which I did with some difficulty. When the food arrived and it consisted of traditional dishes that did not appeal to any of us, we left, much to the displeasure of the staff; instead we dined at the Sheraton, where the food was cooked Benihana-style on grills in front of us, which was very good. Looking back, though, I'm ashamed of walking out of that first restaurant – not least because later in life, Japan would come to hold a special place in my heart. I now understand how to enjoy the dining experience and how good the local food actually is.

Japan is a beautiful country, especially in cherry blossom season. It has a fascinating history and countless amazing places to visit. Nita in particular didn't find it much to her liking and was uncomfortable with the heat, but purely in business terms, the trip was a resounding success. Before we left, Barry went to meet with Jackson's people to firm up the tour arrangements while Nita and I visited a local temple.

★

We came back to the UK with an agreement in place that we would officially promote Michael Jackson's European tour, including dates in London and three or four other UK cities. Barry would also be in charge of working with promoters across Europe, to whom he would in effect subcontract the touring rights.

The album *Bad* had debuted at number one in the USA, selling 2.25 million copies in its first week before going on to reach number one in twenty-four other countries, including the UK. The *Bad* tour was pulling in record audiences during its first month in Japan, which totalled around 450,000 people, so we were confident that we could fill Wembley several times over. The highest number of people that any musical act had previously achieved on a similar tour was around 200,000. We immediately began the process of planning the UK dates, which we would be directly promoting ourselves. We had almost a year to prepare and it would occupy vast amounts of our time – I'll tell you more about that later, but in the meantime, business had to continue as usual elsewhere in the Apollo Group.

By this time, we had further expanded our portfolio of venues. Notable new additions were the Bristol Hippodrome, the Playhouse in Edinburgh and the Empire Theatre in Liverpool. These were all good acquisitions that enhanced our nationwide appeal. The Bristol Hippodrome did particularly well for us over the years because of its great location – people would travel there from all over the South West and also from across the border in Wales. That deal came about after we received a tip from a theatre producer called Duncan Weldon, who was friendly with Lionel.

Duncan's company, Triumph Theatre Productions, had a good track record of staging serious dramas and he enjoyed a close relationship with the Theatre Royal in Haymarket. This put him in a strong negotiating position with leading thespians, because appearing at the Theatre Royal was considered to be a great accolade. Lionel believed Duncan could boost the theatrical side of our business, so we entered into a number of joint ventures together. I once went to see him at his London office and found myself being welcomed by Leonard Rossiter, famous for playing the rotten landlord Rigsby in the TV series *Rising Damp*. Rossiter had just been cast in one of Duncan's productions and together they'd decided it would be a laugh for him to greet me as if he was the new office tea boy. Duncan was in the background ordering him about: 'Come on, ask our guest what he would like to drink!'

Duncan did us a good turn by passing on the news that Louis Benjamin, MD of Stoll Moss, was thinking of selling the Bristol Hippodrome. I rang Louis to ask if this was true, and he confirmed it was. We agreed a price of £600,000 and arranged that I would go to London the following Monday to tidy things up with him.

I arrived at his office in Cranbrooke Mansions on the edge of Leicester Square. The building resembled a dusty old bank. His first words to me were, 'I cannot do the deal! Have you seen today's *Telegraph*?'

I had. The newspaper had run a piece mentioning that David Land, a theatre producer who'd previously worked for the impresario Robert Stigwood, had just bought the Theatre Royal in Brighton for £750,000.

'My board will not let me sell Bristol for less than that figure. We'll need to match it,' stated Benjamin.

I argued that we simply had no more money available. I was also concerned that Bristol's pantomime for the coming season didn't look particularly good, meaning the advance cash from ticket sales might well be less than in previous years. In the end, I agreed that we would pay Louis £600,000 up front plus another £50,000 a year for the next three years in order to shake on the deal.

Duncan and I went our separate ways soon after that. Our association with Triumph Productions hadn't really delivered for us, although there were certainly some memorable moments during the partnership. There were productions with Charlton Heston (known as 'Chuck' to Duncan) and we also presented Al Pacino in his one-man play, which sold out for several weeks. I recall that we won a couple of awards from the Society of West End Theatres while working with Duncan, which was a nice honour.

The Liverpool Empire was yet another magnificent old theatre that was facing difficulties when we took over its management. The building dates from 1925 and is another impressive work by William and Thomas Milburn, the brothers who designed Oxford's New Theatre and the Dominion in London. The Empire is an imposing Liverpool landmark with a grand stone facade and neoclassical pillars. Despite its rich history, it struggled in the late '70s under its original owners and was eventually taken over by the county council. When the Thatcher administration decided to reorganise local government, the theatre again found itself under threat. Derek Hatton, the militant deputy leader of Liverpool City Council, was very vocal in the press about Tory cuts, so the future of the Empire had the potential to become a hot political issue. It was against that background that we received an approach from the Arts Council, who asked if the Apollo Group would care to take a look at the Empire.

We were a bit nervous at first, given the political turmoil in the city, but the Arts Council said they would support us with soft deals on ballet and opera productions if we were willing to take on the risk. The upshot was that we agreed to take over management of the theatre, with ownership of the building being passed to the Liverpool Empire Theatre Trust.

PLANES, TRAINS ... AND MICHAEL JACKSON

I had a number of contacts in Liverpool going all the way back to my time in Southport. Among the people I knew was Terry Smith, who held the licence to operate the city's hugely popular radio station, Radio City. Terry was very active on the local cultural scene and he was a co-founder of Mercury Press, a successful local news agency that supplied news items to all the national papers. He was also close to the club secretary of Liverpool Football Club, Peter Robinson (who later became chief executive of the club). Terry agreed to join the board of the Empire Trust, which was chaired by a gentleman called Philip Carter (later Sir Philip), who was chairman of Everton Football Club. Together, we therefore had a great network of contacts. Despite our initial reservations, the Empire went on to become a success – so much so that we eventually became partners in extending and extensively refurbishing the building a decade later, in its seventieth year, after which it was reopened by the Queen.

My ongoing relationship with Barry served us both well. We enjoyed booking summer seasons at major resorts over the years with many of the best UK light entertainment acts including Les Dawson, Cannon and Ball, Freddie Starr, Little and Large, Michael Barrymore and Jim Davidson, as well as musical acts like The Nolan Sisters and Lulu. Our arrangement in the new company was a simple fifty-fifty ownership split between Barry and the Apollo Group, but it was something that we kept in the background. When we were booking international stars like Barbra Streisand or Neil Diamond, this often meant my name didn't appear on the billing.

I recall doing a poster for a Streisand show, a co-promotion with Harvey Goldsmith. We agreed that the billing on the poster would be 'Barry Clayman and Harvey Goldsmith present . . .' Harvey asked if I was to be included as well, but I said no; I didn't think Barry would want it known that we had a fifty-fifty venture. Apollo Leisure Group would still be at risk if ever there were to be huge losses, but we did not have many of those. Barry had a unique skill – whenever we were on the way to making a loss, he would start cutting costs so that we always stayed in profit on any given project. The first thing he would do was estimate how much we needed to charge for tickets. He would typically then go and sell as many as possible to ticket agents in advance, and it was up to the agents to ensure they sold their quota – an arrangement that reduced our own risk.

★

Wembley Stadium seemed like the natural place to host Michael Jackson. At this point it was still unusual for an artist to perform in a football stadium, but that began to change after the success of the Live Aid concert in 1985, when live images of Wembley in full swing were beamed around the world. Our plan was to promote at least seven shows there for Jackson, five of which would be in July of 1988, with at least another two dates to follow in August. There would also be shows in four other UK cities and they too, given the huge demand, would need to be held in stadiums or parks rather than at provincial theatres.

We arranged dates at Cardiff Arms Park in Wales, the Milton Keynes Bowl, and Roundhay Park in Leeds. The final concert of the UK tour was due to follow those dates and was pencilled in for mid-September (which would also be the last date in Europe as a whole before the tour took a break). It made sense that at least one city on the tour should be in the north of England, preferably in the North West. With the football season traditionally starting in August it would be difficult to reserve a club stadium, but one venue on Merseyside that did have acres of space was Aintree Racecourse. With that in mind I decided to call my friend Terry Smith at Radio City. If anybody had the contacts and necessary clout in Liverpool to make this happen, it was Terry.

'How do you fancy working together to promote Michael Jackson at Aintree Racecourse?' I asked him.

Terry had a keen sense of humour and at first I think he assumed I was joking, but when I explained the background to my call, I had his undivided attention. I told him we needed a quick decision.

'Michael Jackson playing live at Aintree? I'd get behind that one hundred per cent,' he said.

With Terry on board, life was easier, because not only did he have the connections but we could also rely on Radio City for marketing support. Originally we hoped we might be able to hire Aintree's main grandstand, but the MD of the racecourse vetoed that; I think his colleagues were nervous about the impact tens of thousands of pop fans might have on their course facilities. However, they were happy to come to an arrangement for us to build our own temporary facility elsewhere on the site. We constructed a huge open-air arena in the centre of the grounds with room for many tens of thousands of people.

In Japan we had been somewhat remote from the proceedings, but in the UK we were in constant liaison with Jackson's management. Our initial plan was to put 70,000 tickets on sale, similar to the capacity for rock concerts at Wembley. The Wembley dates had been relatively easy to organise in comparison to Aintree because the stadium had previously already hosted concerts. Aintree, as the home of the Grand National, was used to handling big crowds, but this was a very different type of event.

Security was a serious consideration. A substantial perimeter was constructed in order to keep people safe inside the open-air arena, as well as to keep out uninvited guests and ticketless fans. The stage and gantry needed to be purpose-built at every site on the tour in order to meet the various technical requirements. Jackson's road crew had developed an ingenious system for ensuring that this ran smoothly. They actually had two identical stages and sound systems so that if necessary they could be constructing the facilities for the next concert in advance, before the previous stage needed to be dismantled.

When tickets went on sale, the Wembley dates sold out instantly, so I had high hopes that it would be a similar story at Aintree. Thankfully, we were no longer manually processing tickets in our office at Boars Hill, as the company had expanded significantly since those days. Radio City joined us as co-promoters and announced details of the Aintree concert in a special bulletin in April: *'It's official! Radio City is bringing pop superstar Michael Jackson to Liverpool!'*

Ticket sales at various locations were being coordinated by Paul Latham, general manager of the Manchester Apollo (who later became the UK president of Live Nation). Paul promised to keep me updated, so when he called me I was eager to hear about the level of demand.

'We've sold all 70,000 tickets. I think we should put another 10,000 on sale,' he said.

'Very good, let's do it,' I replied.

Apparently, many fans across the North West had being queuing all night. The next call brought further interesting news: 'They're still selling. I think we need another 10,000,' said Paul.

I knew that we potentially had the capacity to go even higher, although it would require careful management. Crowds of 80,000 regularly attended the Grand National in those days, and we were making use of a bigger part of the site. I felt I should share the good news with Barry, but his initial reaction when I rang him was incredulity.

'We're up to 90,000 tickets,' I told him.

'You must be fucking mental!' he exclaimed.

'Well, I think we should keep going. Let's get on with it,' I replied.

Barry was nervous because nobody had done a concert of this size before; but we had huge demand and we had the capacity, so why not sell more? In the end, we continued to sell until we reached an upper ceiling of in the region of 130,000. In fact, we could probably have sold even more. It was going to be one hell of a concert.

The media interest in the tour was relentless and it reached near hysterical levels when the Wembley shows opened in July. The first date fell on a Thursday and Scotland Yard issued a warning to fans not to attempt to buy tickets from touts outside the stadium – police feared that as many as 13,000 fakes would be on offer. As it turned out, though, all the Wembley dates went ahead without any major incidents, including a show on 16 July that was attended by Prince Charles and Princess Diana. The concerts at Cardiff, Milton Keynes and Leeds were all equally spectacular in their own ways. A review of the Cardiff show in the *Western Mail* stated: 'Circus seems the only word suitable for the day Michael Jackson came to Cardiff. Hundreds of police officers, ticket touts, security men and 55,000 adoring fans turned the capital city into the big top for one of the greatest thrillers it had ever seen.'[4]

In Leeds Jackson played two dates, the second of which was attended by 90,000 people. In Milton Keynes, tickets sold so quickly that the local TV station ran a special report on the fact that additional tickets had to be despatched to the Milton Keynes Bowl in a security van. However, in my opinion the most spectacular of the dates was Aintree. Certainly, in terms of the crowds that flocked to Liverpool it was on an unprecedented scale for a pop concert. The local television station pointed out that the concert would involve the biggest police operation on Merseyside since Pope John Francis II's visit in 1982. The police themselves were content that they would have enough officers on duty to keep everyone safe. As the local Chief Superintendent put it: 'We don't anticipate major disorder, because people who attend Michael Jackson concerts are generally well behaved and they are here to enjoy themselves.'

We anticipated that the vast majority of people would travel to the concert by public transport, but we also made provision for coaches and cars containing 25,000 people to park up on site. When the weekend of the concert arrived every hotel, guesthouse and restaurant in the city was fully booked from Friday onwards, even though the concert wasn't until the

Paul Gregg presents Her Majesty Queen Elizabeth II with a teddy bear on behalf of the Variety Club.

Margaret Thatcher with Paul, Nita (far right) and fellow guests at a Variety Club function in 1990.

Paul with actress Shirley MacLaine.

The Duke of Edinburgh with Paul at a Variety Club charitable function.

The interior of the Lyceum Theatre during restoration work carried out by the Apollo Leisure Group, 1993-1996. Excavations at the front and below the stage were required to make room for an orchestra pit.

The rear of the Lyceum also required extensive excavations to include double dock doors and a 100ft+ fly tower for moving set and scenery on modern productions such as The Lion King.

HRH Prince Charles (now King Charles III) at the newly restored Lyceum accompanied by Paul Gregg (holding brochure).

Left: An interior photo of the Lyceum auditorium during renovations. Right: Steve Lavelle, Property Director of the Apollo Leisure Group.

Andrew Lloyd Webber (right) raises a toast to the restoration of the Lyceum accompanied by Sam Shrouder (centre) and Adrian Leggett of Apollo (left).

The state of the roof and ceiling was a primary concern during the restoration work at the Lyceum. Despite appearances the main structure was still intact.

Work in progress as the new Lyceum begins to take shape during restoration work.

HRH Prince Charles (now King Charles III) with Paul Gregg (centre) and Steve Lavelle (right).

An artist's impression of the proposal for a 55,000-seat waterfront stadium for Everton FC at Kings Dock. The ground would have been equipped with a sliding roof and retractable pitch so that the arena could be used for different types of events.

Much of the restoration work at the Lyceum had to be painstakingly done by hand to ensure features were restored to their original state.

Above: An aerial photograph shows the extent of crowds during Michael Jackson's live performance at Aintree Racecourse in September 1988. Around 130,000 people attended the concert.

Left: Michael Jackson pictured on stage at Aintree during the UK leg of the Bad Tour.

A crowd scene during the Michael Jackson concert at Aintree.

Ross Taylor (left), Petula Clark and Michael Jayston as Captain Von Trapp in The Sound of Music at the Apollo Victoria Theatre. The show achieved a record weekly audience of any British musical production at the time.

Queen Elizabeth II is greeted by Andrew Lloyd Webber and Sarah Brightman at a Royal Gala for Starlight Express at the Apollo Victoria Theatre. Nita Gregg appears in the centre of the frame . . . in possibly the greatest ever example of what is today known as 'photo-bombing'.

PLANES, TRAINS... AND MICHAEL JACKSON

Sunday evening. There were stories about enterprising locals who rented out their spare rooms to Jackson fans who needed a bed for the night.

In addition to the 600 police officers who would be on duty that day, we also employed an army of 1,100 private stewards. They spent the few days prior to the concert playing cat and mouse with various groups of ingenious individuals who were determined to find a way of getting in without tickets. We had constructed a double perimeter wall with a sterile area in the middle, patrolled by guards. This didn't prevent the gangs from removing metal bolts from the fence panels during the night and replacing them with temporary fastenings. Presumably their plan was to return during the concert and remove the panels. It was like *The Great Escape* in reverse, with people trying to break in.

On the morning of the show, the roads were gridlocked and the atmosphere was reminiscent of a huge carnival. Many people simply camped outside the racecourse, with or without tickets, in the hope of catching a glimpse of Michael Jackson when he arrived.

There was an enormous queue of vehicles lined up waiting to get into the car park. A man with a peaked cap and satchel walked up and down taking payment in advance from motorists and coach drivers before handing them what appeared to be a chit for the car park. Much to the drivers' annoyance, they later discovered that this enterprising individual had no connection to the concert – he'd simply been chancing his arm at raising some spare cash before walking away from the scene of the crime with their money.

Jackson arrived by helicopter at Speke Airfield, disguised in an anorak and a red polo neck, before being whisked to the Atlantic Tower hotel, where he checked into the Port of Liverpool suite overlooking the waterfront. He then apparently spent the early part of the day watching boats arrive and depart through a telescope before heading over to Aintree. He was, as has often been noted, a very private person – I didn't meet him in person while he was in Liverpool, although we did meet briefly at one of the Wembley shows. He was very polite and quiet, relying on his minders and managers to do most of the communicating.

In total, we had sold over a million tickets at £16.50 to £17.50 each, depending on the venue. Commercially it was a great success, and Barry was invited to do further work with Jackson in the future. After so many months of hard work I was looking forward to the show, which Nita and I attended together. We sat in some VIP seating on a raised platform we had created at the back of the arena. The *Bad* tour was sponsored by Pepsi, so there were enormous stacks of canned soft drinks everywhere you looked. Of course, Michael Jackson was fantastic as always, although the scenes around the perimeter were a little wild at times. From where we were sitting we could see over the fence into the gap between the two perimeter walls, which resembled a kind of no man's land patrolled by guard dogs. Every so often, one or more individuals would scale the outer wall and attempt to find a way inside, only to be confronted by security. I wondered if they would eventually succeed in bursting through, but thankfully the stewards were mostly able to contain the situation.

PLANES, TRAINS... AND MICHAEL JACKSON

I later learned that one group of men had started throwing stones over the wall at the stewards and been arrested. There were also reports that a large number of fans had been treated for crush injuries, although the police subsequently said the numbers involved had been greatly exaggerated. 'I think that's a bit of nonsense really,' insisted the Chief Superintendent. 'In a situation like this there are always people who are overcome by the heat, by the hysteria, by the crushing, because it is crowded towards the stage area.'[5]

In fact, the local TV station later confirmed that only four people had been treated in hospital. Of course, even one injury is too many, and some people may have felt that we were lucky to maintain control. But the local residents made a point of saying afterwards that future concerts would be welcome at Aintree.

What I remember most about that day is the endless sea of happy faces in the crowd.

Variety is the Spice of Life

The sun shone brightly in a cloudless blue sky as I prepared to make a short boat trip across the Caribbean Sea in order to stay on Richard Branson's private island. Five years had passed since the day Nita and I watched Michael Jackson perform live at Aintree. We were now travelling with a group of twenty friends to Necker Island, the private paradise where Branson had chosen to locate his personal retreat in the British Virgin Islands. The island was available to rent on an exclusive basis (assuming you could afford the fees, of course). Today, as I write, the advertised rate is $128,000 per night, although I recall it was substantially less back in the 1990s.

As I looked out across the warm turquoise waters, I reflected that life was good. We were about to celebrate Nita's fiftieth birthday in style and I was looking forward to some lazy afternoons on a secluded beach before dancing the night away under the stars. In the half-decade since the Jackson tour we'd acquired further venues including the Dominion Theatre and the Hammersmith Apollo in London, as well as the Point Theatre in Dublin. Among the guests joining us on Necker was the Irish tycoon Harry Crosbie, who had become our business partner in Dublin. Harry had a reason of his own to celebrate:

he was planning to marry his lovely fiancée, Rita, while we were gathered together on Necker.

We were all in good spirits as we boarded the boat to make the final leg of the journey from a neighbouring island that had an airfield. As we approached Necker from sea level it was a beautiful sight, with its gentle green slopes rising majestically from calm waters. Its beaches are pure white sand – what else? – and scattered around the coastline are a small number of buildings with open-air verandas, surrounded by tropical gardens and shady pools where you can enjoy a piña colada. Towards the middle of the island, in the lush uplands, is a structure resembling a Balinese temple, which was used by Branson. *This certainly feels a long way from Scarborough Pier*, I mused to myself.

In addition to Harry and Rita, our party included David Rogers, Barry and Linda Clayman, Sam Shrouder and his wife Freda along with their young son, Ben, plus a number of other close friends and associates of the Apollo Leisure Group. I'd met Branson briefly in the past when he'd toyed with the idea of opening some theatres, but Nita was keen to make the booking on the understanding that we would have exclusive access to the island, although I forgot to specify this at the time. However, we anticipated Richard himself was due to vacate Necker while we were there.

We were greeted on the beach by the island's hospitality team, who were impeccably friendly. They offered us cocktails and carried our bags to our accommodation while we relaxed in the shade. Throughout our stay, a private chef would be catering for all our needs, and whenever we wandered onto a deserted beach there was always a member of staff nearby with a coolbox to keep us refreshed. In addition to relaxing on the beach or at the side of a pool, we'd planned a range of activities to keep everyone entertained: a volleyball match, tennis tournaments, various water sports and a sand sculpture competition.

Perhaps the nicest thing of all about being here, though, was the feeling it gave you of being cocooned from the rest of the world in your own private paradise. Nita was in her element. 'It's wonderful to be the only party here on the island,' she glowed.

However, our much-desired solitude was about to be interrupted by the unexpected arrival of a helicopter. We were relaxing by the pool when we heard the distant *woomph-woomph* sound of its rotor blades. I assumed at first that it must be en route to another island, but the noise got steadily louder as it approached until it eventually touched down on Necker.

'It's Branson! What the hell is he doing here?' exclaimed Rita.

Within a short time, Richard Branson had arrived at the pool and was smiling and shaking hands as he introduced himself to everybody, including all the ladies. He was with his wife Joan and their children, Holly and Sam. Richard himself was like a huge puppy dog, full of energy and clearly in the mood to party. At first we thought he must just be making a flying visit (quite literally), but I soon realised that since his family was with him, that probably meant he was here to stay.

As the afternoon wore on, there seemed to be no sign of Branson getting back into his helicopter, and he let slip in conversation that he was planning to be around for a few days. Most of our guests seemed pleasantly surprised to meet him, although I sensed that Nita was slightly perturbed, with some justification. Nice as it was to meet Richard and his family, I regretted that I had neglected to specify that we wanted the place to ourselves. Perhaps I was being uncharitable, but it was similar to how you might feel today if you booked a break via Airbnb and found that the property owner was still living there during your stay.

Branson's arrival certainly changed the dynamic of the holiday. Sam Shrouder's son Ben became instant pals with the tycoon's young son, and together they had fun launching water-pistol raids on the sunbathing ladies in our group. Meanwhile, Branson appeared intent on remaining the life and soul of the party. Sam Shrouder said he found him witty and entertaining. It's probably a bit of a churlish exaggeration to say that during the evening he popped up everywhere we looked, but that was certainly how it felt!

'Don't worry. I'm sure he'll leave us in peace tomorrow,' I reassured Nita, who by now was grim-faced at the prospect of her milestone birthday celebration being hijacked.

The following morning we were awoken by the children climbing on the roof with their water pistols, much to the annoyance of several guests who were trying to sleep off the drinks from the night before. Later on Branson turned up again, whereupon several guests were promptly chucked in the pool in the name of 'fun' (which caused further consternation).

'This is *your* fault,' Nita told me angrily. 'You should have told him not to come while we were here.'

I tried to explain that I'd believed I was making the booking on an exclusive basis, but there was no pacifying her. I generally took the view with Nita that 'a happy wife equals an easy life' – whereas if she was unhappy, immediate action had to be taken.

It was time for me to have a word with Mr B.

I must have been a strange sight as I marched up to him in my shorts and flip-flops, slightly pink from too much sun and trying my best not to scowl.

'I'd like to speak to you in private for a moment,' I said. 'It was very nice of you to introduce yourself to our guests, but I don't think you should be here all the time. It's a private party.'

Branson seemed genuinely taken aback. He muttered something about how he was only staying up in the temple and that he hoped it wouldn't be a problem. I'd obviously made a mistake when I made the booking, which had led to confusion. Looking back, I think I may have hurt his feelings, because it had probably never crossed his mind that we might object to his presence. If you're reading this today, Richard: we just wanted a bit of down time on our own, so please don't take it personally. It was a great place for a holiday!

★

Thankfully, Harry and Rita still enjoyed their wedding on Necker enormously. I had originally met Harry in Dublin several years earlier while looking for an opportunity to extend our reach into Ireland. One of the things we had previously achieved at Apollo was to take major West End musicals to venues outside of London. The first example of this was when *Cats* by Andrew Lloyd Webber opened at Blackpool Opera House in 1989. Until that time nobody had considered doing such a thing, presumably because they wrongly believed that there would be no market for high-end productions like *Cats* in the provinces. I hoped to do something similar in Ireland. After all, I thought, Dublin is a thriving capital city – why wouldn't a West End show also flourish there?

To start with, it had been an uphill battle to get the producers of *Cats* to come to Blackpool. Barry and I had a good relationship with the opera house after being asked many years earlier to manage the bookings for its summer season attractions. We had similar arrangements with independent theatres at piers in Bournemouth, Great Yarmouth, Scarborough and Torquay. This further enabled us to foster good relationships with artistes and their agents, as well as the theatres, because we could book high-profile acts for key dates at many different venues. It was a lucrative endeavour and the public got to enjoy great shows by stars like Cannon and Ball, Les Dawson, Freddie Starr, Little and Large and Michael Barrymore, all of whom had big followings thanks to their television work. They were class acts. I have fond memories of persuading Barrymore to tour (a nicer gentleman you could not hope to meet). His agents told him it would help to make his bank manager his best friend – and you never know when you might need the money!

If you wanted to book a real star, you generally also had to take a lesser-known support act from the same agent. It was a system that enabled a lot of up-and-coming acts to get exposure alongside household names. However, the big stars were also in demand for TV work, so it could be a challenge to find a summer act for a venue like Blackpool Opera House, which required an artiste to commit to a full season of up to twenty-six weeks. Hence my idea, which I hoped would alleviate this problem. People were queuing up in London to see upmarket musicals like *Cats* and *Phantom of the Opera*, so why not try some of those shows as summer attractions in Blackpool?

At first, many people thought this was a crazy suggestion. They couldn't envision a northern town – the kind of place often associated with donkeys on the beach, fish and chips, and lots of beer – as a natural fit for a posh musical. In my opinion this was plain old snobbery; after all, I'd booked plenty of ballet and opera during my time in Southport. So I decided to explore the idea further. I went to see Brian Brolly at Andrew Lloyd Webber's Really Useful Theatre Company, and I was pleasantly surprised to discover that he was receptive to the idea of taking *Cats* to Blackpool.

After some persuasion, Cameron Mackintosh – to his credit – agreed to produce the musical at the opera house. He did a spectacular job. In order to accommodate the physical aspects of the production we had to remove the royal box, which as far as I know has never been replaced. The people at our advertising agency initially struggled to get their heads around how to market the show in the North, but we nonetheless achieved good advance sales at the box office. On opening night, I admit that I had some minor feelings of trepidation. I spent the interval wandering around the theatre, checking the takings in the bars and listening to comments from the audience. 'It were OK, but I'd no idea what the bloody hell it was all about,' said one Northern gentleman to his wife.

I knew that this comment probably represented the view of many others in the audience that night, but overall the evening was a success. We continued to sell tickets steadily, and we were surprised at how well the production did over the course of the season. Most importantly, we had challenged the traditional view that summer season was the exclusive domain of headline acts with a background in light entertainment. We had demonstrated that major musicals could be successful at large venues outside London. Later on we were also able to take *Cats* to Manchester and Edinburgh, and we enjoyed similar positive outcomes with *Phantom of the Opera*.

It was during a trip to Dublin for a film festival that I decided to check on the possibility of adopting a similar approach in Ireland. I'd heard about a venue called the Point, which Harry Crosbie had just opened on the site of an old railway shed. I arranged to meet him there one afternoon before I was due to see a film with Nita. As Harry showed me around, I was impressed by what he had achieved. He had created the Point as a place for live rock concerts but I could see that it would be easy to convert into a venue for musicals.

'Look, Harry, I've been searching for somewhere to bring a big musical show to Dublin, but there isn't anywhere. I want to bring *Cats* here,' I confided. 'If we put seats down the middle of your auditorium and rejig the stage area, the Point would be accessible for that kind of show.'

I could see I had his full attention. 'How much do you think it would cost for the whole project?' he asked.

'I don't know exactly, but my guess is probably around two and a half million quid, including hosting the show,' I said.

Harry agreed to think it over, so I went off to meet Nita.

At about six thirty that evening, he rang me at our hotel. 'Can I see you for half an hour?' he said.

'We're just about to go to dinner, but if you can come to meet me now we can get together,' I replied.

Harry came over and we ordered a drink.

'I want to do it together,' he said. 'We'll put in two and a half million between us, and we'll own it fifty-fifty.'

It was a deal. Our first joint project was to bring the Bolshoi Ballet to Dublin, which would later be followed by *Cats*. The Point also hosted the Eurovision Song Contest three times. However, our biggest success came about almost by accident. It was after we'd been to Necker, while I was in Dublin to attend one of the Eurovision events, that I saw a live act showcasing traditional Irish dancing. It was a joy to behold the dancers moving in perfect synchronisation to Irish folk music. This act later became known all over the world as *Riverdance*, but at that stage nobody outside of Ireland had heard of it. It was an instant hit with the audience and it stole the show that night, even though it was only staged during an interval in the main event.

At the after-show party I got chatting to the act's producer, Moya Doherty.

'This show has got real legs,' I enthused (pardon the pun!). 'I'm sure we could do something great with it. It deserves to be much more than a segment at Eurovision.'

Harry was in complete agreement, and eighteen months later *Riverdance* opened in Dublin. On the first night we chartered a plane from London to bring over a group of VIPs, but the flight was delayed. In desperation, I arranged for somebody to phone ahead. Thankfully, disaster was averted when the flight arrived with what seemed like only minutes to spare. The Gardaí were waiting at the airfield and arranged a blue-light escort, driving at suitably fast speed straight to the Point! The rest, as they say, is history. That night cemented a long and happy partnership between Harry and myself.

Another business associate with whom I developed a productive friendship was the American theatre tycoon Jimmy Nederlander. This relationship came about when the Dominion Theatre was put up for sale in London. Barry and I had previously arranged for a number of acts to appear at the Dominion while it was operated by the Odeon Group. The building had since fallen dark, but it was another example of a fine old theatre that was crying out to be rescued, rather than left to rot. Like the Oxford New Theatre and the Liverpool Empire, it had originally been designed by the Milburn brothers; the building was listed, which meant that it would be expensive to renovate, but we nonetheless decided to offer in the region of £5.5 million. To our surprise, it turned out that we had a rival bidder – Jimmy Nederlander. Rather than get into a bidding war, I saw this as an opportunity to share our risk with a partner, so I contacted Jimmy through his New York office.

'Let's stop fighting and do this together. We could approach the Dominion as a joint project,' I suggested.

Jimmy was an astute guy who knew the market very well in America, and he also had interests in the UK which included London's Adelphi Theatre. Through his UK lawyer, he agreed to split the ownership of the Dominion 70–30 in his favour. This was on the basis that the Apollo Leisure Group would handle all bookings for the theatre. I was happy with the arrangement because it expanded our footprint in London at a reduced cost. The renovations were indeed expensive, but not excessive. It was worth the investment in order to partly own such a beautiful old theatre in a prime location, situated at the bottom of Tottenham Court Road near the junction with Oxford Street.

The first act we booked at the new Dominion was Cannon and Ball, who we knew would go down well there because Barry and I had previously booked them for a Christmas season at the Dominion when it was run by Odeon. That run had consisted of two shows a day, six days a week. Many people feared it would be difficult to sell 2,000 seats twice a day, so we had placed a full-page advert in the *London Evening Standard*.

'Nobody has ever taken a full page in the *Standard* for a show like this,' complained Robert De Wynter, the boss of our ad agency, Dewynters. Robert, who had helped us to launch *The Sound of Music* at the Apollo Victoria some years earlier, was a trusted friend and a dapper dresser who liked to do business over a cup of tea and a slice of cake.

'Well then, we'll be the first to do it,' I said.

The show instantly sold out, which left me very confident that the new 70–30 split with Jimmy would enable us to do a lot of great business in the future.

Another significant theatre acquisition that we made during this period was the Hammersmith Odeon. It had originally opened in 1932 under the Gaumont banner, in an art deco building designed by theatre architect Robert Cromie (who also worked on the Prince of Wales Theatre in London). The Gaumont Palace, to give it its full original name, was primarily used as a cinema and became the Hammersmith Odeon in the early '60s. It had a seating capacity of nearly 3,500 and a large stage capable of hosting fully staged musicals.

The MD of the Odeon Group was my old friend Jim Whittell, from my Sheffield days. He and I still spoke on the phone from time to time and I always used to jokily ask if he wanted to sell any of their buildings. Jim always politely declined – until on one occasion he rang me back and told me that his board was indeed minded to sell the Hammersmith site. We eventually agreed a price and the Odeon later became the Labatt's Apollo Hammersmith. From memory, we paid approximately £495,000, but we later deducted around £160,000 of that for repairs that were required to safely remove asbestos.

The combined effect of these acquisitions was to greatly increase our firepower, although some people still wrongly regarded us a company with a background limited to light entertainment. I suppose in some respects we were a disruptive influence, always keen to drive innovation and change – but at the same time, we genuinely loved to restore traditional old theatres and cinemas.

*

The Dominion turned out to be a very good investment. Not only were we able to host wonderful family shows like *Grease* and *Scrooge: The Musical*, but the theatre also became the home of the Royal Variety Performance in aid of the Royal Variety Charity for five years during the 1990s. The Royal Variety Charity is a wonderful organisation that in those days had the Queen as its patron (a role now fulfilled by King Charles). Its events at the Dominion were glittering affairs organised in conjunction with the Variety Club of Great Britain, of which I was privileged to be a member of the executive crew. I had been invited to join by an interesting guy called Jarvis Astaire, who was one of the UK's top boxing promoters and a member of the board of Wembley Stadium. Jarvis worked on behalf of heavyweight champions like Frank Bruno and had also previously masterminded ITV's wrestling coverage (which had been enormous during the '70s and early '80s). Our paths had crossed because we had some contacts in common, and also because many of the sports personalities he represented were also available for pantomime work (including Bruno, whom audiences loved on stage). The Apollo Leisure Group had been a long-time supporter of the Variety Club, which provided 'Sunshine' coaches and wheelchairs so that ill or disabled children could enjoy days out.

The Variety Club was managed by 'the crew', which consisted of around sixteen people who were well connected in the entertainment industry. Among the prominent crew members were Eric Morley (the Miss World organiser) and my Odeon contact, Jim Whittell. Others included John Jarvis, the boss of Jarvis Hotels and chairman of the Prince's Trust, as well as many other directors of prominent companies within the leisure sector. The one thing they all had in common was a desire to give something back to society by helping children who found themselves in unfortunate circumstances.

The Variety Club raised its funds in a number of ways, including organising events such as an annual dinner and ball, plus tribute lunches for famous artistes and sports personalities. There were also lots of awards ceremonies, charitable film premieres and theatre previews, many of which were supported by members of the royal family.

I was elected as co-chairman of the dinner and ball, as well as co-chairman of the annual Christmas lunch. I also organised tribute lunches for personalities including Cliff Richard, Cilla Black, Shirley MacLaine, Tom Jones and many other stars. We operated a simple policy, which was that we avoided spending on anything other than ballroom hire and catering – everything else that we needed for an event had to be begged or borrowed in the name of charity. Over the years we raised millions of pounds. The Dinner and Ball alone could raise as much as £400,000 on a single night, during which we would hold an auction of donated items that included holidays and tickets for the theatre or sporting events. I would sometimes get to meet some of the children and young people whom we helped and it was often a very humbling experience. I remember being introduced to a sixteen-year-old girl who faced life in a wheelchair after being involved in a car accident, which was terribly sad.

The charity had a close relationship with the millionaire author Lord Archer, who hosted the ultimate auction operation and always gave his time and travel for free. (This was before he landed himself in trouble with the law over an unrelated matter. All I will say is that Archer was always a gentleman during all our dealings). The chair of the Board of Trustees at the Club (which is nowadays called 'Variety, the Children's Charity') is referred to as the 'Chief Barker' and is responsible for leading the charity. During the club's fortieth anniversary year I was deeply honoured to be elected to that esteemed position, which resulted in some very happy experiences while raising money for an important cause.

VARIETY IS THE SPICE OF LIFE

One memorable event I helped to organise was a gala at the Guildhall in London for the Great Ormond Street Hospital for children. Our guest of honour was the prime minister, Margaret Thatcher. The event took place shortly after Iraq had invaded Kuwait, which triggered the first Gulf War. When the PM arrived in reception, I noticed that she seemed to be drinking quite heavily from a glass of whisky. However, she was in full command of her faculties. It was my job to greet her.

'What are you going to talk about when you introduce me to the audience?' she asked.

I would never write a speech beforehand on occasions like this. It always seemed better to capture the mood of the moment by speaking off the cuff.

'I'll just give a general introduction, Prime Minister,' I replied.

'No, tell me what you are actually going to say,' Thatcher insisted.

'Well . . . I'll talk about how grateful we are to you for coming here, especially while there is a possibility of a forthcoming war,' I said.

When Thatcher rose to address the event, I was expecting her to make a short speech. She began by making a joke.

"What is a politician doing here?" she asked. "Well there's more in common between politicians and music hall stars than you might think. After all, I do a matinee every Tuesday and Thursday."

She was referring to Prime Minister's Question Time in the Commons, which was twice-weekly at the time. She then spoke long and eloquently about how the West could not allow

Saddam Hussein to win in Iraq. Normally I was not a fan of politicians, but she changed my view and I came to respect her enormously (I was furious when she was turfed out of Downing Street the following November).

The Apollo Group was also a keen supporter of the Make-A-Wish Foundation, another charity that provided help and support for children. Its patrons included a brilliant marketer called Leslie Rose, who had been among the friends who joined me on Necker Island. Leslie was involved in promoting Children in Need on behalf of the BBC, where he created the concept for Pudsey Bear. Other interesting characters at the Make-A-Wish Foundation included Ricci Obertelli (director of operations at the Dorchester hotel group) and Jimmy Quill, who had previously run the Blind Beggar pub in the East End of London during the Kray Twins' reign of terror.

During my time as Chief Barker, we held a charity premiere at the Odeon Leicester Square with the Queen as our special guest of honour. The film, called *Mister Johnson*, was a drama directed by Bruce Beresford. The Variety Club had adopted a teddy bear called Beni as a mascot of our own. I was delighted to present one of them to the Queen. I still have a treasured photo from the event.

Our various sports dinners and awards ceremonies often also enjoyed the support of HRH Prince Philip, the Duke of Edinburgh. One such event was held at the Painted Hall at the Old Royal Naval College in Greenwich. History repeated itself, because Nita was involved in another near calamity that saw her urgently needing to go to the loo before meeting a royal.

This time we travelled together by car, all the way up from Oxford and then onwards across London. We arrived with only moments to spare and Nita had to rush off to the toilet before joining the line-up to meet the Duke.

'Where have you just popped up from?' he asked quizzically.

When Nita answered (with remarkable frankness), the Duke just gave a wry smile before moving on down the line. I suppose variety is the spice of life, as they say.

However, perhaps my most memorable occasion was a Royal Variety Performance at the Dominion that was attended by Prince Charles and Princess Diana in 1992. The royal couple arrived in the Prince's burgundy Rolls-Royce, to be greeted by cheering crowds gathered behind the crash barriers beneath the streetlamps outside the theatre. Diana had a broad smile on her face and looked stunning in a full-length cream dress, decorated above the waist with a discreet paisley pattern. Charles was equally elegant in a black tie outfit that seemed almost radiant by the light of the camera flashbulbs. Once inside, the couple shook hands with the traditional line-up of artistes who were due to appear in the show. It was a great bill that night, including international stars like Barry Manilow and Gloria Estefan as well as British TV personalities, plus the cast of *Cats*. Charles and Diana seemed remarkably at ease throughout the evening, just like any other couple comfortable in one another's company. I found this quite intriguing; the press had been full of speculation all year that their marriage was on the rocks, yet they showed no obvious hint of discord that night.

'Perhaps the papers have it all wrong. They looked like a happy couple to me,' I said to Nita the following day.

The date of the Royal Variety Performance that year was Monday, 7 December – and it turned out to be unexpectedly significant, because it was Charles and Diana's last joint engagement. Two days later, on 9 December, Prime Minister John Major stood up in Parliament and made a sombre statement.

'It is announced from Buckingham Palace that, with regret, the Prince and Princess of Wales have decided to separate,' he told a hushed House of Commons.

I was just as shocked by this announcement as everybody else, but I had to admire Charles and Di for graciously presenting a united front so as not to spoil our charity event. Perhaps one of the reasons they had looked so relaxed was because they knew they were about to escape from the stress of being in an unhappy marriage. It just goes to prove the old adage: you should never judge a book by its cover.

Into the Lyceum

You might think, given our track record of turning around ailing theatres, that the Apollo Group would have been welcomed with open arms when we stepped in to buy and renovate the Lyceum – but in fact the opposite was true. Our chief antagonists were the noble gentlemen of the Theatres Trust, who initially led a chorus of disapproval against us. Apparently they considered us unworthy of the task, despite our history of rescuing other grand theatres that had fallen dark, and there were plenty of others who joined the fray. Suddenly it seemed as if everyone had a strong point of view on the Lyceum, a building about which nobody had cared much for fifty-seven years until we offered a million pounds for the lease.

The recent history of the Lyceum had been characterised by neglect and apathy. In 1939, it had faced demolition after being acquired by the local authority in order to build a new roundabout and offices. That plan was scrapped and in 1945 it reopened as a ballroom, with the seats in the main auditorium being ripped out to create room for a dance floor. It fell dark again in 1985 and the lease was sold to the Brent Walker property group, who planned to demolish and rebuild it with apartments on top. The scheme might well have gone ahead were it not for the fact that Brent Walker went bust in 1991. While the bankruptcy administrators for the company were happy to accept our offer of £1 million, the sticking point was the Theatres Trust, which held the freehold to the land. We received a formal letter from the Trust in which it threatened to block the transfer of the lease. I found this mightily upsetting, given the scale of the resources we were willing to invest in order to restore the building to its rightful grandeur.

If you go onto the Theatres Trust website today, there is a section that states: 'The Lyceum is a building of outstanding national importance, architecturally and theatrically.' While that is undoubtedly true, I think it also goes some way towards explaining why the Trust initially fought against our plans. The organisation is an official body that was founded by an act of Parliament in 1976 in order to 'promote the better protection of theatres for the benefit of the nation'. In my opinion, the Trust had done a pretty poor job of protecting the Lyceum so far, based on the fact that the theatre had been left to decay and that it now required millions of pounds' worth of investment to make it fit for purpose. I assumed that certain people at the Trust felt it would be embarrassing if a commercial company like ours were permitted to outshine them.

So I was furious when I read their letter of objection. It contained a nonsensical argument that basically boiled down to the fact that the gentlemen at the Trust felt we did not have the correct level of integrity to carry out the work. I must confess that this prompted me to use some ungentlemanly language when I later discussed the matter with David Rogers.

'How dare the bastards question our integrity,' I raged. 'I want you to hire the best lawyer we can find and tell the Trust to go fuck itself!'

One of the reasons I was so angry was that we had always prided ourselves on ensuring our theatres were maintained to the highest standards. An interviewer from *The Times* once asked me for the secret of Apollo's success. I replied that it was probably more to do with being sentimental about buildings, rather than the shows within them.

'The role we've created for ourselves is to provide the facilities and make it easier for people to see good shows – and to try to make a profit out of it,' I told the interviewer.[6]

Many people saw these old buildings as a liability, but I never took that view. I would look at the asking price of a million for the Lyceum, or £750,000 for Bristol Hippodrome, and conclude that actually it was fantastic value. Some people might say, *Why do you want to spend a million on something that will become a liability?* My answer would be that it was in fact an opportunity to acquire a unique and priceless piece of history. This way of looking at things had served us well over the years; I reminded myself that we'd hosted royal galas and worked with some of the best up-and-coming producers of a generation, like Andrew Lloyd Webber and Cameron Mackintosh.

Yet despite all of that, some members of the theatrical establishment still treated us as outsiders. The theatre world was a bit of an old boys' club in that respect. Its members regarded themselves as the custodians of the industry, whereas we were perceived to be from a different background. There may have been times when we were too commercial – I don't know.

On the other hand, every theatre in the world needs to have a commercial aspect in order to survive. It was often public bodies, including certain local authorities, that failed to understand this point. Liverpool City Council and the Arts Council had happily collaborated with us over the Liverpool Empire, but elsewhere we were occasionally met with a distinctly cool attitude. We'd previously encountered opposition in both Birmingham and Southampton when trying to acquire venues.

In London, the Theatres Trust had belatedly woken up to the fact that the Lyceum was on a par with the Theatre Royal and the London Palladium in terms of importance. I think they perceived us as a bunch of blokes from up North who had wandered backstage and somehow, unexpectedly, purchased the theatre from under their noses. I wondered if the people at the Trust believed that the administrators would eventually have given the lease to them if no buyer could be found. They could then have arranged a deal of their own and I'm sure they would, in those circumstances, have preferred to offer it directly to Lloyd Webber or Mackintosh. If so, we'd just walked into the middle of things and screwed up the plan!

My attitude was that we should fight fire with fire, which if necessary would include pursuing the matter through the courts. We had a proven history of renovating struggling theatres and I was confident that we would easily be able to overcome any arguments that we didn't have the right skills, or that we were too populist and therefore incompatible with the arts.

The irony was, the Lyceum had historically always prided itself on running popular entertainment alongside the heaviest Shakespearean drama. There had been a theatre on the site since

1774, predating the grand facade constructed by Samuel Beazley after a fire in the 1830s. After reopening, the theatre established itself as a venue for an eclectic range of entertainment, offering everything from Shakespeare to popular circus acts like General Tom Thumb. It was later managed by the great thespian Sir Henry Irving, the first actor ever to receive a knighthood. Irving apparently claimed to have seen the ghost of a woman holding a severed head in the stalls. Among others employed at the theatre was Bram Stoker, who is said to have used Sir Henry's mannerisms and demeanour as inspiration for his 1897 gothic horror novel *Dracula*. The Lyceum was partly rebuilt in 1905, with a new auditorium designed by theatrical architect Bertie Crew, after which it went through a period of staging variety shows that included elephants riding bicycles and other exotic attractions. The venue has also enjoyed a long association with pantomime – Queen Elizabeth II (or Princess Elizabeth, as she was then) saw her first panto there in 1934, when she was eight years old. The young princess reportedly joined in with the singing and leaned over the royal box to ask for an encore. The reality was that the Lyceum had survived for over two hundred years by catering for a wide range of different tastes and audiences.

★

The complexity of the task that lay ahead seemed to increase exponentially by the day. In addition to dealing with the objection from the Theatres Trust, we found ourselves wading through a mountain of paperwork from the likes of English Heritage, the Royal Fine Art Commission Trust, and Westminster Council.

We also faced a major headache over how we were going to fund the project. Our main bankers made it clear they didn't have the appetite to get involved, which was a blow. It was obvious that the project would require two to three years to complete, so there was no prospect of boosting our cash flow in the short-term through advance ticket sales.

However, I was still confident that we had the necessary expertise. It was very much a team effort, with Steve Lavelle taking on a central role in his capacity as Director of Property and Development. David Rogers handled financial and legal matters, while I continued to coordinate the strategy as best I could. In the meantime, we all had our normal day jobs to get on with as well, so it was a very busy time. Thankfully, we also had good people like Sam Shrouder, Paul Latham and our production manager Adrian Leggett around us to help oversee the rest of the company.

Our first priority was to fight off the challenge from the people at the Theatres Trust, who I suspected did not have the finances for a major legal battle (which I was certainly willing to give them). Upon the recommendation of our solicitors, we engaged an eminent barrister who later went on to become very senior in the judiciary. The barrister's opinion was that despite the Trust's fine words, their case would not stack up in court: the administrator was perfectly entitled to sell the lease to us. Our lawyer drafted a brilliant response explaining what would happen if the matter went to court. He laid out the Trust's concerns point by point and then stated why they would lose. It was drafted along the lines of: 'You will argue this . . . [etc., etc.]. In which case, my client will argue this . . .'

Our response had the desired effect of bringing the Trust to the negotiating table. A fair compromise was reached, whereby we agreed to give undertakings that the renovation works would be carried out to the highest standard. We also agreed to pay a peppercorn ground rent to the Trust in lieu of the freehold; and we pledged to give the Trust access to a small number of valuable house seats in the Lyceum when it reopened. Eventually we established a working rapport with the Trust's director, Peter Longman.

By now we'd also received endless lists of demands from a host of other interested parties. The building had been granted Grade II★ listed status in 1973 – this is a separate designation from 'normal' Grade II, without an extra asterisk. Only about 6 per cent of listed buildings fall into this category, which requires a vast layer of additional written consent before works can commence.

'Everyone thinks they have a stake in what we're doing here,' complained Steve. 'We've been inundated with studies and architectural opinions. Some are worth taking on board, but others are from crackpots!'

The paperwork file of demands from Westminster Council alone was already four inches thick – and according to Steve, that was just the tip of the iceberg! Not only did this magnify the workload, but it also had financial implications. Steve's initial cost estimate of £9 million for the renovation was beginning to look conservative. We planned to be up and running within three years, by late 1996. It was an ambitious target, but thankfully Steve had a very experienced property team he could rely upon. However, our financiers were very uneasy about the situation. Our main bank was HSBC, who told us that the project did not meet their lending criteria. We were able to fund some of the initial work from our own reserves, but additional finance would be required in order to meet the final bill.

David suggested we talk to Jimmy Nederlander, our partner in the renovation of the Dominion Theatre. I called Jimmy and offered him the chance to partner with us again in the Lyceum. He was probably the biggest private theatre owner in America at that time, with interests on Broadway and at key theatres through the United States. I was surprised when Jimmy said he didn't want to be involved. He was concerned about the scale of refurbishment and I sensed that he felt uneasy about how we would eventually fund everything.

'I wish you every success, but this one is not for me,' he said diplomatically.

Plenty of people were sceptical about our plans, but it was Jimmy's reaction that worried me the most. I didn't care if a few crusty bankers lacked the vision to back the project, but he was a seasoned professional who knew the theatre industry like the back of his hand. Were we making a mistake?

With Jimmy declining, David Rogers was forced to cast the net wider. Eventually we were able to secure the funding we needed from the Bank of Scotland and the Royal Bank of Scotland, who agreed to share the risk between them. There was also the possibility of receiving support from the National Lottery. Given the cultural importance of the building, we applied for an Arts Lottery Grant of £3.25 million.

Although we needed to borrow a significant amount of money to finance the renovation work, I hoped that we would be able to quickly recoup the cost by offering the newly refurbished Lyceum to the Royal Opera as a temporary new home. The Royal Opera House had been in need of urgent renovation for some time. In 1994 it had been decided that the building would be extensively upgraded, which would potentially cost hundreds of millions of pounds. The opera house rebuilding work was expected to start in late 1996 and take almost four years, with the refurbished venue due to open in the year 2000. I believed that my plan to offer the Lyceum as a temporary venue (which we would continue to manage) made good financial sense for everybody. We estimated that it would generate around £4 million a year for us as the new owners of the building – hence, we hoped to receive around £16 million during the four-year period, enabling us to recoup our investment with a healthy return on top. The Royal Opera would benefit by being able to continue to host as many productions as it pleased, just a stone's throw away from its usual home. It all made perfect sense, at least on paper.

When we approached the people at the Royal Opera, they were initially very positive and for a while it looked as if the plan would go ahead – but what I failed to take into account were the politics involved. The General Director of the Royal Opera House was Sir Jeremy Isaacs, a former TV executive from Glasgow with a reputation for being a tough operator. It transpired that Sir Jeremy and his team were also considering an alternative proposal of their own to build a whole new temporary theatre near London Bridge. Meanwhile, the government was keeping a close eye on the situation due to the cultural importance of what was at stake.

We were willing to go above and beyond the original scope of our own renovations in order to make the Lyceum as attractive as possible as an operatic venue. This included installing two sets of dock doors, so that any given production could be brought in through one set of doors while an outgoing production was being removed at the same time, through the other set. It would also be essential to have a full-sized orchestra pit, which would require us to carry out extensive excavations beneath the front of the stage in order to make room for at least 120 musicians.

'We will give you everything that you need,' I told Sir Jeremy and his team. 'There will be no expense spared.'

Despite my assurances, the negotiations seemed to drag on. Sir Jeremy's team would talk endlessly about their beloved Royal Opera but there seemed to be very little movement towards getting final sign-off for the arrangement. We even considered offering them the keys to the building as part of the sub-lease, but I was reluctant to do that after all our hard work.

It was at this point that I received an interesting phone call from Andrew Lloyd Webber. 'I want to put *Jesus Christ Superstar* into the Lyceum as the first show when it reopens,' he told me.

I was flattered. Andrew's show, which is loosely based on the Gospels, had been an enormous international success as a stage musical. It would be perfect for a return to London, where it had previously enjoyed a long run. However, I was still faintly clinging to the hope that we would land the opera deal.

'That would be fantastic – but I want to see how our negotiations go with the Royal Opera,' I said.

His reply was along the lines of, 'I can tell you now, the Royal Opera will never come to the Lyceum.'

INTO THE LYCEUM

Andrew seemed categorically certain, and of course history proved him right: the Royal Opera did indeed eventually choose an alternative plan. In 1995, the Royal Opera House received a grant of £55 million from public funds, and it later received a further £78 million from its own application to the National Lottery in order to renovate the existing site in Covent Garden (at an eventual total cost of £216 million).[7]

The fact that the Opera was no longer interested in coming to the Lyceum was a real blow, which for a period of time put us in a very precarious position. There was also some other worrying news to digest.

'Our own lottery grant application has been turned down,' Steve told me. 'It was supported by the Arts Lottery Assessor but it was the first application they'd received from a private company, which may not have worked in our favour.'

By this point, our anticipated costs had escalated to eye-watering levels. 'There are now around £5 million worth of additional improvements, over and above our original plans,' added Steve.

These extras included a new elevation on the Exeter Street side of the building, which needed to be in keeping with the style of the original structure. The work on the orchestra pit and the double dock doors would also now require extensive excavations to the small car park located at the back of the building. The Lyceum had, quite literally, become a money pit, but it was too late to turn back the clock – besides, by now we were fully wedded to the idea of restoring it, for better or for worse.

★

Andrew Lloyd Webber had the good grace to stand by his offer regarding *Jesus Christ Superstar*, and we signed terms for the show to open at the Lyceum in November 1996. As part of the deal we also agreed to settle a minor dispute with the Really Useful Theatre Company over advance ticket sales for *Starlight Express*. The settlement involved us making a one-off extra payment of £75,000 towards the advertising costs for *Starlight*.

Having Andrew on board helped to persuade our bankers to give us further breathing space, as it meant we would be able to hit the ground running as soon as the Lyceum was ready to reopen. We now had around eighteen months to complete the renovation work, which from this point onwards became as much a labour of love as it was a commercial project. Steve later described it as an epic adventure that involved a copious amount of sweat and tears. Among those with whom he worked closely were an architect from Holohan Associates called John Murphy, and a talented interior designer called Amanda Fletcher. John later recalled: 'When I first saw the Lyceum it was running damp and knee deep in rubbish, but even then I could see what fantastic potential it had. It seemed dreadful that such a beautiful and historic building should be rotting away in the middle of London.'[8]

Our vision was that patrons would arrive through the 1834 portico and sit in a beautifully restored 1904 auditorium, but would then enjoy shows in facilities that were designed to meet the demands of the twenty-first century. This required the installation of a brand new electricity substation beneath the theatre with enough output to power half of the Strand. Backstage, we created a cavernous fly tower (the area used to move scenery and change sets). This was over one hundred feet in height and included an eighty-bar flying system and a scene dock lift that was capable of lifting a double-decker bus straight from the street onto the stage. It was a remarkable feat of engineering, since it also involved creating the ability to suspend twenty-five tonnes of equipment from a new superstructure that was built into and behind the decorative plasterwork of the theatre. Over three hundred tonnes of steel were used in the fly tower alone, which was manufactured off site and then assembled in situ like a giant Meccano set. At one point we had around four hundred construction workers, craftsmen and women working on the site. The structural engineer was Brian McCann from Thorburn Colquhoun and the quantity surveyor was Mike Crowe of Crowe & Nicholas.

The decorative fixtures were carefully restored in order to ensure an authentic level of detail. Willmott Dixon's project manager, Ron Maylon, oversaw a specialist team that was employed to work on the ceiling of the auditorium, which had been damaged by decades of exposure to tobacco smoke.

'Some of us spent two months lying on our backs on the top of a huge cage of scaffolding,' he recalled afterwards. 'All the beautiful mouldings have been painstakingly repaired and repainted, and the seven-foot-high cherubs are looking chubby and charming again!'[9]

Elsewhere, fragments of original wallpaper were recovered so that Amanda could incorporate the patterns into her designs for the new wall coverings. The excavations at ground level, meanwhile, unearthed some unexpected surprises. A theatre programme for *The Three Musketeers* dating from 1915 was found nestling beneath a floorboard in pristine condition. A team of archaeologists was commissioned to sift through other findings, which included 520 kilograms of animal bones. These were believed to be from a Saxon butchery that dated from the seventh century. In total, earth weighing the equivalent of 1,750 African elephants was excavated to form the basements of the new structure. The portico at the front of the building also required special attention. Its six Corinthian columns were in a sorry state, having been obscured by 135 years of paint, pollution and bird droppings – all of which had to be removed before the restoration work could begin.

In tandem with that work we also needed to install modern facilities, including 150 extra toilets for women (I can assure you that ladies' loos are always in higher demand at theatres!). These new conveniences were discreetly located so as to minimise queuing in busy areas such as the bar. A number of seats were removed in order to ensure perfect sight lines towards the stage, which was expanded to a surface area of 208 square metres to accommodate even the most complex of modern productions. The interior decor included 1,000 rolls of handmade wallpaper and 5,000 square metres of new carpet.

We had a bit of an internal debate about the final colour scheme our designers had chosen. The shade they'd selected for the auditorium was a burgundy red, but I wasn't sure it was right; I wondered if we needed something brighter. That said, it did create the right atmosphere and it was true to the original. We also paid a huge amount of attention to upgrading the catering facilities to include a fully equipped first-class restaurant, called Irving's in honour of Sir Henry Irving. Finally, we ordered a number of books of gold leaf for the two date stones that read '1834' and '1996' on the front facade.

'It's hard for me to put into words what I feel at the end of this project. The sense of job satisfaction that I have is overwhelming,' commented Steve as the completion date approached. 'To see this building come together after so many years of sweat and tears will be an extraordinary moment. There is something wonderful in the permanence of what we are doing here . . . The work we are finishing could still be here in 250 years' time. It will be with the residents of London long after I am gone.'[10]

It had been a long and difficult journey but when the renovation works at the Lyceum were finally completed, the results made everything worthwhile. The final bill was £14.5 million, every penny of which was paid for by the Apollo Leisure Group. Realistically, if you were to undertake a project of a similar size in central London today, you'd be hard pressed to expect any change from £100 million. Even the critics who had doubted our ability to deliver the project were now magnanimous with their praise. I gave a wry smile when I saw that the Theatres Trust was now happy to let the public know about its role in facilitating the transfer of the lease. Peter Longman, director of the Trust, was quoted as saying:

> In so many ways the Lyceum Theatre can be seen as a symbol of much of the work the trust does today; in its triumph of achievement in the face of considerable adversity, in its 57 years in limbo . . . Apollo have exceeded our expectation in their determination and commitment.

A lot of people have sat back, done nothing, sniped away and waited for Apollo to fall flat on their face over this one. Well they haven't, and the Theatres Trust has been delighted to see the private sector operating at this level of professionalism and with such integrity.[11]

I was grateful for his kind words. It had been an epic adventure, but although I didn't realise it at the time, with hindsight I could see that the project had taken a heavy toll on my domestic life. The Lyceum had occupied my thoughts and dreams for nearly three years, and this coincided with a period during which my marriage to Nita began to deteriorate. Like all couples, we'd occasionally had our ups and downs, but now we found ourselves arguing constantly. For her part, rightly or wrongly she felt that I had been spending too much time at work, rather than at home with her and the children.

The reopening of the Lyceum was certainly a watershed moment for the company, one that we were determined to celebrate in style. I approached my Variety Club colleague John Jarvis, who was still chairman of the Prince's Trust, to ask if the Prince of Wales would be interested in visiting the Lyceum for a preview before it reopened to the public. A great deal had been written about Prince Charles's views on architecture, with him famously once describing a proposed development of the National Gallery as 'monstrous carbuncle'. It would be interesting to see what he thought of our efforts at the Lyceum. I was pleased when John called me back a few days later.

'His Royal Highness would be delighted to accept your kind invitation,' he told me.

INTO THE LYCEUM

It was agreed that the future king (as he was at the time) would attend the theatre on 31 October 1996, in advance of the opening of *Jesus Christ Superstar*, which was provisionally pencilled in for the 9th of November. I'd been privileged to meet members of the royal family many times in the past, but this was probably the most intimate occasion, as there were no members of the public present. We agreed that Steve Lavelle, David Rogers and the other senior members of the renovation team would be present, along with a number of invited guests. The plan was to escort Prince Charles on a tour of the building in the morning, followed by a lunch in aid of the Prince's Trust in Irving's restaurant and then a private preview of scenes from *Jesus Christ Superstar*. The chairman of the Arts Council, Lord Gowrie, would also be in attendance to make an introductory address (this raised another wry smile, as it had been the Arts Council that blocked our application for a lottery grant).

The first thing Prince Charles did upon arrival on the big day was to pause at the front of the building for several moments and gaze up in fascination at its colonnaded portico, which was now once again looking truly magnificent. I asked a friend to take a few photos, with the Prince's permission. There's a wonderful shot of the Prince with Steve and me: we're stood next to him with our hands clasped in front of us, all looking upwards like a trio of happy choirboys! We then moved inside, where Charles spent a bit of time admiring the terrazzo flooring in the foyer before being escorted on a guided tour. Charles was genuinely engaged. He seemed to adore the newly restored ceiling of the auditorium and the rich, warm colours of the marble balustrades. His strongest praise was for the attention to detail throughout the building. Afterwards, when Charles met the cast of *Jesus Christ Superstar*, he seemed completely at ease in his surroundings.

The press tried to make a bit of an issue over the choice of *Jesus Christ Superstar* as our opening show. Many felt that it was not really in keeping with the Lyceum's traditions of Irving and Gielgud. 'Shakespeare it ain't,' wrote one rather pompous scribe from the *Independent*.[12] However, there was no doubt that in commercial terms, *Jesus Christ Superstar* turned out to be the right choice for the Lyceum, attracting the biggest potential audience. We received 24,000 advance registrations for information about the show. From these, over 12,000 people immediately purchased advance tickets, which continued to sell steadily afterwards. Since that time, the Lyceum has never fallen dark again – which proves that the commercial choice was also the best choice for the theatre itself.

Jesus Christ Superstar ran for two years, during which time I entered into negotiations to bring an even more spectacular musical to the Lyceum. There had been rumours for some time that Disney was planning a musical stage version of *The Lion King*. The film version of the story had been an enormous hit in 1994, both in terms of its critical acclaim and box-office appeal. It grossed $763 million in its first year and remains the highest grossing traditionally animated film to this day. Disney had previously attempted to turn *Beauty and the Beast* into a stage show with only limited success, but *The Lion King* had far more potential. I'll explain later how we managed to bring the show to London – for now, it's enough to say that when it opened at the Lyceum it was an unrivalled success. To this day it continues to run there, still playing to packed houses.

When I look back over everything we achieved at Apollo, the renovation of the Lyceum – and subsequently, hosting *The Lion King* – is the memory that brings me the most happiness.

The Balloon Bursts

The glow we acquired by breathing new life into the dark shell of the Lyceum may have been a high point for the Apollo Group, but ironically it was also the beginning of the end of our wonderful journey as an independent company. At the same time as we were basking in the warmth of the goodwill that completing the project created, there were fault lines developing within the business. Commercially, we were an enormous success, but perhaps we had outgrown our old way of doing things.

We had always relied on a close working rapport between a small group of individuals at the top of the company: David Rogers, Steve Lavelle, Sam Shrouder and myself. We operated as a family business that was majority owned by Nita and me, but we had expanded at such a pace that there were now 5,000 people employed in that 'family'. In the meantime, the cracks in my relationship with Nita that had started to develop during our renovation of the Lyceum were now a deep chasm. This eventually had a significant impact on the business. Our marriage had always been a partnership, but now there were times when the friction between us clouded my judgement. Within three years of that magical day when Prince Charles had visited the newly renovated Lyceum, we made the surprising decision to sell the company I loved so dearly.

It was while we were in the final stages of preparing to open *The Lion King* that we began to receive attention from a number of parties expressing an interest in buying the Apollo Leisure Group. I suspected that the timing was no accident, since it was obvious that *The Lion King* had the potential to be a runaway success in London. It also emphasised that Apollo was now a major player with global contacts, capable of bringing the biggest musicals in the world to the UK. I'd first heard about the forthcoming stage production of *The Lion King* from my old colleague Peter Schneider, whom I'd met many years earlier when he was acting as general manager on our production of *One Mo' Time*. Peter and I had also worked together on *Camelot*, after which he had gone on to become head of Disney's animation division in the USA.

The film version of *The Lion King* had not only been a smash hit at the box office but had also featured brilliant music by Tim Rice and Elton John, including incredibly catchy hits like 'Circle of Life' and 'Can You Feel the Love Tonight'. It was the first ever animated soundtrack to be certified by the Recording Industry Association of America as achieving 'diamond' status (the equivalent of an album going platinum, times ten). If ever a film looked set to make a great stage musical, it was *The Lion King*.

You can imagine how fast my ears pricked up when Peter invited me to a preview of the new production that was due to debut in Minneapolis. I couldn't wait to jump on a Concorde to New York before catching an onward flight. While I was in

THE BALLOON BURSTS

Minneapolis I caught up with an old friend, Vince Egan, whom I'd worked with on live projects in the past; he had masterminded live productions of *Sesame Street* and stage spin-offs from *The Muppet Show*.

I enjoyed a wonderful time in Minneapolis, the highlight of which was the privilege of being among the first people in the world to see *The Lion King* on stage. It delivered everything that the movie had, and more besides. The production was due to open on Broadway later that year. If there was one thing I knew, it was that I was determined to bring it to London.

'It's magnificent,' I told Peter. 'I'll sign a contract to host it at the Lyceum whenever you're ready.'

However, our negotiations with Disney were very complex and dragged on for many months. Every time we were ready to sign, there seemed to be yet another set of hurdles to overcome. I think it nearly drove David Rogers to exasperation, as he handled the finer points of all our contractual agreements. One of the main sticking points was that Disney's marketing people weren't sure when they would be happy for a version of the show to be staged in London, hence they were unable to give us a date.

In the meantime, Disney invited me to attend the Broadway premiere of the show. It was a lavish event at the New Amsterdam Theatre on 42nd Street. Disney had recently acquired the lease to the building and had spent millions of dollars on renovations in order to transform it into a palace. The premiere was billed as a star-studded event, with Elton John and Tim Rice among those who were expected to attend. It was obvious that Disney was throwing everything including the kitchen sink at

The Lion King in order to make it a success. Nita and I flew to New York together for the event and despite the problems in our marriage we had a spectacular time, of which I have some happy memories.

I repeated my offer to sign a contract with Disney whenever they were ready, but in the meantime I had to fill the Lyceum with something else. This risked placing us in a slightly precarious position, but the important thing was that Disney indicated that the Lyceum was by far the best venue in London to host the show. I was relieved when we were able to fill the gap with a Cameron Mackintosh production of *Oklahoma!* that had previously enjoyed a great run at the Royal National Theatre. Better still, to our great delight, Her Majesty The Queen graciously chose to mark the occasion by paying her own visit to the Lyceum. In fact, she visited the theatre twice in the same day, first in the morning to meet the cast and then in the evening to see the show. The *Daily Mail* marked the occasion the following day by publishing an amusing cartoon that depicted the Queen and the Duke of Edinburgh getting into a black taxi, with a caption along the lines of 'Don't complain, this is how everybody goes to and from the theatre!' I later bought the original of the cartoon, which now hangs proudly on a wall at home.

Hosting shows like *The Lion King* and *Oklahoma!* at the Lyceum was a vindication of our decision to spend all those extra millions on a huge stage area, double dock doors and a sophisticated high tower. Without those facilities, it would simply not have been possible to host a production as complex as *The Lion King*. Although we still had no firm date, we were at least able to put tickets on sale on the basis that people could

THE BALLOON BURSTS

reserve their place. I recall that we banked in the region of two million pounds up front, which was actually no surprise. The show was already a hit on Broadway and it went on to gross a record amount of over $1 billion at the box office.

I think the fact that we had agreed to sign a deal without a date was a significant factor in securing the show for us, because it meant we effectively put Disney in a position where they could no longer raise any further hurdles. Interestingly, I'd recently read a book by Michael Eisner – the former Disney CEO who became president of the Walt Disney Company in 1998 – in which he described how he expected his team at Disney to negotiate their deals. This often involved changing the terms of an agreement even after details had been provisionally agreed. I was later introduced to Eisner at one of Andrew Lloyd Webber's parties.

'Your book was most useful,' I remarked to the Disney chief. 'It helped prepare us to use exactly the same negotiating tactics on your people!'

Thankfully, this made him smile. Needless to say, *The Lion King* continues to enjoy great success in London to this day and I think it's highly significant that the Lyceum has never again fallen dark.

★

My relationship with Nita showed no signs of improving. There were still periods when we could get along together, but these were growing increasingly few and far between. We could now afford an affluent lifestyle, but it seemed to make little difference.

Ironically, we'd actually been closer back in the days when we'd struggled to afford the deposit on a mortgage.

Our main home at Boars Hill was beautiful, having benefited from many improvements over the years. It was equipped with everything we needed; it even had a purpose-built panelled room just to accommodate Nita's huge collection of shoes and handbags. We also owned two properties on Marco Island in Florida, one of which was a superb beachfront retreat called The Hideaway. It had a carport at the front, so it was possible to drive right up to the house, step out and enjoy stunning views across the Gulf of Mexico. The other Florida property was a smaller place that we had purchased as an investment. We had come such a long way, and yet none of this made us happy when we were together.

We often argued about my work and the manner in which the company was managed. For many years Nita had been content for me to make most of the decisions about it, while she concentrated on bringing up Debbie, David and Simon. However, we had always split the ownership of our various assets between us. Apollo was a family business that we had jointly founded and built together, and Nita had been a director of the company since its inception. With the children now fully grown up, she wanted to become more involved in the business; but we often found ourselves arguing over petty things like who should get the best company mobile phone, rather than issues that actually mattered.

I loved Nita in so many different ways, but despite all her highly creditable contributions to our married life and to the company, she seemed increasingly unhappy. Her health began to

THE BALLOON BURSTS

be plagued by niggling chronic conditions that persisted despite seeing a number of therapists. She developed dental problems with her bite and suffered constantly from a bad back. Although she regularly saw a chiropractor in London and a private dentist in Bristol, neither condition seemed to clear up.

One source of disharmony between us was that she was frustrated by the amount of time I spent away from home, visiting different parts of the business. 'Oh, I see you're going off for another nice trip to the theatre, then?' she would say.

I'd do my best to explain that it was a necessary part of the job, but perhaps I should have listened more closely to the warning signs.

'When I go to one of our theatres, I'm not buying a ticket . . . I am working,' I would insist. 'I'm meeting producers, plotting and planning the next tours. I am keeping an eye on the business and always looking for something new, whether it's a show or a star.'

In the end, I suspect that Nita feared I was seeing other women, but that wasn't the case. Even if I'd been that way inclined – which I certainly wasn't – it would have been impossible to hide. The theatre world is a very small, close-knit community in which everybody gets to know everyone else's business. Nevertheless, the seed of doubt remained in Nita's mind, perhaps because in those days there was still a perception that a casting couch mentality existed in some parts of the industry. People worked long hours together and sometimes affairs would start and finish. Nita and I had a row over the fact that we'd previously decided to build some flats into the newly redeveloped Dominion Theatre site. It made perfect sense, both commercially and operationally. It added value to the property and also meant there was a place for production staff to stay if needed. Nita had a different view.

'We're not running a bloody knocking shop!' she complained, after becoming concerned that the flats could be used for illicit purposes.

We also clashed about the ownership structure of the business. Nita felt that she should own 51 per cent of company shares as a way of ensuring that she would continue to have a real say in the business. Our sons, Simon and David, also became shareholders after I agreed to forego some of my own holding. Perhaps by this stage I should have realised that the writing was on the wall for our marriage. It might have been better if we had simply agreed to divorce and split everything fifty-fifty, but for the sake of peace I agreed to her demands. Unfortunately, I failed to anticipate the repercussions that this would have later on.

★

We finally agreed a date with Disney for the grand opening of *The Lion King* in London. It would take place in the autumn of 1999, three months before the start of the new millennium. The halo effect of that and our many other projects led to a number of approaches from people who were interested in either buying the company or merging with us.

One interested group we spoke to were the people behind the London Trocadero entertainment complex at Piccadilly Circus. The property magnates Nigel Wray and Nick Leslau, who owned the site, were interested in exploring the possibility of

THE BALLOON BURSTS

a merger. However, we felt that our respective operations were too different from one another for it to be a realistic proposition. Another interested party was the sports magnate Jarvis Astaire, whom I'd come to know well through our mutual association with the Variety Club. He was keen to merge with us to avoid a sale of the stadium to the Football Association. That was an exciting prospect, but ultimately we couldn't see enough value in the deal for Apollo. Personally, I felt that we already had great partnerships with wonderful people like Jimmy Nederlander through the Dominion and Harry Crosbie at the Point in Ireland.

I wasn't particularly interested in selling the business, although I did wonder whether doing so would give Nita and me the opportunity we needed to start a new life away from the company and heal our differences. Our marriage problems had reached the stage of having a real negative impact on the business. Sam Shrouder later indicated to me that he had sensed Nita's growing dissatisfaction with life at Apollo. One thing that surprised him, and caused a great deal of disruption, was when she suddenly told him out of the blue that she no longer wanted him and his team to work from the office suite at Boars Hill. Sam was abruptly ordered to get out within two weeks and find a different base within the business. The upshot was that he and I were no longer working in the same building and we saw a lot less of one another.

The fact that Nita now had 51 per cent of the company's shares empowered her to act unilaterally. There were also times when she angrily aired her views about perceived shortcomings in front of senior people within the company like David Rogers and Steve Lavelle. The final blow as far as I was concerned was when she informed me that she wanted her interests to be independently represented on the board by John Jarvis of Jarvis Hotels. Perhaps it was indeed time to sell the business, in which case Nita and I could at least attempt to start a new life together living at the beach.

We even considered the possibly of a stock market flotation when we were approached by a large American company called SFX, founded by the broadcasting tycoon Robert F.X. Sillerman. He had diversified into promoting live entertainment and SFX was growing at a phenomenal pace; its management had grand ambitions to acquire a global network of promoters and tour operators. They were interested in taking over the Apollo Leisure Group as part of these worldwide expansion plans. It was an interesting proposition and I was willing to listen with an open mind, especially if there was a chance of me being able to continue in a new role at SFX. We signed a non-disclosure agreement and opened up confidential negotiations about a possible sale. Nita's representative, John Jarvis, was tasked with structuring a potential deal. We all knew and respected John, so I was happy for him to play a key role in exploring possibilities. We made a couple of trips to New York to discuss matters in more detail and eventually John negotiated a deal worth in the region of £150 million, minus net debt. It was a huge sum of money for a company that had originally been founded off the back of a single lease for a struggling venue in Manchester.

David suggested that if the deal went ahead, I should ask to become the new European chairman of SFX. It was a tempting opportunity because we would become an integral part of a global powerhouse – and Nita was very much in favour of selling. However, I still had reservations at the back of my mind as to whether or not it was the right thing to do. After all, it would mean giving up Apollo as an independent business. I decided to ask Jimmy Nederlander, my trusted colleague in the States, what he thought of the proposal. He was aghast.

'Paul, do *not* do this deal,' he told me bluntly. 'You have assets like the Lyceum, the Dominion, the Apollo Hammersmith and the Apollo Victoria. You will never get another opportunity to own magnificent theatres like those again.'

Jimmy was somebody I liked and respected. We shared a passion for wonderful old buildings, and I valued his advice.

'But they're willing to offer a lot of money,' I said, trying to convince myself just as much as Jimmy.

'What do you need money for?' he replied. 'You've already got enough money to stay at the Four Seasons, you eat in the best restaurants and you travel by Concorde. But if you sell the company, you'll always miss the things that you own today.'

His comments made me feel uneasy, but another part of me still hoped that it could work out for the best if we sold. After all, I'd have a new role at SFX, so I would still be working for the company that owned those wonderful theatres. What did it matter if Nita and I no longer actually owned them? Everything would be OK, I told myself.

An army of lawyers was appointed to draft an agreement and for a while I felt genuinely excited about the proposed deal. David Rogers had worked his socks off to reduce our net debt over the years, which meant we would receive in the region of £120 million from the proceeds of the sale. David also helped to negotiate a package including new roles at SFX for Steve Lavelle, Sam Shrouder and himself. Finally, SFX agreed to our proposal to make me European chairman, and in addition we would receive generous share options.

It was now time for SFX to prove they had the funds available. Their founder, Mr Sillerman, was not my favourite kind of person (a bit too pushy perhaps), but I knew that in future I would have to respect his views. Interestingly, SFX initially said they did not wish to include BCC (Barry Clayman Concerts) in the deal — but they later agreed to buy it for an extra £5 million, which Barry agreed to. Looking back, I think it would have been better if we'd kept BCC, which would at least have left me owning a significant foothold in the industry.

On the day the deal was expected to go through, I awoke with an uneasy feeling in my stomach. Nita was in Florida but I was due to meet John Jarvis, David Rogers and others in London, at a temporary boardroom in the Park Lane Hilton, to sign the paperwork.

When I arrived, I had an overwhelming feeling that my worst fears were about to come true and I would end up regretting the sale. I told David and John that I no longer wanted to go through with it. However, John and my son Simon said that Nita had agreed to sell as majority shareholder, and they suggested I should get on with signing the contracts.

I spent the next hour frantically trying to call Nita and let her know that I thought we should pull out. No matter how many times I rang, my calls remained unanswered.

'How much are we liable for in legal costs if we scrap the deal right now, at this moment?' I asked David.

THE BALLOON BURSTS

There was a pause as, with a strained expression, he estimated the lawyers' bills in his head.

'About half a million dollars,' he said quietly.

John and Simon reminded me again that Nita had issued full and final instructions to sell. Even if I were to pull out now, she would still have the right to redraft the agreement and unilaterally sell her controlling stake in the business. I had run out of options.

We signed the deal.

★

That evening, a group of us who had helped to build Apollo over the years went for a meal of fish and chips together at a restaurant in Marylebone called the Sea Shell (which was owned by Jim Whittell). For a group of people who were about to share the spoils of a multi-million-pound deal, with new jobs and share options in one of the world's biggest entertainment groups, we were strangely subdued. There was no popping of corks or wild celebrating. Instead, we chatted quietly on that summer evening about what the future might hold. It felt as if the balloon had burst – and Nita and I were the ones who had stuck a pin into it. We all did our best to put a brave face on things that night, but in my heart I feared we had made a dreadful mistake.

News of the deal was announced the following day. The *Evening Standard* ran a prominent story announcing that the sale of the company had sent shockwaves through the West End. It pointed out that SFX was already the world's largest operator of live entertainment in the USA, with eighty-two venues; in the past year alone it had staged over 13,000 events attended by 37 million people. Its acquisition of the Apollo Leisure Group would mean it was also the biggest theatre operator in Europe, with enormous power at its disposal. Robert Sillerman had issued a statement describing Apollo as the perfect complement to SFX's existing interests in music, theatre, sport and family entertainment.

Reading the article made me feel slightly better about things, and I began to see a future with SFX in a more positive light. After all, I was still in a position that most people could only ever dream about. The money we had received would also, I hoped, open the door for me to pursue new business interests of my own.

One such project that I was keen to develop was the Thomas Tucker popcorn brand, owned by a snack food business that had supplied Apollo with snacks for our cinemas and theatres. The founder of the popcorn business was a woman called Barbara Cheslyn-Curtis, who had started the company several years earlier. Since then it had expanded into other cinema groups, resorts and holiday parks throughout the UK. Barbara was interested in selling her company, so I agreed to buy it with a view to further expanding the business.

Later on, I also invested in starting up a private jet company that purchased a private plane which was available for hire. In the future we would also diversify into supplying pilots, and the electronics tycoon Alan Sugar would become one of our clients. We helped him to source his own private jet, which we then leased out when he wasn't using it. Alan was a tough negotiator,

THE BALLOON BURSTS

but he was always as good as his word. However, private jet rental is a difficult way to make money. In my experience the majority of wealthy people either want a plane of their own, which they own outright, or else they're quite happy to save cash by flying with EasyJet.

Despite these side projects my primary focus continued to be theatre and entertainment, even though I was now looking at that world through the eyes of SFX. I didn't yet know that within the space of a few months my life was going to take another unexpected turn, into the world of Premier League football – a whole new ball game for me, quite literally!

'Welcome to Everton'

The world was preparing to celebrate a new millennium as the year 2000 approached. During the build-up to New Year's Eve there was great excitement about what the twenty-first century might hold; it felt like a watershed moment for humankind. There was optimism about the future, but also a hint of trepidation. The newspapers were full of unfounded fears that computers would malfunction due to the so-called 'millennium bug', resulting in chaos and aeroplanes falling from the skies!

The general mood reflected my own personal situation; the previous year had been a watershed for me too. Although I was delighted with the price we had received for the Apollo Leisure Group, I still had some doubts about whether we'd really done the right thing in selling. My new role as European chairman of the enlarged SFX group meant I still had a say in the theatre empire we had built from nothing, but in my heart I knew that the new owners were the ones calling the shots. On the other hand, I had the time and the financial resources to pursue new business opportunities, even if I wasn't yet making the most of that.

While I was relaxing at home in Oxfordshire over the Christmas period an interesting item appeared in the press about Bill Kenwright, an old colleague of mine from the theatre world. Bill had always been an excellent theatre impresario and our venues had hosted many of his stage productions, but this newspaper article I'd spotted was about something different.

'Do you remember Bill Kenwright? It looks like he's finally agreed to buy Everton Football Club,' I said to Nita over breakfast. We were still just about on speaking terms at this point.

The news about Bill was an interesting piece of gossip, but it represented little more than that to us. We certainly didn't anticipate that it would be the start of six years of mayhem that would later see me drawn into a bitter public war for control of one of the country's most iconic football clubs. I should point out here that if you are reading this book but are not a fan of football, the next few chapters might seem like a bit of a rollercoaster. Don't worry if you can't follow all of the names. Just stick with me, and hopefully you'll still appreciate the ride.

Bill was a Merseysider and a lifelong Everton fan who had been on the board of the club since 1989. I knew he'd been trying to buy out its majority shareholder, Peter Johnson, for more than a year. It looked as if he was finally about to be successful, with a formal bid worth in the region of £20 million for Johnson's holding of approximately 68 per cent of Everton's shares. However, there was still a faint question mark over the funding arrangements, which not only required sufficient cash for the shares but also due diligence with regard to the club's debts, reportedly in the region of £17 million. With costs and fees, it would take the total to around £22 million for the acquisition of a majority share in the club.

I decided to give Bill a call on New Year's Eve to wish him a happy new year and applaud him for what appeared to be more or less a done deal.

'Congratulations about Everton. You must be delighted,' I said.

Bill was very upbeat. He was clearly excited, laughing and joking about what lay ahead. Everton had thumped Sunderland 5–0 at Goodison Park on Boxing Day, which seemed like a good omen. The local press on Merseyside had greeted the news with enthusiasm and the majority of Everton fans seemed to be delighted.

'Well done – now all you've got to do is make sure you've got the twenty million or so that it will cost!' I joked. I wished him well, rang off, and didn't think much more about it until he rang me back the following week.

'Remember our discussion on New Year's Eve about Everton?' he said.

'Yes, what about it?' I replied.

'Well, do you want a piece of it?' he asked.

This wasn't what I had been expecting, so I was caught off guard. Bill was inviting me to become part of the consortium that would soon own the club. It might have seemed like a mad idea – after all, unlike him, I didn't have any previous associations with Everton – but over the years I'd learned never to be too quick to dismiss an opportunity when it came my way. I might not be an expert when it comes to football, but I had been involved in plenty of interesting projects on Merseyside. I've known ever since my days back in Southport that the people in that part of the world are warm and welcoming, and they love their football. Along with my colleague Steve Lavelle at Apollo, I had also worked closely with the local authority in Liverpool to save the Liverpool Empire; so between Steve and myself, we had excellent contacts in the city. The Empire was still a great venue, which had recently hosted a successful run of Bill's stage production of the musical *Blood Brothers*.

The papers were full of speculation about how Bill was planning to restore Everton to its former glory. The Premier League was by now in its eighth season, having been founded in 1992, and it was already obvious that it would continue to grow financially at a phenomenal rate. Football had broken free from most of the problems that had tarnished the game during the '80s and '90s. It was family entertainment with a hard commercial edge, which is where I felt my own expertise lay. I knew I had plenty of business skills that would be useful if I joined Bill on his mission and I also felt, having worked with him in the past, that there was a mutual trust between us. I wasn't sure how much of the purchase price was being personally put up by Bill, but in a partnership situation I often favour the idea of having joint skin in the game. That was the way he and I had always handled things in the theatre when I'd invested in his shows.

I considered my options and then gave him a quick answer. 'Whatever you are putting in, I will put in too.'

Bill said he was currently in for approximately £7.5 million.

'I'll have the same as you, so call it £7.5 million,' I said.

That was how it started – I was on board. Looking back, I should have fastened my seat belt on the spot, because it would turn out to be an extremely bumpy ride.

'WELCOME TO EVERTON'

★

My first impression of Everton was that the club itself was like a grand old lady who had temporarily lost her way and stumbled. All that was needed was somebody to lift it up and give it some TLC in order to restore 'the Toffees' to their former glory. Everton had been a major force in English football during the 1980s and before then, it had also enjoyed a proud history. The team were league champions seven times between 1891 and 1970. The club then went on an upward trajectory after appointing Howard Kendall as player-manager in May 1981. Everton finished in eighth position in Kendall's first season at the helm – a big improvement on the previous year, when they had finished fifteenth. The following season, they were seventh. After that, in 1983/4, things really began to take off. Everton finished seventh in the league once again, but there were also epic cup runs that galvanised the fans. The first ever all-Merseyside Cup Final occurred in March 1984, when Everton and Liverpool drew goalless in the League Cup Final at Wembley. Everton lost the replay 1–0 at Maine Road. However, they made amends in the FA Cup by beating Watford 2–0 in the final to lift the club's first trophy in fourteen years.

By the following season Everton were eager to mount a serious challenge for the league title, but they were beaten by Spurs 4–1 at Goodison Park on the opening day. However, in October, they beat Liverpool 1–0 at Anfield in the Merseyside derby, and a week later they celebrated by crushing Manchester United 5–0. Everton were now a force to be reckoned with and the fans adored their beloved 'Blues'. They were crowned league champions at Goodison in early May with five games to spare. It looked as if they might pull off a treble, having also reached the finals of the European Cup Winners' Cup and the FA Cup. Everton outplayed Rapid Vienna in Rotterdam to win their first European trophy, but missed out on the FA Cup by losing 1–0 to Manchester United.

By rights Everton should have competed in the European Cup the following season, but they were denied their place after English clubs were banned from Europe following the Heysel disaster. Domestically, Everton finished runners-up in the league behind Liverpool in 1986. A year later, they were champions again in 1986/7 and this time it was Liverpool's turn to be runners-up. It had been a remarkable run of success, but sadly it was also to be the end of Everton's glory days.

Looking back, it's easy to see why the blue half of Merseyside welcomed the Kenwright bid to acquire the Toffees in January 2000. Apart from a solitary FA Cup victory in 1995, Everton had failed to lift another major trophy for thirteen years. Goodison Park, which had originally been constructed during the heyday of standing terraces, was now an ageing stadium with an all-seated capacity of around 40,000. Other leading clubs such as Arsenal and Manchester United were already planning to substantially boost their crowd capacities. In the case of Arsenal, they had recently unveiled plans to quit Highbury altogether and move to a new stadium.

Bill had originally tried to buy Everton back in 1994 but on that occasion he'd been beaten by Johnson, a successful entrepreneur who ran the Park Foods empire. By the time Bill was in a position to attempt to buy the club again, Everton had been through a particularly turbulent period. Johnson had become chairman but resigned four years later amid controversy. By then, Howard Kendall had been sacked after his third spell at Everton and replaced by Walter Smith, formerly a hugely successful manager at Rangers in Scotland. However, there was a major row during November 1998 when Johnson sold off star player Duncan Ferguson to Newcastle United in order to pay off some of Everton's debts. Smith was reportedly unaware of the deal and the fans were furious. In the furore that followed, Johnson quit and was replaced as chairman by Sir Philip Carter (who had previously been chairman during Everton's glory days in the '80s).

While Johnson was no longer chairman, he was still the majority shareholder with a 67.9 per cent stake in the club. Kenwright had spent the year since then desperately trying to buy Johnson's shares. He had almost succeeded after putting together an earlier bid with backing from HSBC, only for the bankers to terminate discussions after the bank reportedly became concerned by the club's debts. Having had his dreams shattered on that occasion, Bill was taking nothing for granted this time around. A deadline to complete the financial arrangements and all necessary due diligence was set for the 25th of January. Together with his fellow investors, Bill had made a formal offer in the region of £857 per share, valuing the club at around £30 million. That might sound like a snip at today's prices but it was a considerable sum at that time, especially for a club with an enormous overdraft and an ageing stadium.

'My mum and my partner Jenny still think I'm mad,' Bill told the *Liverpool Echo* in late December. 'It has been very difficult,' he continued. 'The HSBC bank pulling out was a huge blow.

But you just have to stay there and fight for it and in the end it was worth it.'[13]

In the days and weeks that followed, as the deadline to complete the deal in late January approached, Bill and I had several meetings to discuss our next steps. In addition to myself, his other major backers were Jon Woods and Arthur Abercromby, both of whom already had strong associations with Everton. Woods, who had made his fortune in computer software, was a lifelong fan and a member of the Everton Shareholders' Association. Abercromby, a successful building magnate, was already a director of the club and had been involved in Bill's attempt to buy Everton in 1994. The newspapers also speculated that the backers of the current deal would include the retail tycoon Sir Philip Green, but that was not the case. However, Bill and Sir Philip were indeed close friends and Bill would often turn to his good pal Green for advice, as I would later come to learn.

By the time the deadline arrived, the due diligence was completed and all the necessary paperwork was in place. We formed a limited company called True Blue Holdings, which would effectively be the managing majority equity partner in Everton Football Club, leaving a raft of minority shareholders also in place. I had initially misunderstood how things would be structured, because I'd assumed Bill and I would purchase our respective shareholdings directly, but instead we agreed to put the funds into True Blue Holdings. The consortium of Bill and myself, along with Woods and Abercromby, were named as the directors of the new company. It was a slightly messy arrangement because we didn't own the shares as individuals, which would complicate things later on. Instead, Bill and I each had approximately 33 per cent of True Blue Holdings, with Woods at 25.6 per cent and Abercromby at 7.3 per cent. In total, True Blue Holdings acquired almost 25,000 shares, which included all of Johnson's holding plus around a thousand shares from smaller stockholders. Bill and I put up the majority of the cash, each contributing the agreed £7.5 million, with Woods and Abercromby contributing the remainder.

In total, the four of us stumped up in the region of £21.5 million in order for True Blue Holdings to acquire over 70 per cent of club's shares (which was slightly more than Johnson had owned). The majority of the remaining shares were controlled via the Everton Shareholders' Association, which represented the raft of smaller shareholders. The upshot of all this financial planning was that through True Blue Holdings, Bill and I each effectively owned approximately 23 per cent of Everton Football Club. The relevant point to note was that no single individual among us controlled the magical 51 per cent of True Blue Holdings that would be required to unilaterally control the club. Instead, we were able to achieve control by acting together as a consortium through True Blue Holdings.

The success of our takeover bid was met with great jubilation on Merseyside. 'IT'S A DEAL! Kenwright's dream finally comes true,' screamed the front-page headline of the *Echo* alongside a picture of Bill arm in arm with his partner, actress Jenny Seagrove.

It was a remarkable achievement for Kenwright, who, as the newspapers were always keen to point out, had begun watching his beloved Everton from the terraces when he was a small boy.

How could we possibly turn that into an own goal?

★

There was no doubt in my mind at the time that there was enormous potential for us to transform Everton's fortunes. Not only did the club have a magnificent history, but it was what I regard as a 'family club'. By that I mean that Evertonians are collectively like a big community closely concentrated in and around the city, whereas Liverpool FC has more of an international support base. Of course, vast numbers of Reds fans (whom I also highly respect) live in Liverpool, but fans of the Blues are very much at the centre of the beating heart of the community. The club is revered and respected within the city as well as in the wider world of football, in a similar way to how Arsenal is regarded in London. David Moyes once described Everton as 'the people's football club' and was famously quoted as saying that the majority of people you met on the city streets were Everton fans.[14] That may or may not be completely true, depending on what end of Stanley Park you favour, but I would certainly agree with the sentiment. Furthermore, during the talks in the early '90s that led to the formation of the Premier League, Everton were regarded as one of England's 'big five' clubs alongside Manchester United, Liverpool, Arsenal and Tottenham Hotspur.

Everton were arguably no longer in that same position by the turn of the millennium, but our strong belief was that with the right plan we could restore the club to similar heights and beyond. However, in order to achieve our collective goal it was obvious to me that Everton needed complete modernisation. The first time I arrived at the club on a match day after we took control, it all felt chaotic. The fans in were in a buoyant mood and Bill was in his element, meeting and greeting everybody. He seemed to adore being seen and waved at by the supporters – I got the impression that he was revelling in the attention. It was my first chance to have a really good look around Goodison Park.

The club was clearly steeped in history but I couldn't help but think it was stuck in a bit of a time warp. Sir Philip Carter was among the group I joined for lunch that day. I'd previously come into contact with Sir Philip through his work as chairman of the Liverpool Empire Theatre Trust, and he struck me as a very traditional operator. He was a jovial, white-haired chap in his early seventies who had been around at Everton in one guise or another for well over two decades, having first been appointed as a director of the club back in 1975. I got the impression that he liked to conduct matters in much the same way that the club had always done things in the past. That was understandable, given that he had presided over Everton's mid-1980s heyday, but it seemed to me that what the club really needed was to be dragged into the twenty-first century.

One thing that caused me to raise an eyebrow was the fact that men and women were seated at separate tables in the directors' dining room. Sir Philip and his wife, Lady Rita, would greet all the guests upon arrival.

'Welcome to Everton,' Sir Philip would say, rather grandly.

The men would then be ushered to their table while Lady Rita organised where the women would sit. It all felt slightly pompous. Guests were later offered a slice of an Everton cake, which was decorated with blue-and-white icing (I later discovered that a similar cake was ordered for every match). It all struck me as being more like a scene from a period drama than a modern-day football club in the elite Premier League. Looking back, it reminds me a little of a scene from *Downton Abbey*.

Airs and graces aside, the club itself was in a financial mess. It had been living beyond its means, borrowing and burning through its financial reserves. By the close of the financial year at the end of May 2000, Everton had accrued annual losses of over £11 million, which came on top of a £10 million loss the previous year. The club's overdraft stood at £15 million, despite previous efforts to lower it by selling players. The annual interest alone on the overdraft came to over £1 million. For a club with a turnover at the time of just £28 million, the Annual Report and Accounts made grim reading that year. As for any worthwhile budget for new players, forget it. I could only hope and pray that we hadn't spent too much on those blue-and-white cakes.

★

I noticed right away how close Bill was to Walter Smith. The first thing Bill had done, even before the ink was dry on the final deal to buy the club, was to offer Smith an extension to his contract as team manager. In announcing it to the press, Bill was careful to manage the expectations of fans. He asked for their patience and said it would take time to turn the club around. Kenwright spoke to the *Liverpool Echo* again in January, two days after we acquired the club. He gave a long interview that praised Smith and made it clear that the Scot was to be the foundation stone of Kenwright's blueprint for restoring Everton to greatness. Bill also spoke about how close they were, praising Smith's sense of humour and even commenting that the Scot had a 'twinkle in his eye'.

The paper pointed out that Smith had been the one who had doomed Peter Johnson by flushing out the truth over the Duncan Ferguson transfer, leaving the door ajar for Bill to buy the club. The article also made it clear that there would be no big transfer bankroll in the near future.

Privately, I didn't always share Bill's enthusiasm for Smith, although I felt the manager was a decent man. He had a fantastic track record in Scotland, but there would be difficult financial decisions ahead and I wasn't sure it was healthy for Bill to be so personally close to the manager. At the end of Smith's first season in charge Everton had been in the relegation zone with just six games to go, although they eventually managed to finish in 14th place. The team's performance had improved since then, but I knew that unless we could turn things around relatively quickly there was only a certain amount of time that we could reasonably expect fans to be patient. Meanwhile, Bill would invite Smith to the openings of his glamorous theatre shows and on one occasion the pair even travelled to Las Vegas together. They had developed a friendship, as opposed to a business relationship between the owner of a club and a team manager. I was concerned that if things were ever to go drastically wrong on the pitch, Bill's closeness to Smith could become an issue.

'I think you should consider putting a bit of professional distance between yourself and Walter,' I later said to Bill. 'If the fans ever turn on him then there's a risk you'll go down with him.'

Bill shrugged this off and replied with words to the effect that he would look after the footballing side of things, including the relationship with Smith, while I should concentrate on improving the business aspect of the club. Of course, Bill and I still had a good relationship at this point. We had traded together during my time with the Apollo Leisure Group, working on shows that we had jointly promoted and put into theatres. Our initial conversation about Smith didn't amount to much, but later on, when things started to get tougher, it would become more of an issue. When I was previously in Southport I was friendly with Peter Robinson, the chief executive of Liverpool FC at the time, and he used to invite me to go and watch the odd game, so I had an interest in football – but there was no point in me pretending to be an expert about matters on the pitch. So it did make sense for me to concentrate on the commercial aspects of the club.

I discovered that Everton employed around a thousand people, the majority of whom were part-time staff working on match days. However, the club's full-time staff included a team of nearly sixty people who were described as 'management and administration'. It seemed to me like a large number to cover a relatively limited set of duties back then compared with today. I seem to recall that, among other things, these duties included ordering the black bin liners. I was also concerned about the number of company cars and mobile telephones that seemed to be in existence. When I raised issues like this with Bill, he seemed fairly relaxed about it. He probably felt it would take time to fix, but I was surprised at his total lack of concern. In his theatre dealings, he had always struck me as being fantastically on top of financial matters, studying the figures morning, noon and night. He would insist on receiving several updates a day about his theatre ticket sales.

We had only just acquired the club, but I felt we should take action as soon as possible. However, I suspected that first and foremost Bill was more interested in the romantic aspect of owning a football club. He simply adored being Mr Everton and there was never any doubting his passion for the club. Unfortunately, you can't run a multi-million-pound business on passion alone. To begin with it wasn't too much of a problem, as I was more than happy to get stuck into dealing with the harsh commercial realities that we faced; but there were niggling little doubts in my mind about how things would unfold.

★

Away from the boardroom, the team enjoyed a decent cup run on the pitch early that year, eventually reaching the quarter-finals of the FA Cup when we were drawn against Aston Villa at Goodison Park. This brought in a minor cash windfall thanks to the extra gate receipts and an additional £300,000 in fees from Sky TV, but it was really just a drop in the ocean. I knew that what Everton truly needed was a complete overhaul of the club's finances. We finished in 13th place at the end of the 1999/2000 season: hardly a spectacular achievement, but at least it was comfortably above the drop zone by seventeen points. Besides, by the end of the season in May we were already working on a new plan for something spectacular, with the potential to truly transform our financial position. Everton needed a new home – and I was soon to discover that there was a golden opportunity on the horizon.

A Stadium Fit for Kings

One thing the city of Liverpool is renowned for today is its rich cultural heritage. Its history can be traced to the year 1207, when King John ordered the creation of a new borough called 'Livpul'. The first ever commercial wet dock was completed on the River Mersey in 1715, and it's estimated that by the beginning of the nineteenth century, 40 per cent of all global trade passed through Liverpool's waterfront.

The bustling port included King's Dock, which opened in 1785, and Albert Dock, which opened in 1846. During the 1960s, Liverpool revolutionised the global music and fashion scene as the birthplace of The Beatles. However, prosperous times rarely last forever. By the 1980s, the fortunes of the city had changed and it was associated with social deprivation and poverty. Liverpool struggled to shake off the impression created by the Toxteth riots in 1981, which were followed by a period of political turmoil in the middle of the decade when the city council clashed with Margaret Thatcher's government. By the year 2000 Liverpool had lost its status as the region's leading commercial centre, having been overtaken by Manchester.

However, Liverpool's reputation for social deprivation was only one side of the story. The city still had much to offer and as the new millennium approached, the council made an effort to boost its image through a number of contemporary arts projects. These included a biennial festival of visual arts that was launched with the support of the Littlewoods family (who had previously enjoyed a long association with Everton Football Club). The festival became the largest of its kind in the UK, rivalling similar events in Venice and Sydney. My own company, Apollo, had played a role in the cultural renaissance of the regional arts scene by taking over the Liverpool Empire, which hosted a production of *Les Misérables*.

Most importantly of all, in January of the year 2000 the city council announced an ambitious proposal for a massive regeneration plan. This aimed to reverse the economic decline of Merseyside by delivering investment of £1.5 billion, of which £500 million would come from public funds. The combined effect of all this activity would not only transform the city, it would create a once-in-a-lifetime opportunity for Everton to build a magnificent new stadium in a prime position on the city's historic waterfront.

The council and its development partners were keen to make the dockside as desirable as possible as a destination for visitors and international cruise ships. Hence, a new sports and entertainment arena equipped with world-class facilities was designated as a flagship project within the official regeneration plan. It was estimated that the plan would create in excess of 10,000 new jobs in tourism. The council had previously announced in November 1998 that Liverpool would also bid to become the European Capital of Culture. A target year of 2007 was set for this goal, aiming to coincide with the 800th anniversary of Liverpool being granted its borough status (although the target was later revised to 2008). The council hoped to emulate the success of Glasgow, which had seen a 40 per cent jump in tourism after becoming a European Capital of Culture in 1990. Glasgow built upon that to become the UK's third biggest tourist destination, after London and Edinburgh.

Looked at from the perspective of my own background in arts and entertainment, Liverpool City Council's strategy was intelligent, thoughtful and highly credible. It had the potential to generate enormous opportunities for future generations of Liverpool residents. It also had the potential to be a game-changer for Everton Football Club.

★

It was clear that Everton needed to either vastly expand its old home or find a new stadium altogether. Redeveloping Goodison was simply not viable; the practical challenges and constraints were too great. During the 1966 World Cup Everton had been selected to host five games including a semi-final, but the grandeur of the stadium had long since faded despite the addition of a three-tier main stand in 1971. Prominent areas of the stadium were starting to look tired and dated. It was telling that during the Euro '96 tournament, Goodison did not host a single game. What the club needed more than anything, to enable it to keep pace with its rivals, was a new home. A modern stadium in the right location would enable Everton not only to expand its capacity, but also to develop new revenue streams in addition to traditional gate receipts.

The Premier League was already growing fast as a commercial entity, and clubs like Manchester United and Arsenal were planning a future in which corporate facilities at larger stadiums would dramatically increase their revenues on match days. In the case of Everton, a new stadium presented an even bigger financial opportunity than just corporate entertaining. If the project could be aligned with the city council's plans to redevelop the city, then Everton could locate itself at the heart of the regeneration zone. This would benefit everybody connected with the club, not just the so-called 'prawn sandwich' brigade to which Roy Keane famously alluded.

On 27 January 2000 – two days after Bill and I successfully completed the purchase of Everton – the council released details of its regeneration plan to the public. It included a proposal for a 'world-class cultural and leisure facility' on the site of King's Dock, which had closed in 1972. There were also plans for a new financial hub on the waterfront along with improved links between the city's Pier Head and Albert Dock, plus upgrades to the main shopping centre along with redevelopment of the area around Lime Street. The council intended to apply for funding from the European Union under the Objective 1 programme – a huge pool of cash set aside for the development of regions that, in the view of the EU, were 'significantly falling behind the rest of Europe'.

The proposal for a cultural and leisure facility at King's Dock was highlighted as a priority. King's Dock is approximately four miles from Goodison Park and located close to the city centre. So my view was, why not incorporate a new football stadium into the leisure complex on the same site? It made perfect sense.

A STADIUM FIT FOR KINGS

The cherry on the cake from Everton's point of view – incredible as it may seem today – was that a substantial amount of the cost of a new stadium could potentially be paid for from public funds that were set aside to rejuvenate the city as part of the regeneration plan.

In addition to top-flight football, the plan could create an opportunity to use the stadium for other world-class events on non-match days. It would be a grander version of the strategy I had adopted during my time at the council in Southport, where building a new theatre alongside other leisure facilities in an entertainment hub had helped to transform the fortunes of the town.

I decided to call my old colleague Steve Lavelle, who had done such a magnificent job at the Lyceum. Together at Apollo, we had specialised in developing and redeveloping entertainment venues, so it was a no-brainer for us to explore the possibilities at King's Dock.

'Can you come up to Liverpool and take a look at the council's plans to redevelop the city centre?' I asked him. 'I think it might create an opportunity for Everton to benefit.'

In the days and weeks that followed, Steve made meticulous enquiries and discreetly spoke to his Merseyside contacts. When he reported back, he was in a positive mood.

'It would obviously require significant investment, but in principle there is definitely enough space for a fantastic new stadium at King's Dock,' he told me.

Meanwhile, the city council's leadership were throwing all their weight behind the regeneration programme. They had reached out to every MP on Merseyside, along with MEPs and the Government Office for the North West.

In the past, Everton had voiced an ambition to expand Goodison Park into a 55,000-seat stadium, but with the benefit of hindsight those proposals were doomed. They became bogged down in red tape, planning issues and objections from local residents. The possibility of moving to a new stadium had first been flagged up in 1996, when Peter Johnson suggested leaving Goodison. His comments stirred up a hornet's nest and led to the formation of a supporters' group called 'Goodison for Everton', which voiced strong objections. Ironically, Sir Philip Carter was chairman of the Merseyside Development Corporation until 1998 and might have been in a good position to help the club navigate through the stadium issue, yet somehow Everton made zero progress.

I felt it was time to have a more detailed discussion about the matter with Bill Kenwright. I had huge respect for Bill and everything that he has achieved in the theatre industry, but I was unsure what his reaction would be. At Everton, he was always very focused on trying to win the next match and celebrating afterwards, but I sometimes feared that could be a distraction from the long-term picture. He was always keen to sign great players and there's no doubt that his sentiments were admirable from a fan's perspective. However, in my view the best way to build lasting success on the pitch was by creating a sustainable long-term financial structure. To be fair to Bill, when I sat down with him to discuss a way forward with regard to the stadium he was very positive and open-minded.

'We need to do our homework and put together a detailed proposal,' I said. 'I think we should seriously consider relocating to King's Dock. It would potentially make a perfect home for

Paul Gregg and Yoshiko pictured together on their wedding day at the Kamikawa Shrine and temple on Hokkaido island in Japan.

Paul and Yoshiko pictured together on a visit to a summer festival at Asahikawa in Hokkaido, Japan.

Paul Gregg and Yoshiko on their wedding day with guests on Hokkaido island in Japan, pictured by Oleg Mikheev.

The restored auditorium at the Lyceum begins to take shape.

Left: This image shows the extent of space required in order to create the fly tower at the Lyceum.

Right: Fallen dark . . . the Lyceum Theatre boarded-up prior to renovation work in 1993.

Above: The England football team for the 1990 World Cup with Paul at a Variety event.

Above: A booklet designed by Paul Gregg during lockdown dedicated to his 'Japanese princess' Yoshiko.

Left: Andrew Lloyd Webber accepts a Variety award.

Knockout . . . Boxing champ Frank Bruno at a Variety event during Paul's time as Chief Barker of the charity.

Margaret Thatcher is presented with an award by Paul at a black tie dinner in 1990.

Paul Gregg (right) shakes hands with a Chang Beer executive as they show off a new Everton shirt in front of a portrait photo of Wayne Rooney during a contract signing ceremony in Bangkok in July 2004.

Prince Charles chats with David Rogers (centre) and Adrian Leggett of Apollo Leisure Group.

HM Queen Elizabeth II arrives for the opening of the newly renovated Scarborough Outdoor Theatre in May 2010.

The Lyceum as it is today. The Lion King has continued its run for nearly 25 years and is still going strong.

The upper levels of the Lyceum Theatre following completion of restoration work by the Apollo Leisure Group.

The lower level of the auditorium, facing towards an orchestra pit and stage.

Artwork designed by Paul in *Lockdown Love*.

Everton and the cash it could generate would eventually enable you to buy all the players you want.'

Bill had previously witnessed the negative reaction when Johnson had hinted at a move, so he was keen to tread with caution; but I think that in his heart he probably knew that the club would eventually need to leave Goodison. From my perspective, I was convinced that unless we moved, Everton would languish in the wrong half of the table for the next twenty years.

'However, if we build a stadium as part of a world-class complex then it can also be used for things other than football. It will help to create a mountain of cash for the club and the community,' I mused. 'We could be talking about rock concerts, conferences, exhibitions – you name it. I think we need to meet with the city council as soon as possible and commission a team of architects.'

Bill was impressed by the concept and we agreed to open a formal dialogue with the council and Liverpool Vision, an urban regeneration company that had been formed to implement the strategic development framework for the city centre and its waterfront. In addition to the council, the other major parties involved in the Liverpool Vision project were the North West Development Agency and English Partnerships (which owned the site at King's Dock). If Everton were to win the right to build a new stadium on the waterfront, it would be necessary for the club to put forward a formal bid to become the city's preferred development partner. In order to ensure all other options were explored, Everton also commissioned a feasibility study about what the future might hold if the club decided to stay put in its current home.

In the meantime, Bill wanted to make some cosmetic improvements to Goodison Park, which made good sense for the benefit of fans. We agreed that I would manage all of the logistical and technical aspects for the specification of any new stadium, assisted by Steve Lavelle. In order to get the ball rolling Everton appointed a company called Houston Securities, which Steve and I had formed after selling Apollo to SFX, to compile the King's Dock bid on behalf of the football club. This would leave Bill free to liaise with Walter Smith about more immediate matters. Bill and I still had a great rapport at this stage of our relationship, so it was possible for us to make good progress. Our respective shares in True Blue Holdings meant that when we were in agreement we could potentially make quick decisions in order to work towards a bright future.

★

It was a busy summer. Walter Smith needed to put together a squad that could improve upon a disappointing finish to the previous campaign. Unfortunately, the only way the club could realistically afford to bring in new players was by selling existing talent, which defeated the object. We certainly wanted to avoid having to sell Nick Barmby, who was arguably our best player. However, any such decision was made for us when Barmby himself told Smith that he wanted to quit in order to join Liverpool. This was regarded as sacrilege in the eyes of Evertonians – and it presented Bill with a major headache. He was forced to spend a day in London trying to agree new terms with Barmby and his agent, but the lure of a rumoured £30,000 a week at Anfield under Gerard Houllier was too great. Barmby had started more games at Everton than any other player the preceding season, and he was the second-highest scorer that year (behind Kevin Campbell), but Blues fans would never forgive him for his decision.

'It was hearing he had used six of the worst words in the English language as far as Everton fans are concerned. He had said: "I want to play for Liverpool," Bill told the BBC.[15]

In truth, Barmby probably did us a favour. His contract only had a year or so left to run, yet we received a fee of £6 million, which at least gave Walter Smith some breathing space to look for new signings. Interestingly, it was Barmby's third multi-million-pound transfer in the space of five years. Middlesbrough had signed him from Spurs for £5.25 million. He later arrived at Everton for £5.75 million and he was now off with another huge deal. This merry-go-round in the football transfer market was new to me. It was something that, later, would come to frustrate me a great deal. I felt that agents in general had far too much influence over clubs and players, although it was clear that Barmby had left Everton by his own free will.

I continued to have my reservations about Smith. Barmby's departure seemed like a case in point: there didn't appear to be a great deal of mutual respect in his relationship with the manager. However, Smith did at least put the cash towards signing some players who looked as if they might show promise. They included Alessandro Pistone (for £2.75 million), Steve Watson (£2.5 million), Thomas Gravesen (£2.5 million), Niclas Alexandersson (£2.2 million) and Alex Nyarko (£4.5 million). The biggest headline-grabber of all was the return of Duncan

Ferguson, who transferred back to Everton from Newcastle United for £3.75 million. Finally, Paul Gascoigne, England's 1990 World Cup hero, joined on a free transfer. Gazza was by now in the twilight of his career, but the move at least gave fans plenty to talk about.

Meanwhile, Everton raised £2 million by selling John Collins plus a further £2.5 million for Don Hutchison, who had fallen out with Smith over his contract.

The new season therefore started with reasonably high hopes owing to the fact that it was the club's first full campaign under our new ownership. Bill promoted Everton's club secretary, Michael Dunford, to the new role of chief executive (which in reality was not much different to his old role). Dunford attempted to set the tone in a newspaper interview with *The Evertonian*, commenting that the next two or three years would be make or break for the club.

'It doesn't bear thinking about if we cannot achieve some success in the next three years,' he said. 'It frightens me to death. Not being successful is just not an option for the club.'[16]

This was a valid point. During the summer, Bill had somehow managed to authorise Smith to splash out over £18 million on players. Unfortunately, despite having sold a number of players, the club's overdraft and bank loans continued to rise. In order to make up the shortfall the club was hoping for a windfall deal with the US internet giant NTL, which would have considerably eased the financial situation. NTL had already agreed to pump around £235 million into English football by signing deals with ten other Premier League clubs, including Liverpool. Bill had a team negotiating with NTL, but sadly the deal fell through at the last minute, leaving yet another hole in our finances.

We were forced to talk to bankers, who agreed to be patient with us. By the end of the financial year in May 2001, Everton's Annual Report and Accounts stated that the club had spent a net £10 million on strengthening the playing squad, having eventually raised a sum of £10.7 million from player disposals). However, overall losses for the year were nearly £3.7 million. Worryingly, the amount owed by the club in bank loans and over-drafts had by now swollen to over £18.5 million (a year-on-year increase of over £3 million).

Nor was there eventually much to cheer about on the pitch. Everton stayed in the bottom third of the table for most of the campaign due to injuries and poor performances, eventually finishing in 16th position. Sir Philip Carter later acknowledged in his chairman's statement that Smith's injury-prone team had failed to deliver.

'It is clear that we under-achieved; to suggest that there is plenty of room for improvement would be to understate things,' he wrote.[17]

Thankfully, it wasn't all doom and gloom. The King's Dock proposal continued to gather pace – and the good news was that the city council confirmed it was willing to throw its weight and money behind the new stadium.

★

The recently appointed chief executive of Liverpool City Council, David Henshaw, was nobody's fool. He was a Liverpudlian by birth and had previously been council chief in Knowsley, where he'd attracted investment from corporate entities such as Jaguar and QVC. He had a friendly demeanour, with a rounded face and a stubbly beard, but beneath the welcoming smile lurked a steely determination. His brief was to implement change and regenerate the city with the support of the elected council leader, Mike Storey. Henshaw was extremely competent and his role would later earn him a knighthood. He became a great ally in Everton's bid to relocate at King's Dock.

From our early meetings with Henshaw, it was obvious that the council's leadership was obsessed with ensuring that its bid for European Capital of Culture was successful. Their vision for King's Dock was to create something unique that didn't exist at the time in the North West: a multipurpose arena that would act as a magnet to draw people to the region. From the council's perspective, combining Everton's new stadium with a cultural and entertainment hub at King's Dock was a winner. It would add enormous appeal to King's Dock as an anchor destination and bring people into the cultural complex on a regular basis.

The original designs for what we hoped would become Everton's magnificent new home were breathtakingly beautiful. The *Liverpool Echo* described the concept as a 'stadium fit for kings'. The intention was to build the UK's premier venue: a brand new 55,000-seat stadium, with a huge glass-fronted facade that faced the waterfront. The stadium was equipped with a sliding roof and a retractable pitch so that the arena could be used for multiple different types of event. When not being used for football, the pitch would glide away on a rolling platform into a protected area outside of the main stadium, where ground staff could nurture the turf within a landscaped garden. The manner in which the pitch retracted reminded me of *Thunderbirds*, the TV series in which a swimming pool on Tracy Island slides away to enable a rocket to take off!

'They're also building a retractable pitch at Schalke in Germany, so we'll need to go out there to take a good look at how it works,' Steve Lavelle explained. 'There's also a multi-purpose arena at Ajax in Holland, but nobody in the world has done anything quite as ambitious as what we're planning.'

In addition to the new stadium, there was plenty of room at King's Dock to locate new housing nearby, including next to the protected gardens where the pitch would be stored. I imagined that Evertonians would love the idea of watching from their bedroom windows while the magical turf was rolled in and out of the stadium! The council's strategy called for a 'major attraction of international significance', which was exactly what we planned to deliver. Steve and I knew from our experiences at Apollo and SFX that if any international stars wanted to play in the north of England, they were currently choosing the Manchester Arena (which had a capacity of around 21,000). SFX had links to 75 per cent of the world's major rock acts, but I knew from first-hand experience that Liverpool was simply not on the map at that time as far as the world's biggest names were concerned. However, a stadium at King's Dock, which could convert into an indoor arena with a capacity of 55,000, had the potential to change that forever. It was a point that I was keen to impress upon Bill.

'We'll be able to grab attention from Manchester by pulling in all the biggest acts,' I explained. 'Instead of playing three nights in Manchester, the biggest stars in the world will reach the same audience in a single night at King's Dock. It means that Everton can play Arsenal one day, and the stadium can host a concert by Madonna the following day.'

The halo effect would build the appeal of Everton as a brand internationally and add enormous muscle to our marketing power. I could visualise the impact of an international rock star performing an encore wearing an Everton hat or scarf, with the subsequent images flashed all around the world!

The plans also included provision for international athletics events, with the lowest tier of seating removable to make room for a running track. Beyond that, we intended to use modern technology to make the match-day experience as enjoyable as possible for fans. There would be interactive TV screens on the back of every seat, similar to the ones used on planes. Fans would be issued with season tickets in a format similar to a credit card, the idea being that you could then use your card to check in at the game and order food and drinks for half-time via the screen. That would also create an opportunity for club sponsors to connect with fans, maximising the club's marketing and merchandising revenue. While relaxing before a game, you might also want to place a bet, order some club merchandise, or even watch the highlights of last week's game. The possibilities seemed endless.

We did our initial research privately to establish the viability of the project, but in June of 2000 our hand was forced into publicly sharing details while we were still at an early stage. Rick Parry, the chief executive of Liverpool FC, announced that Everton's closest rivals were considering a move of their own to a new stadium (which would have seated 70,000). Their plans eventually

A STADIUM FIT FOR KINGS

came to nothing, but it led to a rash of speculation about what Everton might do. There was a perception that we were being left behind and Bill reacted to this by confirming that Everton had met with David Henshaw to discuss various options, including a brief mention of a potential site at King's Dock. Bill's tone remained cautious, implying that he didn't necessarily want to leave Goodison Park, but that a move might be a last resort.

A week later, another big story appeared in the press containing the first tangible details of our proposal for the stadium at King's Dock, including the retractable roof and pitch. Once again the official tone was cautious, with a senior source at the club stating that Everton's priority was still to try to expand its current home. In fact, there was no chance by this stage of redeveloping Goodison Park. The feasibility study we had commissioned made it clear that any redevelopment would be fraught with problems. Unless we could find a new home, Everton risked being left further behind by Manchester United and Liverpool. It was true that leaving Goodison would no doubt be a wrench for every Evertonian, but even the Goodison die-hards were beginning to change their views. Our fears of a backlash proved unfounded, and a newspaper phone poll of the fans showed overwhelming support for the King's Dock proposal.

From this point onwards, Bill became a public champion of the scheme and Steve and I generally enjoyed a good working relationship with him. Steve and I were assigned to be the driving force for delivering the bid to become the preferred development partner of Liverpool Vision. Together we put in an enormous amount of work and engaged with all the major parties involved in the decision, including English Partnerships and the North West Development Agency. We faced stiff competition from a number of rival bidders – including a proposal to turn King's Dock into a Venice-like network of canals around a multiplex cinema – hence we were determined to do our very best. Steve and I were, of course, still colleagues together at SFX (which later became known as Clear Channel Entertainment), which meant that we had access to some of the best experts in the field. A few months earlier we had travelled to Germany on SFX business to meet with a team of architects at a company called HOK Sport Venue Event (remember that name, I'll tell you more about them later). HOK were involved in a proposal to enhance Munich's Olympic Stadium, which had hosted the 1974 World Cup final, so that it could also be used as a venue for concerts and events. The Munich proposal was kicked into the long grass due to local issues, but it meant that HOK had an enormous amount of knowledge that we were able to draw upon. They were completely confident that they could create a football stadium that would double up as a home for Everton and an arena that could host up to two hundred major events a year.

In addition to HOK, we employed the very best property and project management consultants. These included Franklin & Andrews, JLL Property Valuation, and Amsterdam Arena Ltd in Holland. The Dutch team were also leading experts in specialist arena projects and were involved in developing a home for Ajax at the Johan Cruyff Arena. Other partners included Bovis Lend Lease and a local leisure property company called Neptune. Altogether, we had created a world-class task force with formidable expertise. The plan was to deliver the 55,000-seat stadium by June of 2006. We initially hoped the cost would be in the region of £125 million, but by the time the bid was formalised this had been adjusted to £155 million. That included the retractable roof and pitch, enabling the venue to host everything from rock concerts to American-style motorsport events featuring 'monster trucks'.

In July of 2001, we achieved a major victory when it was announced that our bid had secured us the status of preferred development partner. We now had a period of up to a year to further refine our plans before submitting them for final approval.

To say that we were ecstatic would be an understatement. 'Bloody hell – we've won!' was my first reaction.

Bill and I celebrated by jumping on a plane to Germany with Steve for an update on the progress that FC Schalke were making with their own efforts to install a retractable pitch. The mood back on Merseyside was jubilant. The leader of Liverpool council, Mike Storey, told the press the development was 'great news for Everton and the entire city'.

Our next task was to put together a detailed business plan and an overview of the funding proposals. The final plan for the King's Dock development also included a state-of-the-art cinema complex, commercial offices, a family entertainment centre, a wellbeing clinic, a nightclub, shops, bars and restaurants, not to mention a large housing development. The total cost of the entire development, including the stadium, was budgeted at £296.8 million. (Details are contained in the tables below.) The new stadium would be held on a 999-year lease in the name of a new public–private company called the Waterfront Stadium and Arena (WSA Ltd), which would be a joint venture between Everton and the three public bodies involved in Liverpool Vision. Initially, it was proposed that Everton's ownership stake in WSA would be 49 per cent, along with English Partnerships (25.36 per cent), the North West Development Agency (12.82 per cent) and Liverpool City Council (12.82 per cent). We later suggested this be amended to a straight 50–50 split between Everton on the one hand, and on the other, the three public bodies, who would own 50 per cent of WSA between them. In order to provide fairness to the taxpayer, Everton would pay an affordable rent based on number of games and 10 per cent of ticket sales. Hence the club would technically be both partially a landlord (through its 50 per cent share of WSA) and also a tenant, with a lease to play at the stadium. It offered the peace of mind of jointly owning the stadium through the public–private company.

Development costs (for whole of King's Dock)

Multi-purpose Arena	£155 m
Cinema (including Fit Out)	£4.3 m
Commercial Offices	£20.5m
Family Entertainment Centre, Wellbeing Clinic, Nightclub	£4.3 m
Retail – including Restaurants and Bars	£7.8 m
Residential	£83.5 m
Hotel (excluded)	n.a.
Service / Infrastructure Costs	£7.7 m
Design Fees	£13.7 m
Total Estimated Cost Source: Franklin + Andrews	**£296.8 m**

Funding sources for stadium

Public Sector Partners – EP, NWDA, LCC	£30 m
Everton FC	£30 m
Commercial Mortgage	£25m
Private Sector (Guaranteed Minimum)	£35 m
Objective 1 ERDF	£35 m
Total (Guaranteed Maximum Price) *Source: Houston Securities*	**£155 m**

A substantial share of the £155 million cost of building the stadium would be paid for through grants and public funding that amounted to £65 million (£30 million of which was to come jointly from English Partnerships, the North West Development Agency, and Liverpool City Council – with a further £35 million coming from the EU's European Regional Development Fund). Another £35 million would come from private funding (primarily from the profits of the residential element of the scheme) and £25 million from a commercial mortgage.

Everton's share of the costs was to be a relatively modest £30 million. In return for this sum, the club would become the largest single shareholder in the stadium through WSA Ltd and the club would acquire a 125-year lease that granted it the exclusive right to play football in Everton's new home.

It was the deal of the century. Not only was it a golden opportunity for Everton, it was a chance to put the whole of Liverpool on the front foot in terms of international tourism. I said as much in an interview with the local media in which I stated: 'We could say to every major rock artist in the world:

"Come to the home of The Beatles. Play in one of the best arenas in the world."[18]

Our future as a club was looking very bright indeed – or so I thought.

A Disaster for Everton

The situation with Walter Smith reached crisis point in March 2002. Everton had begun the season with a victory over Charlton, but by Christmas the team had managed just six wins. On Boxing Day, Smith's side lost 2–0 at home to Manchester United. From that point onwards, Everton continued to languish in the bottom half of the table for the rest of the season.

Smith's tactics and transfer dealings continued to be called into question. The summer had seen the departure of two of the squad's most promising players, Francis Jeffers and Michael Ball, after they became embroiled in contract squabbles. Their sale raised a much-needed £14.5 million, which meant that for the time being the club's overdraft didn't expand. Many fans said they found Smith's tactics messy and confusing, as was his decision in February to sign David Ginola (who was regarded as well past his prime) on a free transfer from Aston Villa. By now the Everton supporters were no longer prepared to accept any more excuses about injuries or lack of funds. It was clear that the team was going nowhere, and we began to receive a large amount of criticism aimed directly at Smith and the board.

Our progress with regard to King's Dock had at least given everyone a lift, but the earliest date on which a new stadium could be delivered was still three to four years away – and many people at the club were running out of patience with our performance on the field. My own public profile at Everton was relatively modest at this point compared with the attention Bill received, but I nevertheless started to receive regular letters from fans demanding that something be done. Many of the notes came from angry women who were fed up with the impact of the club's problems on their families. They would write things like, 'My husband works as a joiner. He is awake in the night because he is worried. He can't sleep and it's affecting his work. You need to get a grip on things.'

I may not have been a born and bred Evertonian, but those letters helped to give me an understanding of just how much the club meant to the local community. It wasn't just a handful of letters, it was a sack full – and Bill must have been receiving double or treble the number that reached my desk. They all basically expressed similar sentiments, ranging from 'Get rid of Smith' to 'Sack the board'. I knew that Bill would probably be loath to remove Smith, but in my view the time had come for a change.

'Walter Smith isn't delivering. If you don't get rid of him now, then the fans will turn on you,' I reasoned. 'You'll be the one to go, because the fans won't have it!'

Despite my protestations, Bill remained reluctant to act. There was simply too much water under the bridge shared between him and Smith. Bill's loyalty to his friend was admirable, but I feared it made it difficult for him to be objective. The pressure on the manager eased slightly when the team enjoyed a brief run in the FA Cup, defeating Crewe in a replay to reach the quarter-finals. Everton were drawn away at Middlesbrough and Smith was now desperate for a result.

'I honestly think it's realistic that we can win the cup this season. We've got to hold out that hope,' he told the *Daily Post* on the day before the big game.[19]

Few among the Everton faithful took him seriously but that didn't prevent the club selling its entire allocation of 5,000 tickets for the tie at Middlesbrough, which was shown live on TV. Unfortunately, the game was a disaster and Everton were abysmal. We were thumped 3–0, prompting the travelling Everton fans to repeatedly chant a chorus of 'We want Walter out! WE WANT WALTER OUT!'

Bill sat with his head in his hands in the directors' box for five minutes after the final whistle. Meanwhile, back on Merseyside there was fury. The humiliation of being torn apart during a televised tie on a Sunday was simply too much to bear. Hundreds of fans began to contact radio stations and newspapers calling for action. The following day the club's switchboard was jammed with angry callers, and they were no longer being polite. The general consensus seemed to be along the lines of, 'Sort it now, for fuck's sake!' One prominent Blues fan, the former MP Eric Moonman, made it clear that many believed the club were doomed to relegation unless it replaced Smith.

'I can't for the life of me understand why he is staying on when his record is so abysmal,' he said. 'The consequences of dropping into a lower division will cut all revenue and Kenwright's dream of the King's Dock will be gone forever.'[20]

Any hope that Smith could survive was gone, although even at this late stage I got the impression that Bill was reluctant to sack him. However, a board meeting was called and Bill finally accepted that the club faced a stark choice between getting rid of his friend or risking its Premier League status. It was time for Smith to go. Loyal to the end, Kenwright issued a sugar-coated tribute to the outgoing manager, and there were rumours of a generous compensation package.

'Walter Smith was, and is, one of the most honest and honourable men in football,' Bill told the press. 'He brought a stability and dignity to Everton when it desperately needed it most.'[21]

Smith himself adopted a more direct tone: 'At this stage it's very difficult to say that I've enjoyed it. There have been highs and lows, there's been a lot of good things I've enjoyed during my time here. It hasn't been easy but overall you feel a sense of frustration, coupled with a level of disappointment.'[22]

A number of observers believed that Smith was made scapegoat by the board, but the truth was he was no longer up to the challenge. However, it would certainly have been unfair to blame him for the previous two decades of malaise at the club. The immediate challenge that Everton now faced was to appoint a new manager at great speed. There was speculation that Joe Royle might return to Goodison, or that Gary Megson of West Bromwich Albion could be an option, but David Moyes at Preston North End was quickly decided upon as the club's number one choice. The difficulty with this was that Moyes had just signed a new five-year deal at Preston over the summer and they were unwilling to lose the man they called their 'crown jewel'. Moyes had a strong track record at Preston, who had ambitions of their own to secure a place in the Premier League through promotion. Hence, the question of compensation arose: Preston demanded a sum in the region of £1 million, but Bill was indignant. He was determined that Everton was not going to pay Preston anything like that amount.

'I think you may find that they have got us by the balls,' I said.

A crazy dance then occurred between the two clubs. Everton initially offered a much smaller amount, but we became increasingly desperate as the week progressed. Things came to a head when Preston threatened to pull the plug on the negotiations, which would have resulted in lots of legal wrangling and costs. Meanwhile, the clock was ticking and Everton faced the prospect of a home game on the coming Saturday against Fulham without a permanent manager. On the Thursday before the game, when Bill decided his only option was to drive up the motorway to meet on neutral ground with our counterparts at Preston, I agreed to accompany him. Together we drove to a hotel just off the motorway, near Haydock Park.

To say that the representatives from Preston were pissed off with the situation would have been an understatement. They were determined to get maximum compensation, but Bill was refusing to budge. The discussion went round in circles for what felt like hours and hours. In the end, the difference between our offer and what they were willing to accept was approximately £100,000. By this stage I was beginning to lose patience. I asked for a short break so that I could speak to Bill in private. We always seemed content to splash out for players, so I felt we should also cough up for a new manager.

'Let's just pay them what they want and we can get on with our lives,' I said bluntly. 'Otherwise we are just sat here wasting our time, while we argue the toss. They want the money. Let's just agree a figure with them.'

Bill agreed.

'OK, gentlemen – we have a deal,' we announced.

Moyes arrived at Goodison that evening, leaving him with just twenty-four hours on Friday to prepare for the match against Fulham. Thankfully, Everton won 2–1.

We finished in 15th place that season, having survived yet another relegation dogfight. In the end, terminating Smith's contract and compensating Preston came at a substantial price. Everton's accounts that year included a note stating that wages and salaries included a bill for compensation totalling over £2 million 'as a result of the termination of Team Management contracts'.[23] It was a hefty sum, but relatively minor compared to the financial catastrophe of relegation.

*

On the opening day of the new season in August of 2002, a bright new star shone during his first team debut in an Everton shirt. He was sixteen years of age and his name was Wayne Rooney. Expectations were high among Evertonians who had followed Rooney's progress through the youth team, where he was regarded as a goal-scoring machine.

Everton drew 2–2 with Spurs that afternoon and Rooney did not disappoint. Despite his age, he was strong, bulky and quick – and he assisted in setting up the opening goal with a precision pass. Perhaps mindful of protecting his young protégé from further hype, Moyes sensibly substituted Rooney in the

A DISASTER FOR EVERTON

sixty-sixth minute. For Evertonians, Wayne Rooney was one of their own. Born and bred in Croxteth, where he lived in a council house with his parents and younger brothers, he was regarded as a true Blue. It wasn't long before he was winning plaudits nationwide. In October, he scored his first Premier League goal with a magnificent curling strike against Arsenal. Thierry Henry later recalled how the Arsenal players had been wary of Rooney even before they arrived at Goodison.

'People talk in the game. We knew there was a young kid who was going to score goals and has the body of a man,' the Arsenal legend later confided in a documentary for Amazon.[24]

Moyes's intention was to use Rooney sparingly. 'There is a bit too much pressure on him at the moment,' he said during a pre-season interview. 'We will look after him, because he is a baby in terms of professional football. We will take care of him at the right times, he will go back into the reserves and the youth team.'[25]

In fact, Rooney went on to make more than thirty appearances in the first team during his debut season. Playing alongside him in midfield on that opening day was another interesting newcomer. He was a Chinese national called Li Tie and his arrival on Merseyside coincided with Everton announcing an international sponsorship agreement with Kejian, a telecoms corporation in China. It was a commercial deal that I had brokered on behalf of the club during a trip to Beijing with Sir Philip Carter. Clubs like Manchester United and Liverpool were in the process of building up their followings overseas, so it made good sense for Everton to attempt do the same, especially given our aspirations to make King's Dock a hub to attract entertainment acts with a global following. When an opportunity arose to expand our commercial appeal in China, I jumped at the chance.

The initial query about sponsorship from Kejian had landed on Sir Philip's desk, in his capacity as chairman. I wasn't convinced that he was the best person to handle any deal that might be in the offing. His grandstanding on match days was all very well when he was performing in front of the Everton faithful, but I didn't trust his commercial acumen. Besides, I was becoming increasingly frustrated by what I perceived to be a dismissive attitude towards me by certain individuals at the club. This included Sir Philip, despite the fact I'd previously worked with him at the Empire Theatre Trust. I'd assumed at first that it was merely because I was a newcomer to the club and that it would pass in time, but after nearly two years it was beginning to wear a bit thin. I wasn't the only person to notice; occasionally, if I brought a guest to a game, they would pick up on it too.

'I got the impression they regarded you as a bit of an upstart who's done well in the theatre, but isn't really part of their world,' one friend later confided to me.

Despite whatever dubious reservations Sir Philip might have, I knew that negotiating with an international corporation was definitely something that fell into my own area of expertise.

'I think we should go to China together at the weekend,' I told Sir Philip. 'If we put together the right sponsorship package, we can agree everything in principle while we're out there. If they're in agreement we can sign a deal in time for the new season.'

A DISASTER FOR EVERTON

I caught an overnight flight to Beijing and checked into a hotel ahead of our meeting with Kejian; Sir Philip had already arrived. I had imagined that we would sit down with half a dozen executives in a private room, but I was in for a bit of a surprise – apparently they did things rather differently in China.

The meeting was being held in a large conference room packed with sixty or seventy people, all of whom seemed to be chain-smoking. The air was filled with the thick, grey fug of cigarette smoke and the clamour of many voices talking loudly into mobile phones. Kejian was a major entity in telecommunications and software, with sales worth $176 million and thousands of staff. I got the impression that Everton was not the only item on their agenda that day, but even so, the Kejian executives who greeted us were polite and friendly. It soon emerged that they were not remotely interested in selling any of their products in the UK or Europe. Their number one priority was simply to get their name and logo visible during televised matches in order to increase their visibility in the Far East. Premier League games were starting to attract large TV audiences in China, and they were keen to turn that to their own advantage.

By the time lunch was served I was feeling tired after my long-haul flight, but the encouraging thing was that Kejian seemed ready and willing to agree a shirt deal. However, they felt the value would be greatly enhanced if Everton were also to sign a player from China. They explained that TV audiences in China would rocket for any game in which a Chinese national was on the pitch. Among the candidates they had in mind was Li Tie, a talented midfielder who was apparently open-minded about an international transfer.

During a break in the negotiations, I went outside to call Bill Kenwright and explain the situation.

'Why don't you just ask David Moyes if he wants to sign Li Tie?' I said. 'It would mean that eighty million viewers in China are going to watch us play – that's what brings the value to the deal.'

At first, Moyes was sceptical. He made it clear that any player would be signed purely on the basis of ability (which was understandable). Later on, however, after doing his research, he would have a genuine change of heart about the prospect of signing a talented player like Li Tie.

After talking to Bill on the phone I returned to the smoky meeting room, where our Chinese hosts announced that they were taking us to another hotel in order to continue negotiations in a quieter environment. Unfortunately, the new venue was not much of an improvement. If anything, the cigarette fumes were even thicker there. The smoke looked as if you could cut it with a knife. That night we retired to our rooms exhausted, but the next morning everything remained amicable with our hosts. Before flying back to the UK, Sir Philip and I promised to investigate further the prospect of signing a player from China.

We later signed a contract for a two-year shirt sponsorship deal that was worth in the region of £1 million a year. As part of the agreement, a centre half from China called Li Weifeng briefly joined us on loan, with Li Tie signing a contract the following month. Li Weifeng played in just one game, but David Moyes was impressed with Li Tie, and during the approaching season the player would go on to appear in more than thirty games for the first team.

A DISASTER FOR EVERTON

★

That summer marked the high point of my time at Everton. In addition to the debut of Wayne Rooney, we had a new manager and a new sponsor; and we continued to make progress with our plans for the stadium at King's Dock. It seemed like there was plenty for Evertonians to feel positive about. Things even improved on the pitch, and towards the end of November Everton were briefly in the top three. The club eventually finished in seventh place, but even that was a welcome improvement on the usual relegation dogfight.

While the team were churning out respectable results, behind the scenes there were a number of fault lines developing at boardroom level. My niggles with Bill over Walter Smith had made me realise that everywhere you looked at Everton, Bill was surrounded by his own friends in positions of influence. This meant that it was often impossible to get anything done without his agreement. I'd invested a substantial amount of my own cash in Everton through True Blue Holdings and I obviously wanted the club to be a success. My interests were therefore aligned with Bill's in that respect, but I felt that he and I were at odds whenever I suggested doing anything new that threatened the status quo. I came to understand that our arrangement through True Blue Holdings – which don't forget also included his long-time pals Jon Woods and Arthur Abercromby – effectively rendered me powerless in the event of a dispute. This was because Bill could always rely on Woods and Abercromby to back him. I may have owned the same amount of shares in True Blue as Bill, but I would always be outvoted.

If I'd invested my £7.5 million directly in Everton shares rather than True Blue, I would at least have had the freedom to work with the independent shareholders, who still owned around 28 per cent of Everton.

I was also concerned about the practice of Premier League clubs paying large sums to football agents, which obviously remains widespread today. I could never understand why we should pay a player's agent in the first place. In the theatre or movie industry, if you want to hire somebody like Tom Cruise you expect to go through his agent, but you don't *pay* the agent. That's the responsibility of the artiste. In football, the clubs are basically paying for somebody to negotiate *against* the club in order to squeeze as much cash out of the club as possible. In my opinion, this is ruining the game. It fuels the ridiculous merry-go-round whereby agents are incentivised to encourage players to constantly move between clubs, even though that's not necessarily in anyone's best interests. If a player is unhappy about the tiniest thing – the position of his seat on the bus or the distance of his hotel room from reception – it can fester in his mind. If clubs are throwing pound notes at agents, then in that situation you can understand why agents suggest a move rather than sitting down with the club to work things out.

We have a situation today where the agent goes to the club and says, 'The player is really unhappy with you.' This creates a negative mood that is not in the interests of players, clubs or the game as a whole. Every time a player is transferred a huge chunk of money is paid to the agent – and invariably it's the club that picks up the bill. It was no surprise to me that figures published by the FA estimated that by 2022, Premier League clubs paid out

£272 million in agent fees in the previous two transfer windows (which included nearly £11.49 million by Everton).[26] Nobody knows how much was being spent on agents before 2015, because there was no requirement to publish any details prior to that date. Ultimately it's the fans who suffer, because every pound spent on agents' fees has to be recouped from somewhere, whether it's ticket prices or the cost of a replica shirt. I was also unhappy that transfer fees could often be staggered over several years, which in my view encouraged overspending.

I urged Bill whenever he went to Premier League meetings that he should raise the issue of agents' fees. 'Will you ask the Premier League to stop clubs paying agents? Clubs should not pay agents. Players should pay agents,' I'd demand.

I knew this would put Bill in a challenging position. Everton couldn't act unilaterally or we'd never have been offered certain players, but I felt somebody should make a stand. Of course, as you can see from the situation in football today, nothing changed.

My relationship with Bill was becoming slightly strained for all the reasons just described, but it took a real turn for the worse when we hit a stumbling block on the King's Dock development. Up until this point, things had gone according to plan and Bovis Lend Lease had been confirmed as our construction consultants. The plans for the 55,000-capacity waterfront stadium by now included 70 executive boxes and 3,000 executive seats. When the rolling pitch and roof were retracted, we'd confirmed that the stadium could convert at the push of a button into an indoor arena with a capacity of up to 24,000. There were also 10,000 square metres of exhibition space and a banqueting facility for up to 3,000 people. By now, we also had detailed plans for the multi-screen cinema, health clinic, state-of-the-art gymnasium and five-star hotel, along with nearly a thousand private homes. When the architect's drawings were publicly displayed at the Merseyside Maritime Museum, they were greeted with great enthusiasm.

'Evertonians who viewed the plans seem unanimous in their admiration of the club's efforts, and their awe for the vision and grandeur of the proposed project,' read one comment on an online forum used by Everton fans.[27]

However, all this grandeur came at a price. The estimated costs of the proposed stadium eventually rose to approximately £193 million. While this was a substantial increase, it was still regarded as great value and should have been a manageable sum. However, the club's private partners in the project were unwilling to stump up any of the extra cash. Unfortunately, by the end of August 2002 a story appeared in the local press stating that Everton was now struggling to come up with the club's own £30 million contribution towards the construction costs.[28] We were informed that we would not get the final go-ahead from the authorities until we could provide a 100 per cent guarantee that we had all the funds in place.

It was still a fantastic deal for an opportunity to own the biggest single shareholding in the world's most advanced stadium. However, it became a sticking point when the accountancy firm KPMG compiled a report concluding that Everton simply did not have access to the money. It was a crazy situation. We'd allowed Walter Smith to blow £18 million in the space of a few months on under-performing players, yet we had nothing in the kitty to pay for a roof over our heads.

Despite this setback, I was confident that the club could raise £30 million in loans via a secondary funding arrangement with new investors, something that is quite common in the business world. Bill understood this but he was against it. He later said that he didn't believe that I could deliver the funding.

I considered personally guaranteeing the cash with an unsecured loan from my own proceeds of the sale of Apollo Leisure Group, but decided against it. Had I done so, it would have meant I was the only individual putting their personal cash into the scheme without receiving any extra security in return. I would have been left with just my existing shares in True Blue Holdings, nothing extra to show for the £30 million and no security against the loan.

'You must think I'm a lunatic if you believe I'm going to sign a personal cheque for thirty million pounds,' I told Bill. I also expressed a similar sentiment when asked about the situation in the press.

In the end, Bill grudgingly agreed that I should further investigate how to raise secondary funding that could be secured against the assets of the club, but he remained deeply uneasy. I think his main concern was that nobody would lend the club that sort of cash without expecting something tangible in return. It wasn't long before it became public knowledge that Bill and I had different views on the matter, resulting in speculation about a boardroom rift. Stories began to appear in the press in which unattributed sources at the club made it clear that Bill would never accept any new terms, claiming that the rest of the board would rather stay at Goodison or find somewhere other than King's Dock. Undeterred, I engaged a funding partner to put together a consortium of private investors who were willing to collectively put up the £30 million. The deal was to be structured in the form of a 'reverse mortgage', which did not require payment of capital or interest until after a certain time period had elapsed. This would have given the club plenty of time to put its long-term financial affairs in order and pay off the reverse mortgage in order to secure its share of the ownership of the stadium.

The club's AGM was scheduled for the end of October and it was inevitable that fans would demand answers after all the speculation in the press, so I was anxious to get things agreed before then. Bill suggested we should get a view about the proposal from his friend Sir Philip Green.

'That sounds fine to me. I'm sure Sir Philip would agree it's a good solution,' I said, mindful that Bill sometimes turned to Green for advice. Bill seemed content to proceed on that basis. Soon afterwards I gave an interview to the press in which I outlined the new funding proposal.

'Bill Kenwright and I have put together a five-year-plan to put Everton into its new stadium,' I said. 'Everton will move into the stadium, where the receipts will be such that they will then buy back their ownership of the stadium. That will enable the club to compete at the top of the Premiership and be at the King's Waterfront.'[29]

Bill and I travelled down to London a few days prior to the AGM to meet with Green at his offices in Marylebone. The retail tycoon was in a buoyant mood when he greeted us. He and Bill clearly knew each other well and were comfortable in one another's company. I explained the proposal in detail over

A DISASTER FOR EVERTON

lunch in his office. Green was interested and open-minded. I felt everything had gone well. I was so confident that we had reached an agreement that I was even quoted in the local press. As far as I was concerned, the funding proposal should have been given the green light. I was now looking forward to the AGM, which was due to take place on the coming Thursday and would be preceded by a board meeting at Everton to endorse the proposal.

The press regarded the board meeting as a sort of 'high noon' scenario which would decide the future of the club. Many of the fans seemed to be divided. Some had been spooked by early misgivings, but plenty were in favour. In fact, there was no need for any further discord, but on the day I was totally horrified to discover that Bill had changed his mind. Instead he proposed a messy compromise, whereby the club would investigate further before committing. I felt angry and upset after all the work I'd put into it, along with Steve Lavelle, the city council and our many partners.

I watched in disbelief that evening at the AGM, as Kenwright and Carter stood up in front of hundreds of fans and shareholders and told them that we had not yet secured the money for the stadium, but that they remained 'fully committed' to the move to King's Dock. In the meantime, they vowed to continue to investigate my proposal and keep it under consideration. I was angry and shocked. As far as I was concerned, the funding *was* in place.

'What the hell do you think you are doing?' I said to Bill.

He simply shrugged it off and gave his usual response about wanting the best for Everton. The impression given to fans was that King's Dock was still very much on the cards despite the hiccup. However, with the deadline for the final planning application approaching, I feared it would be too late to turn things around unless we acted quickly.

The next morning, I phoned David Henshaw at Liverpool City Council. I felt he was entitled to an explanation; after all, King's Dock was the jewel in the crown of the council's regeneration plan for the city, ahead of its bid to become the European City of Culture. I expected that Henshaw would be as angry as I was with the rest of the Everton board.

'They won't approve the £30 million. It's not going to happen,' I told him.

In fact, Henshaw was calm and professional. He was obviously already well aware of what had happened at the AGM the previous night.

His reply surprised me. It was along the lines of: 'Don't worry, perhaps we can investigate a way of building the stadium and you can lease it.'

'What do you mean?' I replied.

Henshaw indicated that he was open-minded about suggesting to the council that, for the good of the city, the council should find a way of helping to provide further finance for the construction costs. It was a clever suggestion that was worth serious consideration by all parties. There were hundreds of millions of pounds of investment at stake, so why risk everything for the sake of £30 million? I thanked Henshaw and then I called Bill. I was convinced that this was a proposal that he would agree had an upside for everybody.

Unfortunately, I was wrong.

A DISASTER FOR EVERTON

I said: 'Bill, I've got the city council to hopefully help with a solution. We'll get the stadium. We just have to rent it for 125 years.'

I was staggered by his reply, which was along the lines of him being concerned that any such deal would leave the club without ownership of the new stadium.

At this point, I finally lost my temper. I am ashamed to say that I used some very colourful language and made some comments that were probably hurtful to Bill.

'Don't be f***ing stupid,' I said. 'That is crazy. The city council are going to deliver the stadium. You can carry on wasting all of the money that you let go through the dressing-room door, but at least you will have an incredible stadium in the heart of Liverpool.' I reminded him that every Liverpudlian would see King's Dock from the city centre. I urged him to consider the benefits to the Everton brand.

'I am not doing it. We have to own the stadium,' he insisted.

'We'd have a 50% share of a 999-year lease on the site and a 125-year exclusive right to play football, which the club will be able to renew in the future. That IS owning it, in my book,' I replied. 'You are going to get the fucking stadium for free, delivered as a turnkey operation. You just have to put the players on the pitch. It's the best opportunity we will ever have.'

Bill refused to budge.

From this point onwards, the King's Dock stadium was now effectively dead in the water, although I continued to fight my corner in the weeks and months that followed. By the end of the year our preferred bidder status was removed, although we were granted a further three-month window to put our house in order. When the club's final planning application was delivered in March 2003, it had been watered down to a pathetic level by the lack of funds. There was no retractable roof, no retractable pitch. We had failed to deliver on our commitment to creating a world-leading leisure and entertainment complex. It was rejected eleven days later and the following joint statement, issued by Everton and the regeneration body Liverpool Vision, appeared on the BBC website on 11 April 2003:

> Over the last year Liverpool Vision and Everton FC have made enormous efforts to deliver proposals for a purpose-built Arena and associated developments at King's Dock. It was a hugely bold, ambitious and exciting plan – one of the biggest developments of its kind taking place in Europe.
>
> However, it became clear that the funding of the scheme had become problematical and on 31 December, 2002, it was decided that Liverpool Vision would end Everton's status as the preferred developer for the site. At the same time, it was made clear that there would be a three-month window of opportunity for Everton to come forward with alternative proposals which would still be considered alongside other options for the site.
>
> The club has recently presented new proposals for the King's Dock site which have been the subject of close and detailed examinations. Unfortunately, it is accepted by both parties that these plans are not now achievable. The sheer scale and ambition of both the original and amended schemes mean that they will not be able to at-

tract the level of funding needed to deliver the standard of development which the city of Liverpool deserves.[30]

I felt the statement was quite cold and corporate – and news of the rejection was a disaster for Everton. It was obvious that the club was unable to move forward while in the grip of True Blue Holdings, which was effectively controlled by Bill. From this point onwards our relationship completely broke down. Whenever I tried to raise a difficult issue he would simply shrug off my concerns. He also developed a frustrating habit of avoiding a discussion by complaining about minor ailments or feeling tired if a conversation became awkward. The upshot of the rift between us was that I was now publicly at war with my old friend.

From Wayne Rooney to a Russian Oligarch

Early in 2004 I found myself in Bangkok, about to be introduced to the prime minister of Thailand – although I wasn't quite sure why. Since my falling out with Bill Kenwright a year earlier, I had stayed away from Goodison Park on match days, but now I felt ready to get back into the thick of things. At home, Everton fans were anxious about the future of Wayne Rooney, whose contract was up for renewal. Bill was handling the details, while I had flown to Thailand to explore sponsorship opportunities.

When I arrived, I was expecting to be greeted by a lowly tourism official. I was bemused by what happened next.

'The prime minister will be here within one hour,' I was told.

I should have realised that something odd was going on when we arrived at the airport in Bangkok earlier that day. I was travelling with Leslie Rose, my good friend and business associate, as well as a go-between who had facilitated a meeting with the office of tourism. When we got off the plane we were slightly tired, but in good spirits. Instead of facing the usual queues at the passport desk in the arrivals lounge, we were pleasantly surprised to find a black limousine waiting beside the steps that led up to the aircraft.

'This is nice – it looks like they're giving us the VIP treatment,' smiled Leslie.

We were driven via the Bangkok expressway to the Mandarin Oriental Hotel on the banks of the Chao Phraya River in the heart of the city's cultural district, where we were staying as guests courtesy of the tourism authority. I'd stayed in many a five-star hotel, but the Bangkok Mandarin Oriental was in a different class. The views across the river were stunning and it was just a short hop by boat to the Grand Palace, the former residence of the King of Siam. Upon arriving at the hotel we discovered that we would be staying in the Presidential Suite.

'This is *very* nice,' commented Leslie.

I have to explain here that, like me, Leslie is not a lifelong Evertonian. In fact, he is a Spurs fan, but don't let that put you off. He is also one of the best brains there is in the marketing sector, and he has unrivalled business contacts.

In my luggage I had a framed, signed photograph of Wayne Rooney in his Everton kit. I'd been intending to give it to our hosts as a gift, but it now felt slightly incongruous amid the grandeur of the hotel. Nevertheless, once we had checked in I took it with me back down to the lobby, where the officials who greeted us explained that we would now travel to a second hotel.

We were ushered outside to another limo, surrounded by what seemed to be an inordinate amount of security. When we arrived at the second hotel, it seemed even grander than the first one. We were shown upstairs to a huge ballroom, empty apart from a single table and six chairs in the middle of the vast space.

I thought we were probably about to sit down with an official and discuss the possibility of sponsorship, as our deal with Kejian in China was due to come to an end.

And that was when our host said, 'Please take a seat, gentlemen. The prime minister will be with you in one hour.'

I should pause here for a moment to explain that the prime minister of Thailand at this time was a colourful individual called Thaksin Shinawatra, whom you may have heard of in the past. Somewhat ironically, he was involved in a public attempt to invest in Liverpool Football Club. Shinawatra was a successful billionaire in his own right, having amassed a personal fortune in the telecoms sector.

'Shinawatra? Isn't he the bloke trying to buy Liverpool? What does he want with us?' Leslie whispered to me.

'I don't know, but we're about to find out,' I replied.

When Mr Shinawatra swept into the room, he greeted us with impeccable politeness. I briefly wondered whether it might all be a big muddle — did he actually think we were from the red part of Merseyside? But he was no fool. He knew who we were. I think he wanted to meet with us partly out of curiosity, and partly because he had a general interest in promoting football in Thailand.

I explained as best I could that Everton were open-minded about any commercial opportunities for sponsorship that might exist. Leslie, meanwhile, seemed intent on interjecting every few minutes to try to convince Shinawatra that Liverpool Football Club would be a poor choice for investment. Tottenham fans have historically held a bit of a grudge against Liverpool, and I think Leslie saw it as his duty as a Spurs supporter to speak up.

I could see that Mr Shinawatra was buying none of it. However, he was impressed enough by my pitch for sponsorship that he promised to introduce us to the chairman of Chang Beer, a hugely successful brand in Thailand despite the fact that nobody in the UK had heard of it at the time. We shook hands, and as he was preparing to leave I remembered the signed photo of Wayne Rooney that I'd brought along.

'Prime Minister – I'd like to present you with this,' I said.

It was a mischievous choice of goodwill gift for somebody who was intent on buying Liverpool FC, but he accepted it with good grace. My gesture certainly didn't harm Everton, because Leslie and I later returned to Thailand on two occasions to meet with the chairman of Chang Beer and his charming wife. They were hugely impressed by the prospect of forming a lucrative partnership with Everton. As for Mr Shinawatra, his bid to buy Liverpool was rejected although as football fans will know, he did later become the owner of Manchester City (before being indicted for corruption).

On the 7th of July that year I travelled again to Bangkok, accompanied by a colleague from Everton, to formally announce a shirt sponsorship deal with Chang Beer. Everton received £1.5 million for the first year, a significant improvement on our previous deal with Kejian. There were also options to extend the deal, which brought the value of the agreement to £6 million over four years. It was not only a substantial and much-needed windfall, but also the start of a long-running partnership between Everton and Chang. The commercial relationship lasted until 2017, having been renewed in 2008 (for a further £8 million) and in 2010 (for a further £12 million). In 2014, it was extended by three years for up to £16 million. It was described at the time as the most lucrative agreement in the club's 136-year history.

★

I returned to Merseyside that summer feeling reinvigorated and refreshed, although the club itself was in a mess. Everton had finished fourth from bottom, escaping relegation by six points. I was now determined to turn things around, even if that meant going head to head with Bill Kenwright for control of the club. My final trip to Thailand to announce the sponsorship deal had coincided with the aftermath of the Euro 2004 tournament in Portugal, where Wayne Rooney had performed magnificently. Unfortunately, the attention he created had come at a high price. Ever since George Best kicked a ball for Manchester United, talented young footballers have found themselves under the microscope both on and off the field. In eighteen-year-old Rooney's case, this scrutiny led to a series of headlines in a Sunday newspaper alleging that he had used the services of sex workers. He issued the following short statement, which was published on the BBC website:

> Foolish as it now seems I did on occasions visit massage parlours and prostitutes. It was at a time when I was very young and immature and before I had settled down with Coleen. I now regret it deeply and hope people may understand that it was the sort of mistake you make when you are young and stupid.[31]

Rooney made the public confession in response to an exposé in the *Sunday Mirror*, which claimed that he had been caught on CCTV at a brothel in the Aigburth district of Liverpool. It was part of a lurid pantomime that was both shocking and tragic in equal measure. It was shocking for Evertonians to see the young England star caught in a national scandal at a time when the club was desperately hoping to convince him to stay at Everton. For Rooney, it was also a personal tragedy. He was engaged to his childhood sweetheart, Coleen, with whom he'd recently moved into a new home in Formby. The newspaper story alleged that Rooney had visited the massage parlour a number of times in 2002, when he was aged under eighteen (according to the unconfirmed claims, he may even have been as young as sixteen). He reportedly signed an autograph as a souvenir for a vice girl after paying her £140 for her services. Meanwhile, a receptionist at the brothel was said to be a forty-eight-year-old grandmother, who wore a rubber catsuit and was known locally as 'the Auld Slapper'. These were hardly the type of details you'd expect to find Sir Philip and Lady Rita discussing in the polite confines of the boardroom over a slice of Everton cake.

The effect on Rooney and his family life would obviously have been devastating, but the whole saga also raised serious questions about the role of Everton Football Club. How the hell had Everton allowed a naive teenage player to find himself in a position where he could repeatedly wander in and out of a vice den, unchecked and unsupervised? Of course, Rooney also had to accept personal responsibility for his own actions – but why hadn't his visits to the massage parlour been on the club's radar? After all, Everton had publicly vowed to protect its young protégé, and I had taken those assurances at face value. In my opinion, it should have been made clear to Rooney that certain temptations were best avoided.

The first thing I did upon learning about the whole fiasco was to suggest a board meeting with Bill Kenwright so that we could discuss the matter, which was the right thing to do.

'Why on earth didn't you have an experienced older player assigned to protect him?' I asked. 'He should have had somebody with him, who if need be could have put him up against a wall and said, "If you do that sort of thing I am going to bash the hell out of you!"'

My outburst may have been slightly harsh, but Bill had always taken an interest in the players and the manager, so it was to him that I looked for an explanation. The truth was that I felt we had all let Rooney down.

Rooney's subsequent further indiscretions over the years have been well documented, but I can't help thinking that if the original story had broken today it would be handled very differently by the media. The club itself would have come under far more scrutiny, given Rooney's age at the time. He would have been visiting the massage parlour at roughly the same time he was emerging as a prominent new talent. I was reminded of David Moyes's comments in 2002, when he had said that Rooney needed protecting because he was 'a baby in terms of professional football'. These days, many people on social media are quick to judge Rooney for his past, but they forget how young he was when he found himself in the limelight. Personally, I think Wayne deserves credit for going on to become a great servant for England and a loving father to his children, despite the mistakes he's made.

Rooney had been a revelation at Euro 2004, scoring four international goals during England's journey to a quarter-final against Portugal. He was injured during that game before England predictably crashed out on penalties, but there was no doubt that Rooney was the hero of the tournament. He was named 'European Golden Boy' in a poll of international journalists, leaving Ronaldo in second place and Fernando Torres in third position. The massage parlour story was published amid feverish speculation about whether or not Rooney would seek a transfer to a bigger club. The furore also coincided with a very public spat between Bill Kenwright and me, beginning in July, over Everton's future.

Rooney's performances for England turned him into a national hero and Manchester United and Chelsea were among the bigger clubs that were circling, ready to pounce. His contract still had two years to left run, but negotiations for an extension began almost as soon as Euro 2004 ended. Everton offered him a five-year deal worth in the region of £12.5 million, which would have taken his wages from £13,000 a week to approximately £50,000 – a phenomenal sum of money for the club at that time.

'That is not a joke offer – that offer is in the contract,' Kenwright told the press.

Rooney and his agents prevaricated and there was talk of Everton being prepared to offer him a get-out clause that would allow him to leave at the end of the season, provided any interested club was prepared to offer the stated market price. Bill had previously hinted that if a transfer were forced upon the club against its wishes, Everton would not let Rooney go for anything less than £50 million. The official position remained that he was not for sale, but it now seemed as if his mind was increasingly elsewhere.

When the massage parlour story broke, it further set the cat among the pigeons. Rooney was badly unsettled and the day after the *Sunday Mirror* published its exposé, he apparently told David Moyes that he wanted to leave Everton. It was around this time that, sitting on the train one day, I received an unexpected phone call. It was from Freddy Shepherd, the chairman of Newcastle United.

'Would you be prepared to sell Wayne Rooney?' he asked.

I'd previously done everything I could think of to try to help the club keep Rooney. While I was in Thailand, I'd telephoned Bill to suggest we reward him for his success at Euro 2004 by buying him a new Mini car in Union Jack livery, which I thought would have been a wonderful gesture. I also called his agent to ask for a one-to-one meeting, but my request was declined. I even suggested to Bill that it might help us to hold on to him if we replaced Moyes with a more charismatic manager. However, I could see that it was now becoming a lost cause and a transfer looked inevitable, so I was prepared to listen to the Newcastle chairman.

'I'd definitely vote to sell Rooney if we got twenty-five million for him,' I told Shepherd.

That afternoon I attended a board meeting in Bill's office, where he opened proceedings by stating that he'd received a telex from Manchester United.

'Well, I've just had a call from Freddy Shepherd,' I replied.

'He asked me if we would sell Wayne Rooney to Newcastle. If Rooney is intent on leaving, why don't we just announce he's for sale? If he's going, we might as well get as much money as we can for him.'

'You can't do that,' said Kenwright.

'Of course we can do that – why not?' I insisted. I knew that we needed every penny we could find. 'If he's going, then he's going. Let's find out who's willing to pay the most.'

Bill's view was that Manchester United would make the best offer.

'OK, which one of us is going to negotiate with Manchester United?' I asked.

'Aaghh . . . we could get Philip Green to do it,' said Bill.

'Why do we need Philip Green? You and I both have experience of booking the world's biggest artistes in the theatre. Why do we need someone else to do a deal for us to sell Wayne Rooney to Manchester United?'

Bill continued to argue that he wanted to involve Green about the approach from Manchester United.

'Then you're a fool,' I replied. 'We don't need him.'

In the end, I don't believe that Green was involved but Manchester United topped Newcastle's offer with a transfer package worth in the region of £30 million. This consisted of £10 million up front, with a further £10 million the following year. There was potentially another £7 million on offer, subject to Rooney staying at United and the number of international caps he would go on to win, plus a sell-on clause. United confirmed that Rooney's agents, Proactive, were due to receive fees of up to £1.5 million. To be fair to Bill, it wasn't a bad deal, but Rooney's mantra of 'Once a Blue, always a Blue' became an ironic slogan for Everton fans.

★

Everton's failure to hang on to Rooney was symbolic of everything that I felt was wrong at the club. Following the collapse of the King's Dock proposal, it seemed as if we had no long-term vision and were going nowhere. The Rooney affair coincided with my own attempts to change things by gaining control of the club.

At this point I need to rewind the clock a little in order to explain.

David Moyes had initially been given a transfer budget that summer of £1.5 million – a fraction of the amount Walter Smith had blown during his spending sprees. Everton's borrowings were in excess of £30 million and rising. Perhaps not surprisingly, when Michael Dunford's contract as chief executive expired in June, I was among those who felt it should not be renewed. In his place the club appointed Trevor Birch, a savvy operator who had previously been chief executive of Chelsea. Birch had also served at Leeds, where he'd helped to rescue the club from financial meltdown. Ironically, he was a former Liverpool player who had once cleaned Kevin Keegan's boots as an apprentice and later sat on the subs' bench during the European Cup Final in 1978. In my opinion, Birch was exactly the breath of fresh air that Everton needed. In the subsequent boardroom reshuffle Bill also took the opportunity to replace Sir Philip Carter by becoming the new chairman in his place.

Trevor Birch set about his task with great enthusiasm, but he was evidently horrified by what he found. To put it bluntly, the club was starving for cash. Birch told Bill in no uncertain terms that Everton was in financial disarray. Drastic changes would be required. The iron grip of True Blue Holdings, with control of over 70 per cent of Everton's shares, had become a straitjacket. The only solution was a radical shake-up of the ownership structure, which I had been calling for since the King's Dock debacle eighteen months earlier. When Birch arrived it was very obvious that the structure of True Blue Holdings was a barrier to attracting new investment. Anybody pumping new money into Everton would be denied any real say in how the club was run, because True Blue acted as a single entity that gave Bill, Woods and Abercromby complete control.

In addition to wanting to dissolve True Blue, I was also in favour of sacking David Moyes. Everton had endured a dismal brush with relegation the previous season when the team finished just one place above the drop, and in light of that I was no longer prepared to leave footballing matters solely to Bill. My family and I had already invested a lot of money in the club; I accept that football is different from many other businesses, but that should never stop a club from being run properly. I therefore felt the time was right for a change of manager, preferably somebody with plenty of experience.

I arranged with Birch to speak informally to Martin O'Neill, who had been enormously successful at Celtic and struck me as a good possible replacement for Moyes. We talked on the phone and O'Neill seemed prepared to listen with an open mind. I suggested that he could help to build a future legacy at Everton, which if necessary could potentially include taking some equity. No disrespect to Moyes (who, many years later, did a good job at West Ham), but at the time I felt that what Everton needed was a manager of O'Neill's profile and charisma. I believed he had the magical attraction that we needed. Hiring him would also send a statement to Rooney and his agents that we were serious about turning the club around, and I hoped it might convince Rooney to stay. However, when I suggested Moyes should be axed, Kenwright was horrified. He said that Moyes had only been at the club for two seasons and deserved more time in the hot seat. I pointed out that a number of top clubs had given managers their marching orders within shorter timeframes, sometimes even after one year, but Bill refused to be swayed.

Moyes may have had the support of Kenwright but it didn't stop him from clashing with Trevor Birch, who was anxious to keep a tight grip on the purse strings. In contrast, Moyes was desperate to free up more cash in order to improve his squad. Realistically, there was zero chance of this happening without a fresh injection of funds from outside sources. Prior to Birch's arrival, Everton had accrued borrowings of around £42 million. In addition to the huge debt pile, Birch also faced the prospect of dwindling season ticket sales, which were significantly down on the previous year. However, he had experience of navigating his way through similar problems at other clubs, and he'd joined us on the understanding that he would be given autonomy to sort out the mess. His conclusion was that the only way to get Everton out of its hole was to sell a sizeable chunk of the club to a new owner, depending on what sort of offer we could attract. This would necessarily have involved disbanding True Blue Holdings.

Birch was also vocal in his support for a proposal that Everton should consider sharing a stadium with Liverpool FC. This was an idea that had been suggested in the past without gaining much traction, but Birch now announced that he intended to formally raise it with Liverpool.

Personally, even though I was a director of True Blue Holdings myself, I was in favour of dissolving it and transferring the company shares into Everton shares (a proportion of which we all would then have received back as direct equity in the club). I therefore publicly announced a plan of my own, which received a large amount of media attention. The ultimate aim of my proposal was to attract £15 million from outside investors, plus a further £15 million by offering 15,000 fans the opportunity to invest £1,000 each in the club. I believed that a new ownership structure combined with a war chest of £30 million would give us the best possible chance of getting our club back on the front foot.

Meanwhile, Birch was becoming increasingly frustrated by the lack of support for radical change, so much so that matters came to a head in mid-July. In what became a major embarrassment for the club, when his demand that True Blue should relinquish control was refused, he promptly resigned. Everton lost one of football's most respected businessmen – just six weeks after he had joined the club! The reaction on Merseyside was one of astonishment and anger. Four days later, Arthur Abercromby stepped down from the board, leaving only three directors in place: Kenwright, Woods and myself. That evening, Everton played in a friendly fixture at Crewe, where the travelling Blues fans voiced their discontent. One banner in the crowd read: 'Kenwright! Enough Is Enough, We Want Success.' The banner also included the club's Latin motto, 'Nil satis nisi optimum' (Nothing but the best is good enough). It was a sentiment I wholeheartedly agreed with, and I blamed one person above all others: Bill Kenwright. That week, I wrote a letter to Bill demanding that he and Woods should resign. My letter began by outlining my intentions to raise the first £15 million in my proposal from new investors, which would have required the appointment of a new chairman and two new directors.

'Obviously to make this progress happen, that would require the current board standing down and hopefully wishing the new board success with their endeavours and ambitions for the club,' I wrote. 'You and I both know that Everton and its fans are bigger than both of us and is a very important part of many lives on Merseyside, and what we now need is a really positive step forward that lets us embrace the ambitions of our supporters and not those wishes of ourselves.'

The story was splashed across the front page of the *Liverpool Echo*, which carried the headline 'STEP DOWN BILL: Call for Chairman of Everton to Quit'. I knew Bill wouldn't go without a fight, so I was prepared to go all out in my attempt to gain control. This included reaching out for support from independent shareholders (e.g. those outside of True Blue Holdings) and various supporters' groups. I knew that many members of the Everton Shareholders' Association (ESA), which represented large numbers of smaller shareholders, were equally keen to see the back of True Blue. The supporters' group was also unhappy with the manner in which the Rooney contract negotiations were being conducted. Its members put together a petition with 220 signatures, the amount required to trigger an Extraordinary General Meeting at Everton. They intended to submit the request at the next board meeting.

In the weeks and months that followed I also met with more than twenty editors of Everton fanzines and supporters' websites, including ToffeeWeb and Blue Kipper. On one particular day later that summer, I hosted seven half-hour meetings in the foyer of the Radisson Hotel in Liverpool. I wanted the fans to know that although I was not a born and bred Evertonian, my intentions were good. I found them all to be thoroughly decent people, who listened with an open mind but were not afraid to be fiercely protective of the club they loved. Many were openly critical of me, but a significant number were supportive. Others were understandably suspicious, but willing to respect my openness about my intention to get rid of Bill. Overall, the majority wanted change in some shape or form, although many remained unsure about whether or not they were willing to back me.

Kenwright reacted to my letter by attacking me in the press, branding my proposals as 'irrelevant and mischievous'. Woods chipped in by calling them 'impracticable and unachievable'. The battle lines were now clear. Together Kenwright and Woods controlled True Blue Holdings, which in turn controlled Everton because it had the ability to outvote all of the independent shareholders combined. My only hope of loosening the stranglehold was to break up True Blue, so I was fully supportive of the attempt by the Everton Shareholders' Association to call an Extraordinary General Meeting.

The next two board meetings at Everton set the tone for the rest of the summer. The atmosphere was fiery and confrontational. I made comments to Bill along the lines of: 'I think you should resign. I think you are just f——ing up the club! You don't make any of the right decisions. I'm not saying I always do, but from a business perspective, the club is badly run and we should be making important decisions.'

Bill and Woods disagreed vehemently. We had reached deadlock and my best hope was that fan pressure would eventually force them to cave in and quit, or at the very least agree to dissolve True Blue. Our war of words continued into early August, when I attended my first game in many months at Goodison Park. It was a pre-season friendly against top Spanish side Real Sociedad. I arrived shortly before kick-off to discover the first row of the directors' box was empty. According to the press at the time, I sat in the seat that was usually occupied by Bill. Also elsewhere in the stadium was Wayne Rooney, who was injured but still with Everton at this point. When Bill arrived, rather than sit in the front row he spent most of the first half stood in the aisle behind, chatting to people. Following the half-time break, he rather comically rushed back out earlier than usual and plonked himself down in his usual place. When I came back into the stand, I decided discretion was the better part of valour and I took a seat further back. The crowd had seen us both taking up our respective seats and began a loud chorus of, 'Sack the board, sack the board . . . Sack the BOARD!' The fans had also unfurled a banner that read: 'From Sir John Moores to Death's Doors.' Feelings were running high.

'See you next season, Mr Gregg,' quipped one fan as I left the stadium that afternoon. He was obviously mindful of my recent absence from the club!

My stance during this period was that my proposal to raise new funding would immediately put cash into Everton's coffers. Bill therefore either needed to accept it for the good of the club, or find an immediate alternative source of investment. The week after the Real Sociedad game, the balance tipped slightly in my favour when the Everton Shareholders' Association was granted its request for an EGM, which was provisionally set for the 9th of September. I felt that if Bill failed to come up with the cash by then it would potentially be game over for him. However, there was no guarantee that the bid to dissolve True Blue would be successful, as it would essentially require the company's board to vote to close itself.

It felt as if the stalemate would go on forever, but then things suddenly tipped back in Bill's favour. He claimed to have secured a pledge for investment in the region of twenty to thirty million, from an international consortium. I was sceptical about the source of this funding, but interestingly Bill seemed to be conceding that True Blue would need to be dissolved in order to facilitate the deal.

Bill announced the new investor as a corporate entity called the Fortress Sports Fund. The majority of the cash was said to be coming from a Russian oligarch called Boris Zingarevich, with the deal being fronted by a Geneva-based financier called Christopher Samuelson. Apparently, Zingarevich later pulled out and was replaced by other private investors. I couldn't help thinking it all seemed a bit too good to be true, so I asked for various documents in order to substantiate matters. The announcement was greeted in public as if it were the answer to all of Everton's problems. Meanwhile, my own credibility had taken a knock in the eyes of the press owing to some confusion about the identity of one of the backers of my proposal.

When the Extraordinary General Meeting came around, I sensed that the only way Bill and Woods would ever agree to disband True Blue Holdings was if the EGM approved their proposal. Besides, my pragmatic view now was that if the £30 million they had talked about really did materialise, it would certainly ease the plight of the club and there would be a new shareholder that I could potentially work alongside in future. The Fortress Sports Fund indicated it would make the investment in return for a large chunk of the club, with the £30 million being paid in return for the issue of new shares. In the meantime, the club had an untouched credit facility for £15 million that had been extended by Bill's pal Sir Philip Green.

'I can confirm we will be dissolving True Blue Holdings as soon as practically possible, hopefully by the next AGM in December,' announced Kenwright at the EGM. 'The deal with the Fortress Sports Fund is an absolute possibility and will hopefully be sewn up within the next few weeks.'

He went on to state that all necessary checks had been carried out on the individuals involved, who had received 'A1' clearance. Bill and I publicly shook hands at the meeting and I agreed that I would no longer attempt to instigate my own proposal while the Fund's offer was in the process of being finalised. After all the anger and public recriminations, our war of words was finally over . . . for the time being.

Goodbye, Everton

Many people predicted that Wayne Rooney's departure from Everton would result in the club being relegated that season, but ironically things actually improved on the pitch. To give David Moyes due credit, for the time being he succeeded in turning things around. By December of 2004, Everton were in second position in the table and playing in front of capacity crowds. Bill was as good as his word, and True Blue Holdings was put into liquidation ahead of the club's AGM. Our respective equity was transferred into Everton shares, which felt like an enormous step forward.

I issued a statement saying I was delighted that the campaign for which the Everton Shareholders' Association and I had fought so hard was a success. But despite the renewed positivity, there was bad news ahead. There was still no sign of the money from the Fortress Sports Fund, despite Bill's hope that the cash would arrive within a few weeks. The club's borrowings had peaked at almost £47 million at the end of the previous financial year in May 2004. The situation had been eased since then by the proceeds from selling Rooney, but even so there was consternation among the fans when the accounts were published ahead of the AGM.

Despite the delay, Bill was still hopeful that the deal with the Fortress Sports Fund would go ahead. However, there was no item on the agenda at the AGM that would have facilitated the issue of the new shares that would have been required. Instead, Christopher Samuelson – the Geneva financier behind the deal – flew into the UK in order to give assurances at the AGM.

The meeting was attended by a couple of hundred people, mostly independent shareholders who were anxious to hear what Samuelson had to say. The AGM began with a routine vote to re-elect Bill as chairman. Those types of vote often go through unopposed, but although the vast majority were in favour Bill seemed disappointed when twenty or thirty people raised their hands to object.

'I didn't think I was that bad!' he quipped.

After being re-elected, Bill introduced Keith Wyness, who had recently been appointed as Everton's chief executive following the departure of Trevor Birch. Wyness had a background in sports management and had previously been CEO of Aberdeen FC in the Scottish Premier League. He had an impressive CV (and later went on to become chief executive of Aston Villa) but I was sceptical that his appointment would be a success. However, to his credit he gave a warts-and-all assessment of Everton's current predicament, which seemed to win over many of the fans in the room.

When it was Samuelson's turn to speak you could sense an atmosphere of anticipation. He was a snappy dresser, immaculately attired and looking very much the part of an international financier. He explained that the Fortress Sports Fund had actually offered an initial cash injection of £12.8 million in exchange for a 29.9 per cent stake in Everton, which could lead to further investment over time. However, he denied that the Fund was seeking a full takeover.

'We are prepared to be locked in and put more money in to help the club grow,' he said confidently. 'We have no intention of taking control. It is not a takeover. We will have two people on the board, so we will be outnumbered, but we want to help.'

He was a smooth talker and the majority of fans in the room seemed satisfied with most of his answers, but somewhere at the back of my mind little alarm bells were starting to ring. If Samuelson and his private investors were so keen to go ahead, why had things been delayed? Mr Samuelson is apparently highly regarded on the international financial stage, where his nickname is said to be 'The Magician'. He certainly gave the impression that there was some conjuring going on when he also claimed to be a lifelong follower of Everton. The Blues fans are a tight-knit community and can sense if somebody is one of their own. At least one mischievous supporter in the room was sceptical. The quick-witted fan responded by firing an unexpected question at Mr Samuelson.

'Who scored the winning goal in the 1966 FA Cup Final?' he asked.

This seemed to catch Samuelson off guard. There was an awkward moment when, instead of answering with the name of the relevant Everton player, he explained that he had been studying in Munich in 1966. My own knowledge of Everton's history might not be encyclopaedic, but then again I had never attempted to portray myself as a lifelong fan.

When I was asked for my thoughts about the Fortress Sports

Fund, I chose my words carefully but honestly. 'I still need to see the facts of the proposal and we need to see the money is in the bank,' I replied. 'If it is in the best interests of the club then it is acceptable, but we have not had a board meeting to discuss it and it is a question of whether it is at the right price.'[32]

Aside from the Fortress Sports Fund, the other topic of significance that arose at the AGM was the issue of a new stadium. There was further speculation about the possibility of sharing a ground, which had been gathering pace after it was announced that Liverpool FC had put in a bid with the North West Development Agency to develop a new stadium in Stanley Park. Bill had previously vowed that Everton would never be a tenant of Liverpool, but the new stadium raised the prospect of sharing on an equal basis. From the point of view of the agency, a shared stadium appeared to be an excellent option. Bill told shareholders at the meeting that the sports minister Richard Caborn had also made it clear that the government was behind the idea of one stadium being shared by two great clubs. Everton was due to meet with the city council for talks in the near future, and one of Keith Wyness's new tasks as chief executive was to assess whether it would be feasible.

Personally, I thought the idea of a shared ground was a great one provided it had the support of the fans. The image of a single magnificent stadium in the park, with one end decked in blue and the other in red, was a powerful one. The idea was that we would build a Goodison Village on one side and an Anfield Village on the other, so that the history of both clubs could be protected. The stadium would have boxes and dressing rooms on one side for Liverpool and the other side for Everton. Each club could therefore have their own 'home end', with an approaching walkway that could be lined with statues of club legends.

The ground-share idea seemed to gather momentum after the AGM. We spoke with David Henshaw at the city council and a meeting was scheduled with the sports minister. Caborn was a high-profile figure in Tony Blair's government, so he certainly had the clout to make it happen if all parties were in agreement. Bill Kenwright, Wyness and myself were asked to attend a meeting with Caborn in Manchester in order to represent Everton. The Liverpool chief executive Rick Parry was also due to attend, so I had high hopes that we could come to a provisional agreement on the day.

When Caborn arrived he got straight to the point. The government was keen to get involved to the extent that they were willing to supply the funding, which could then be repaid to the taxpayer over time.

'I believe Liverpool should be the first city to host a two-team stadium, and we will fund it and get our money back,' he announced.

'That will do. Thank you very much!' I quickly responded, anxious not to look a gift horse in the mouth.

But when Caborn then asked Rick Parry what he thought of the idea, the response made my heart sink. Parry's answer was that Liverpool would *not* share with Everton.

I tried to nudge Bill under the table, to get him to reiterate that we *would* share a stadium, but I don't think he could bear to lose face as an Evertonian by arguing for something that Liverpool had dismissed. I got the impression that David

Henshaw was furious that all the council's hard work had once again come to nothing. In January the idea of a ground-share was officially declared to be dead when the council issued the following statement:

> It is disappointing both sides have been unable to reach agreement on a joint stadium. However, the existing plan for a new Anfield is part of a major regeneration of the Anfield-Breckfield area and we fully intend to help deliver that because of the economic benefits it will bring to an area that badly needs them. Of course, we will also do everything we can to help Everton find a twenty-first-century solution for the club and its fans.[33]

There was further disappointment to come with regard to the Fortress Sports Fund. Christopher Samuelson continued to promise that the deal would go ahead, but each deadline passed without any sign of the cash. Eventually, much to Bill Kenwright's disappointment, the deal simply fizzled out. Samuelson reportedly helped broker deals several years later that were connected to Aston Villa and Reading, so he clearly did have some worthwhile contacts. As for Everton, we were back to square one – with no new stadium and very little cash.

★

I was offered one last roll of the dice in my quest to find a new home for Everton. Through my contacts in the leisure industry, I received an approach from representatives of the Las Vegas

Sands Corporation. This company is one of America's most successful developers of tourist infrastructure; it's the owner of the Venetian hotel and casino in Las Vegas. The people at Sands were aware that Tony Blair's government was keen to open a number of 'super-casinos' in the UK – potentially one in each region. They were interested in developing a site in the North West, and they enquired as to whether Goodison Park might be a potential location.

I couldn't visualise it myself. There may have been enough space, if the car park and some of the surrounding land were included, but it didn't feel like the right spot to place a casino, either for the local population or for Sands. I couldn't imagine people flocking there on a wet Tuesday in November. Besides, the planning situation would have been difficult even with government support.

Stanley Park might have made a better option. The people at Sands had contacts in Boston who were potentially interested in buying Liverpool FC. They suggested that, if that deal went ahead and Sands also partnered with Everton, the two American corporations could then combine forces to build a super-complex which would include a stadium for Liverpool and Everton to share. It was a slightly bizarre idea, but it might have had some merit if it had ever got off the ground.

One obvious stumbling block was that Liverpool FC was not for sale, but we felt there was a possibility that could change. There was a rumour that the club's chairman and majority owner, David Moores, was discontented, perhaps because Liverpool had not lifted a league title at the time since 1990. This perception changed somewhat when they made it to the

Champions League final in May of 2005. The people in Boston felt that if Liverpool were to lose, that might be a good time to swoop with an offer for the club. Of course, Liverpool went on to win spectacularly against Milan on penalties after coming back from being 3–0 down at half-time. The casino idea was quietly dropped, although as we know, Liverpool FC was sold to a different American owner a few years later.

Everton finished in fourth place that season, positioned above Liverpool for the first time in eighteen years. This result also entitled us to a place in the Champions League, although we faced a difficult first tie with Villarreal in order to reach the group stage. The club's debt position had also further improved thanks to extra gate receipts, additional TV money and ongoing attempts to reduce costs and wages. However, the long-term prospects remained challenging, and I was tired of all the infighting. It was true that things were now much calmer but the rift between Bill and me had been too great to recover from, and I felt that the time was approaching when I should consider selling my shares. When True Blue was dissolved, the investment I had made on behalf of Nita and myself had been transferred back to us – half in my name and half in hers – meaning that she had become a director of the club, although from that point onwards it was looking increasingly likely that we would sell up.

Everton lost the tie with Villarreal, which meant we had to make do with a place in the UEFA Cup. We crashed out from that competition at the first hurdle. Things began to stagnate on the pitch, although the team eventually managed to finish in 11th place. At this point I made it known that both my shares and Nita's were for sale. I was informed that the club would be willing to broker a deal and it was suggested that Bill Kenwright and I should meet at Philip Green's office in London to discuss the matter. This didn't strike me as unusual given how often Bill called upon Green for advice, but I was slightly apprehensive owing to my recent history with Bill, so I asked my lawyer to accompany me to the meeting. Nita and I had put £7.5 million into Everton; I had recently been advised that thanks to the increased prominence of the Premier League over the past six years, our stake was now worth more than the original amount. I had also heard through the grapevine that the club had received an approach from an outside investor that would potentially place the value of our holding at £9 million.

When we arrived at his office, Philip Green was in a flamboyant mood. He pulled out his chequebook and slammed it down on the table.

'This is a night in the casino for me!' he joked.

'Well, maybe you'll lose,' I joked back.

We were both smiling, but there was an icy edge to the atmosphere. It transpired that the club was willing to buy my shares for a certain price, which I felt was unacceptable. Before we got into the finer details, my lawyer pointed out that he was here to represent me and asked if the club would like to bring in his lawyer.

Green joked that we didn't need another 'f——ing lawyer' and everybody seemed happy to proceed on that basis.

However, as we discussed the value of the shares the conversation became heated. My lawyer stated what we knew about the potential new investor. This seemed to surprise Green.

'I don't know anything about this!' he complained. (I genuinely believe he had no knowledge of it.) He looked at Kenwright as if to say: 'What the f—— is all this about?'

Bill's reply suggested that he knew nothing about it either, so a telephone call was made to Keith Wyness, who was told to get down to London by four p.m. In the meantime, we agreed to break for coffee and get something to eat. I requested that Bill refrain from talking to Wyness any further until he arrived.

When we reconvened, Wyness stated that Everton had recently received an approach from somebody who was interested in buying the club. I was quietly furious that I hadn't been informed about this, but that oversight was blamed on a breakdown in communication.

'The answer is that we should sell the club, and then we'll get the best value for everybody,' I suggested.

There was a brief discussion about who could potentially handle such a sale, with the names of various brokers being bandied about. I was amazed that Bill seemed to be in agreement that it was time to throw in the towel and sell up. The meeting concluded with me under the impression that the club would now find itself under new ownership, subject to agreeing on a broker. However, later that evening I received a phone call informing me that Bill had now made a decision and that instead of selling the club, he was happy for a new investor to buy me out. We eventually did a deal with Robert Earl, the Planet Hollywood tycoon, whom I never met. We spent the weekend negotiating a price through my lawyer. Eventually we agreed on £9 million, which gave Nita and me a profit on our investment.

GOODBYE, EVERTON

In October 2006, it was announced that my involvement with Everton Football Club was finally over.

★

Looking back, I often ask myself what we could have done differently during my time at Everton. Certainly if King's Dock had gone ahead, I genuinely believe that the club's financial fortunes would have been transformed for the better in the years that followed. Could I personally have done more to make it happen? All I can say to Everton fans – for whom I continue to have immense respect – is that I fought as hard as I could. I also did my best to bring money into the club through our various sponsorship agreements with Kejian and Chang.

However, at the time of writing, the future for Everton continues to look uncertain. It's 17 years since I parted from the club and Everton has continued to run up huge losses in recent years. Like everybody, I was shocked in the autumn of 2023 when the club was deducted ten points for being in breach of the Premier League's financial regulations. This related to the fact that the club was calculated to have made losses of £124.5m for the period ending season 2021/22. Everton intend to appeal and the potential ramifications may clearer by the time you are reading this book.

One thing that seems obvious is that Everton's losses over the years are staggering for such a grand old club that continues to be loved by so many people. Figures published in March of 2022 revealed that Everton made operating losses of over £100 million for three consecutive seasons between 2019 and 2021

283

(which, to be fair, partly coincided with the pandemic). These losses consisted of £111.8 million in the financial year ending June 2019; £139.8 million for the year ending in June 2020; and c. £120.9 million in the year ending in June 2021.

Meanwhile, Everton does at least finally have a new home under construction in the shape of a 52,000+ seat stadium at Bramley-Moore Dock (which has no doubt added to financial pressures). At the time of writing, the club is also waiting for approval for prospective new owners to take over. I hope very much that the new stadium does eventually prove to be the club's salvation. However, the tragedy is that that Everton could have been playing at a magnificent new stadium many years ago. Hence, my lasting regret is that I wasn't able to foster enough support get King's Dock over the line. You may recall that I mentioned HOK, the architects that we planned to use. Today they're known as Populous and they are the international world leaders in stadium design. They have subsequently taken part in completing numerous stadiums for FIFA World Cup tournaments, along with the Emirates Stadium for Arsenal, Wembley Stadium in London, and Tottenham Hotspurs' breathtaking new home. It breaks my heart to think that Everton could have enjoyed playing in similar surroundings as long ago as 2006, for a price to the club of just £30 million (or possibly even less if the city council had stepped in).

As for my old friend Bill, I was obviously sad when I learned that he had passed away in October 2023. Despite our many differences over the years, I never believed that he was a bad person at heart, even though he could be hopelessly misguided on occasions. His passion for Everton may have been a great source of inspiration, but it sometimes made things extremely difficult when an objective decision was called for. I wish we could have worked harder together to achieve the move to King's Dock. Despite our very public rows, I will always admire his achievements in the theatre industry. I like to imagine that he's gone to that great premier league in the sky, where he's watching a performance of Jesus Christ Superstar.

I don't want to be too critical of Bill now that he is no longer here to defend himself. However, I feel that I need to put the record straight regarding certain misconceptions that have appeared online suggesting that King's Dock failed because my proposal to fund it via a reverse mortgage fell through. The truth is that the plan was well funded and ready to go, but Bill refused to go down that route. I think the main reason that he stalled over the King's Dock stadium was because he hated the idea of public bodies sharing in the development. Would that have been such a bad thing? Personally, I've come to realise that whilst a football club is a business that you might own on paper, it never truly belongs to you.

The real owners of a club like Everton are ultimately the fans – and they always will be.

Sweetness and Sorrow

My marriage to Nita was marked in equal measure during my time at Everton by periods of sweetness and sorrow. On the one hand, I loved her dearly for her sassy approach to life and her refusal to be fazed by anybody. From the moment I met her, back when she was working on the food counter of a bingo hall, I had adored Anita for her feistiness. Like me, she came from a relatively humble background, yet she wanted the best out of life and had a strong sense of self-worth. I never once saw her star-struck and she was never afraid to speak her mind. (I still chuckle warmly at the memory of her telling Prince Philip that she'd gone missing from a royal line-up due to an urgent call of nature.)

On the other hand, there was a side to our marriage that became extremely frustrating. While I admired Anita for being headstrong, there were occasions when her behaviour drove me nuts. It seemed like even the smallest things could sometimes trigger an angry outburst. During our early marriage we'd been soulmates and she had seemed happy for me to concentrate on business while she raised the children. But in later years things changed dramatically. I felt as if Nita was trying to overcompensate by demanding control of everything, whether it was related to business matters or our lives at home.

'Why can't you just do as I say and stop bloody arguing about everything?' she would screech at me.

Don't get me wrong, I could be equally stubborn, but I eventually grew tired of fighting and would inevitably cave in to her demands. With the benefit of hindsight, my failure to be stronger was a mistake that helped neither of us in the long run. Our decision to sell Apollo to SFX was a case in point. It was wonderful to be financially rewarded at the height of our success, but my fond memories of the Apollo Group are also tinged with sadness about not having fought harder to hold on to the company. Part of my motivation was that I'd hoped selling up would allow us to enjoy a more relaxed lifestyle, which might in turn help to improve our relationship.

It took me a while to adjust, but there were plenty of positives to enjoy. We'd collectively made financial gains of well in excess of £100 million. As majority shareholder, Nita received 51 per cent of the proceeds and my cut was approximately 25 per cent. The rest was divided between the other shareholders, including our sons, Simon and David, plus members of the management team. I wasn't concerned that Nita's share was greater than mine. I'd always taken the view that it didn't matter how we divided our wealth. I've never been motivated primarily by money (for me, it was always more about the satisfaction of building a great company). I must admit, however, that it's very nice to have piles of cash at your disposal!

Nita was determined to invest by splashing out on various properties. Her shopping list included a place in Chelsea (expensive and large), another house in Oxford (where we still had the huge place at Boars Hill), plus a *third* property in America (where we already owned a beach home and an investment condo).

'I think we should buy another house in Florida for when guests want to come and stay with us,' she told me.

It felt like a crazy game of Monopoly, with real money!

'Why do we need another house, when we've already got a great big place there with four empty bedrooms?' I replied.

Nita was insistent, so it was time to raid the piggy bank. We had friends in the US real estate business and they told me about a place in Marco Island that was coming up for sale. It was a beautiful balconied villa, complete with tropical gardens and pool house. Nita felt it would be perfect as our main residence while we were in Florida, which would free up one of the other properties for friends and family. The asking price was in the region of $8.5 million, which was a hefty sum at the time, but it seemed like a good investment. We funded the purchase by selling some of the share options we had inherited when we sold the company.

'I don't know the current value of our shares, but whatever they are worth is what we can offer you for the house,' I told the property agent.

It turned out that the shares didn't quite match the asking price – in fact, they were worth about a million dollars less – but the agent decided to accept our offer in any case. It worked out nicely because we were able to convert a paper asset into valuable property that would potentially accrue in value more quickly. We were now the owners of three houses in Florida and two in Oxford, with Nita still harbouring aspirations to buy a place in Chelsea as well (which we eventually did).

Meanwhile, my new role as the European chairman of SFX overlapped with my time at Everton. I was delighted that SFX had also hired David Rogers, Steve Lavelle and Sam Shrouder; I hoped this would enable us to recreate the old magic that we'd enjoyed in the past. The 'band' was back together in that respect, even if we were now being asked to play a very different tune. Being part of a global corporation brought its own opportunities and challenges. From one week to the next I could often find myself in a different European city, whether it was Paris, Amsterdam or Copenhagen. There were times when this was exhilarating. My American paymasters were using their financial muscle to snap up promoters and concert operators in whatever country they became available (although, unlike Apollo, they were relatively uninterested in acquiring actual buildings). The downside was that our old team were no longer masters of our own fate, but instead more like cogs in a huge corporate machine. This was further compounded by the fact that SFX was later purchased by an even bigger corporate entity, Clear Channel, which controlled more than eight hundred radio stations along with numerous television stations and over half a million advertising billboards in the USA. In the past at Apollo, we had been able to make quick decisions among ourselves that were generally profitable, but it was impossible for us to work in that way now. Our new employers understandably had their own way of doing things, and we were expected to submit detailed plans for everything in advance.

Unfortunately, despite our epic property shopping spree, my

marriage to Nita continued to struggle. Even when we spent quality time together in Florida things didn't seem to improve, despite the fact that we had everything we could possibly want. We'd go for meals in expensive restaurants in Marco Island or in nearby Naples, but it made no difference. It all boiled down to the fact that we could no longer find happiness in one other's company, regardless of how comfortable we were financially. We drifted back into spending more and more time apart. Sadly, my relationship with our son Simon also began to suffer around this time, as he and Nita often took a similar view of how the family's business interests should be managed.

On the occasions when Nita and I were both in the UK, I would go home after spending the day at Clear Channel or Everton and we would nearly always end up arguing about trivial matters. It reached a point where I'd sometimes storm out of Boars Hill and stay in a hotel. This became a pattern that repeated over and over again. Previously, during our later years at Apollo, Nita had become very controlling in her attitude to the business. The fact that she had a majority shareholding gave her the freedom to call up anybody within the company and berate them. Things were obviously very different now that I was at Clear Channel; Nita had no control over the new company, yet she would still constantly ring the offices in Grosvenor Street demanding to be put through to me. If I happened to be out on business she would become very frustrated.

'Where the HELL is my husband? I want to be put through to him NOW,' she would demand.

Her brusque manner eventually resulted in a number of complaints.

'We need to speak to you about Mrs Gregg,' said one rather embarrassed person from the HR department. 'I'm afraid we've had reports that she has been rude and abusive to secretaries and other members of staff.'

I spoke to her about it, but things subsequently came to a head one afternoon when she came to the office and began shouting at the top of her voice about the trouble she'd had getting hold of me. It led to an unpleasant scene during which, in her fury, she accidently knocked a table lamp to the floor. This seemed to be the final straw as far as Clear Channel was concerned. Soon afterwards, my bosses invited me in for a private conversation.

'We're wondering if, all things considered, you might be happier if you were to think about moving on to somewhere new?' they suggested.

To be fair to Nita, the writing was probably already on the wall in relation to my position. Deep down, I'd been expecting to leave Clear Channel at some point. I'd been striving to do my best and for a time I had enjoyed the role, but in truth I missed the old way of doing things. I'd fallen into a rhythm of dividing my time between Marco Island and Europe, and at the back of my mind I knew it was probably only a matter of time before I decided to leave. Perhaps my new colleagues sensed that I wasn't bringing the same passion to my work as I had at Apollo. But I was sorry to learn that Clear Channel had decided to offer Sam Shrouder a severance package, too. It seemed crazy that there wasn't a role there for a man of his immense talent.

All in all, Nita's fiery outburst in the office probably did me a favour, because it brought things to a head and forced me to think about the future. I realised that I much preferred running my own company, and this sparked an idea. I knew Clear Channel wouldn't want to part with any theatres, but I wondered whether they might be willing to return some of the other assets we had sold.

'Why don't we try to buy back our cinemas and bingo halls?' I suggested to Nita.

We agreed to make an offer to Clear Channel, and we negotiated a price of £22 million for twelve cinemas and four bingo halls. I was delighted when they accepted our proposal. It felt fantastic to be back in business! I was also pleased when Steve Lavelle decided to join us as property director. David Rogers opted to stay on at Clear Channel for a time, although he too would later agree to join us.

I was excited by the prospect of growing the cinema network but I was less sure about the bingo operation, which needed a dedicated management team. We therefore decided to sell the bingo assets and achieved a price of £11 million, which was an excellent deal. The final result was that we walked away from Clear Channel with the cinemas, plus extra cash on top.

I became chairman of the newly reborn Apollo Cinemas and I then approached my old friend Jim Whittell, former boss of Odeon Cinemas. He agreed to become our new MD, so we now had the makings of a great team. The cinemas were virtually debt-free and the company was in a good position to grow. One of the first things we wanted to explore was the possibility of acquiring a prestige site for a new flagship cinema in the West End, so we went to view the old Plaza Theatre in Haymarket close to Piccadilly. It was perfect, so we purchased the lease in order to open the new Apollo West End Cinema. We were once again at the helm of a successful business that was making healthy profits.

In spite of all these positive changes, my marriage continued to be very challenging. Things deteriorated further during a break in Marco Island while Jim and his charming wife, Jenny, were our guests. At one point during the holiday Nita flew into a rage at Jim over a trivial row about the timing of a trip to the hairdresser's. It was a silly argument, but it was a foretaste of the storm clouds that lay ahead.

The cinemas were in Nita's name, which we had been advised was the most tax-efficient way of doing things at the time. Once again, this gave her carte blanche to let rip. After we returned to the UK, she popped her head around the door during a board meeting at Boars Hill while we were discussing whether to have a pick 'n' mix confectionery section at the new Apollo cinema in the West End. Jim attempted to explain the commercial advantages, but Nita refused to contemplate the idea.

'There will NOT be any pick 'n' mix!' she insisted.

Jim became increasingly frustrated with her, and after that they regularly clashed to the point where he eventually resigned. Not long afterwards, Nita and I had yet another huge row. To be honest I can't even remember what it was about, because we had so many fights. I was sick of arguing and needed a break, so in the heat of the moment I stormed out of the house and went to stay the night in a hotel while things calmed down. When I returned home, the locks had been changed.

Our marriage was finally over.

★

The following year, on New Year's Eve in 2009, Nita was taken ill while on holiday in Marco Island. We had been estranged for over a year and I had moved into a flat in London. She was diagnosed with cancer of the gall bladder and was told she had approximately five weeks to live.

I was, obviously, bitterly sad to hear the news. I don't believe it's possible to share nearly forty years of your life with somebody and then suddenly lose your feelings for that person, even if you are no longer in a relationship.

I had spent Christmas in the UK with Jim Whittell, so I heard the tragic news by phone from our son Simon. My first reaction was to say I would immediately fly to Florida, but he told me Nita did not want to see me. I was shocked and told him that this was no time for family arguments with Nita.

'Your mother and I have got things to say to one another after being together for forty years,' I told him. 'I should have a right to see her because we have issues to resolve. If she's dying, we both have a right to try and make our peace, for good or for bad.'

I was half minded to ignore what Nita had said and jump on a plane, but I didn't think it would help the situation if we ended up in a confrontation at the hospital. Simon no doubt felt that he was acting in his mother's best interests by passing on her views, but I was very saddened at not having the opportunity to say farewell.

I spent the next few days calling for updates, but I was unable to speak to Nita in person. I later discovered that she was being flown back to the UK by private plane and would be spending her final weeks in Oxford.

Unfortunately, the message conveyed to me in England was the same: Nita felt it would be better if I stayed away. I contemplated driving to Oxford, but again I had to acknowledge that it would be better to avoid a confrontation and hope for a change of heart by Nita and Simon.

On the 21st of February, ten days after our wedding anniversary, Simon rang to inform me that Nita had passed away.

It was a sad situation for everybody and in the circumstances I felt it was best for everybody if I stayed away from the funeral.

How could it come to this? I asked myself.

I spent the day of the funeral trying to remember the good times Nita and I had shared, before things went wrong between us. I wondered over and over if she had thought about me during her final days.

I learned the answer to that question a few weeks later when I received a heartbreaking letter from lawyers acting for Nita's estate. I assumed it must be a routine communication to tidy up our financial affairs in the normal way, but I was in for a shock. I'd always understood that if either Nita or I were to pass away, then anything we owned would automatically be passed to the other. We were technically still married – on paper, at least – but even if we had chosen to divorce, things would have logically been split fifty-fifty. However, the letter informed me that this would no longer be the case. Nita's last will and testament had been changed while she was in Oxford and signed on the 11th of February (the very day of our fortieth wedding anniversary). It had been her last wish that I should receive nothing from the proceeds of anything that could be perceived as her property. I was cut out of virtually everything.

Emotionally, it was a bombshell. It felt as if forty years of marriage had been erased at the stroke of a pen, presumably in the presence of a lawyer at Nita's bedside. Financially, it was also a huge blow. I'd always regarded the cinema and the properties as part of a family estate, rather than Nita's personal domain. If her will was left unchallenged, I could potentially be left with the Thomas Tucker business (which was in my name) and very little else apart from a share of some of the property.

'Surely this cannot be correct in law?' I asked my own lawyer.

'It would certainly be open to challenge, but I'm afraid that in the circumstances it's likely to be a very complex case,' he replied. 'It would be much better if you could simply come to an amicable arrangement with your son.'

Initially, I hoped I could resolve matters amicably with Simon without having to go to court, but by now there seemed to be armies of lawyers and accountants involved and things degenerated into an expensive family feud that went on for over two years. It was painful and frustrating, but throughout it all, my main emotion was a deeply felt sorrow that I'd been unable to say goodbye to Nita.

A Family at War …
and a New Beginning

I was feeling very low after Nita passed away. Even though we hadn't seen one another for a year prior to her death, I had hoped we would overcome our difficulties, but instead things had broken down to the point where we hated even speaking on the phone. With hindsight, I think she had probably decided many years earlier that our relationship was over. Yet there was a part of me that still loved her very much. She could be headstrong to the point of belligerence, but I know that I too played a role in the demise of our relationship by concentrating too closely on the daily details of my job. Sometimes, it's only when you pause to reflect on your life that you realise how many of the things you hoped for have been lost through conflict.

I began to dwell on the fact that everything that had once been important to me had been sold in an effort to bring some harmony to my marriage. I should have understood that it wasn't the company that was at the root of our problems – it was what we were doing to one another. We had a wonderful business at the Apollo Leisure Group, with a great staff and management team. Jimmy Nederlander's words continued to echo in my mind: *You've already got enough money . . . But if you sell the company, you'll always miss the things that you own today.*

Jimmy had been right, and the realisation hit me hard.

To be frank, I was feeling a bit of a mess in other ways too. About six months before Nita passed away I'd fallen into the habit of living on a poor diet with little or no exercise. I was probably also drinking a little more than was healthy, hence my weight ballooned to in excess of fifteen stone and I had constant backache. Workwise, I still had a number of projects to concentrate upon, but it felt as if something was missing from my day-to-day existence.

Maybe it was time to make a few lifestyle changes?

A friend recommended that I might benefit from seeing a therapist called Yoshiko Yamaguchi, who ran a wellbeing clinic in Mayfair. I was willing to give it a try, so I booked an appointment. When I arrived, I noticed how tranquil the atmosphere felt inside the clinic, away from the bustle of the city. A charming Japanese lady greeted me with a warm smile.

'How can I help you?' she asked.

I explained that I wanted to enquire about physiotherapy for my back and that I might also benefit from some advice on how to lose weight. Yoshiko explained that she practised a holistic approach to wellbeing, which combined modern techniques with alternative medicine such as Reiki, an ancient form of Japanese energy healing. I'd never taken much interest in alternative therapies in the past, but there was something about her calm demeanour that made me listen with an open mind. After that, I started to visit the clinic on a regular basis.

A FAMILY AT WAR ... AND A NEW BEGINNING

This was after Nita and I had parted, so I would also talk about the ongoing issues in my marriage. It was a relief to be able to get certain things off my chest. Yoshiko would listen objectively and she often responded by saying that in her view, I was partly to blame for the failure of the relationship.

After Nita passed away I continued with the therapy sessions, which were a great help to me. However, the relationship between Simon and me continued to deteriorate. Simon had by now been chief executive of Apollo Cinemas for over two years and the company had run up an annual pre-tax loss of around £1 million. The executors of Nita's estate became the new majority owners, so I continued to be locked out of any say over the cinemas. Despite this, I hoped that we had a basis upon which to rebuild a successful business. The company now operated fourteen venues across the country, including the flagship Apollo West End. I hoped I could break the deadlock by offering to take control of the company. My view was that with the help of David Rogers and Jim Whittell, we could restore it to profitability for the benefit of the whole family.

Simon initially offered his support for a settlement that would have resulted in me taking ownership of the cinemas. However, this required placing a formal value on the company, which proved difficult owing to the fact that the finances were in such a mess. Things had become very disorganised on the financial side after Jim and I had stepped back and the company was now wasting cash in a number of areas. It had a perfectly good HQ in Preston, yet it had recently spent a fortune on decorating expensive offices in London (which were in addition to the venue in Piccadilly). I was advised that until I had full visibility over the financial situation, there was a risk that I would actually be taking on a huge liability – hence, I chose not to accept until matters could be fully clarified. With the benefit of hindsight, that was a mistake on my part, because it set off yet another endless cycle of legal bills and forensic accounting. I found it frustrating that such a huge amount of money was being wasted on lawyers and accountants.

My hope for the future was that Apollo Cinemas would come under my control after agreeing a fair valuation and I would then merge the company with the Thomas Tucker popcorn business. This would enable us to streamline our operations into a single profitable entity. However, my dispute with Simon had by now become very acrimonious. I felt very sad that as a family we had not been able to come to an amicable agreement.

Meanwhile, the Thomas Tucker business was facing pressures of its own in the wake of austerity that followed the global banking crash, but I felt that if we could consolidate with the cinemas we would have the makings of another major entertainment company. I hoped that we could develop a new aspect of the business, hosting special events using digital and 3D technology to integrate with live theatre, opera and ballet. We also wanted to encourage Sky Sports to work with us to create cinema events showing live football in 3D. I would still have been happy for Simon to have equity in the company, because if David Rogers and I could recreate the old magic that we'd enjoyed together for twenty-five years then I knew we would build a good company producing strong profits – something from which Simon and his family could potentially benefit for many years to come.

A FAMILY AT WAR... AND A NEW BEGINNING

Aside from all of that, I had plans of my own to help relaunch the historic open-air theatre in Scarborough as part of a £3.5 million renovation, in conjunction with the local council. This project brought back many happy memories from my childhood. The dispute with Simon meant that this was a tough period of my life, but as I've learned over the years, it's often when you are at your lowest – and when you least expect it – that things take an unexpected turn for the better.

In this instance, I was about to experience a new beginning.

★

For a long time, it didn't even cross my mind that my relationship with the charming Japanese therapist I'd met in Mayfair could be anything other than strictly professional. Indeed, it stayed that way until well after Nita passed away; but gradually, things began to change. As the year wore on, I noticed how much I had started to look forward to the therapy sessions with Yoshiko. I enjoyed our conversations but certainly didn't think they would develop into anything beyond a friendly client–therapist connection with this kind and intelligent young woman. I estimated that Yoshiko was aged in her early forties – she was slim and attractive and many years younger than me. I felt foolish when it fleetingly crossed my mind one day to ask her if she would like to come for a coffee. I felt sure she would decline, but then again, there was something about Yoshiko that made me decide to carefully raise the subject by asking what she liked to do when she was not working.

'Have you seen any good movies lately or been to any nice

restaurants with friends?' I asked. 'Perhaps we could go for a coffee one day.'

Yoshiko chose not to accept on that occasion, but I think she must have sensed my disappointment. I was pleasantly surprised when, a few days later, she indicated that she had changed her mind.

'Would you still like to go for a coffee, Paul?' she said. 'Perhaps we can meet later on after I finish for the day?'

I readily accepted and we met that evening. Every moment felt special. I realised how much I admired her eyes and her beautiful smile and her ability to explain things using the meticulous logic that is favoured by Japanese people. Our conversation seemed to flow naturally and I found myself smiling and laughing for the first time in months. We spoke about lots of different things and at one point, when the subject of our age difference came up in conversation, Yoshiko said something in passing that stayed in my mind.

'I wish you were twenty years younger,' she smiled.

Normally in our therapy sessions, part of Yoshiko's role was to help me understand my faults, but this was the first time she had said anything to indicate that she enjoyed my company. Her comment reflected my own feelings.

That night we decided to extend our evening together by going the cinema. It felt slightly strange, but very pleasant after so many months of feeling low. Here I was, at the age of sixty-eight, going out with a beautiful Japanese princess. She was the first woman I'd met in a very long time that I found charming in every way.

During my treatment sessions, I'd previously explained to

Yoshiko that I'd spent my life in the entertainment business and that I continued to have interests in the cinema industry. Yoshiko told me that she had some friends in Japan who were involved in a film called *Jun-Ai*, which told the story of a Japanese humanitarian campaigner who built a school at the foot of a mountain. The film was directed by an award-winning Chinese cinematographer and starred an actress who was a friend of Yoshiko's. During our conversation, Yoshiko mentioned that her friends were keen to arrange a screening in London. I suggested that the Princess Anne Theatre at BAFTA in Piccadilly, where I am a member, would be a suitably prestigious venue. Yoshiko was worried about the cost, but I explained that if I booked the venue we could reserve it at member's prices.

We went ahead, and we discovered that many Japanese people living in London wanted to support the screening. We agreed that any proceeds after expenses would go a children's charity in China. I was delighted to be helping Yoshiko bring the film to London. This project gave us a reason to meet regularly outside of our therapy sessions to discuss the marketing and planning. When we eventually hosted the night at BAFTA, the audience adored the film, with many people crying during the emotional scenes. We were delighted to meet the cast and the director afterwards and we enjoyed a wonderful evening.

Over the weeks and months that followed, my life started to change as Yoshiko and I developed a close friendship. I reduced my drinking and I no longer craved sugary cakes. It felt good that a beautiful young Japanese woman found me interesting in different ways. As the year progressed, Yoshiko told me that her parents would be coming to Europe in the summer to visit

Rome, Venice, Paris and London, after which she planned to go to India for a few weeks.

In the meantime, I was due to attend the opening of the new Scarborough Open Air Theatre. It made me very happy to be involved with such an important project in the town that had given me so many memories. It was everything I had hoped for. The Queen and the Duke of Edinburgh travelled up to North Yorkshire on the royal train for the grand opening, which was staged on a Thursday. The weather was perfect, with the new theatre bathed in sunshine for most of the day. Her Majesty was given a tour of magnificent local gardens before watching a performance by local theatre groups.

The chief executive of the local council made it clear that the new complex would have a significant impact on the town. 'This is truly a historic event of the highest magnitude for a borough that has a tradition of entertainment and attracting many generations of visitors,' he told the BBC.[34]

Most of my family in Scarborough were long gone by now. However, there was one notable exception: my Auntie Marjorie, who celebrated her 100th birthday that year. It gave me a great deal of pleasure to arrange a front-row seat for her at the opening show.

I was due to stay in the North for a few days afterwards and so I texted Yoshiko and asked if she would like to come and meet me in York on the Saturday. I met her on the platform at York Station, where I was struck by the sight of her smile and her lovely eyes. It felt like the most special thing I had done for many years, and I think from that point onwards I began to believe that our relationship might lead to something

A FAMILY AT WAR... AND A NEW BEGINNING

more than friendship. We travelled back to London on Sunday evening, after which Yoshiko was due to fly to Japan to meet her parents. She was then planning to fly back to Europe with them to spend some time in Venice. I arranged to join her in Rome after the family trip to Venice while her parents travelled onwards to Paris.

When I arrived in Italy there was a change of plan, due to Yoshiko's mother feeling unwell and needing to see a doctor. Thankfully it was not serious, but instead of going to Paris her parents decided to travel straight to London so that her mother could rest.

While Yoshiko's parents were in the UK, her mother rested at Yoshiko's apartment while her father made sure that she was comfortable. I suggested to Yoshiko that we should buy him a Japanese newspaper every day and that I would go to the HMV store to see if I could find some movies in the Japanese language. This worked well – he loved being able to share the news from Japan with us, and he and I watched several movies together and started to build a relationship despite the language barrier. The health of Yoshiko's mother began to improve, and we arranged for her parents to see *The Lion King* at the Lyceum and also to attend the Proms at the Royal Albert Hall so that their holiday would be special.

When it was time for Yoshiko's parents to travel back to Japan, both she and I felt sad to see them go. The previous few weeks had been something of an emotional whirlwind for us: we had become very close, but in the pause after her parents went home it felt as if we had a lot of things to consider. Somehow, our age gap and cultural differences didn't seem like an obstacle. We had very different day-to-day habits – for one thing, Yoshiko loves healthy Japanese food like sushi, noodles and rice, whereas I am a Yorkshireman at heart and favour roast beef or fish and chips. None of that seemed to matter. Our relationship grew to a point where we were happy to spend almost all of our time together.

One day while we were talking, the subject of marriage came up, and I suggested that it might be something we should consider in the future. However, in truth, talking about the future felt a bit overwhelming. By the autumn, Yoshiko began to question whether we were doing the right thing by letting our relationship develop; for my part, I also felt hugely responsible for so quickly becoming an important part of her life. Things came to a head in October.

'Paul, I feel we both need a break to give us some time to consider everything. I think that we should spend a month apart,' Yoshiko suggested.

I hated the idea of four weeks without seeing her; I knew that it could mean the end of the relationship. On the other hand, I understood that some breathing space might be exactly what was needed to give us the reassurance we needed and help us feel more confident about our future together. I agreed to her suggestion and we arranged to meet in a month's time for tea, on a Monday afternoon at the Savoy. Yoshiko asked that until then there should be no phone calls, no emails or texts, no flowers or cards – in fact, no communication at all during our planned weeks apart.

At the start of the break, I dropped her off at her apartment and went upstairs for a last coffee, but my feeling of gloom was

A FAMILY AT WAR... AND A NEW BEGINNING

overwhelming. Just as I was leaving, Yoshiko called me back to give me a card with a message saying to take care, and that she would see me a month later. That made me feel slightly better.

I booked a week in the US to sort out loose ends in Florida relating to business matters, taking my brother David with me. David and I had kept in touch over the years, as I had also done with my sister, but I had not been involved in business with my siblings. When I arrived back in the UK, I spent the next two weeks concentrating on trying to find a way forward with Simon over the cinema business, but things remained deadlocked. It was a miserable month. I asked a friend with hotel connections to book afternoon tea at the Savoy, but they had no tables available. However, I did manage to book two tickets for *Romeo and Juliet* at the Royal Opera House in the hope that Yoshiko would agree to come along.

When the month had passed, I arrived at the Savoy early and tried everything I could to persuade the staff to find a table, but there was still nothing available until 6.30 p.m. – which meant Yoshiko and I would need to go for a drink in the bar instead. The Savoy is a big hotel, so I texted her details of where I was sitting. I don't mind admitting that I felt very nervous and apprehensive about the fact that she might choose not to show up. I checked my phone on a regular basis but there were no messages, and there was no sign of Yoshiko. I started wandering around in the hope that I might spot her. As I paced up and down, I began to fear the worst.

Then, suddenly, at around four thirty, there she was. My heart lifted – it was a wonderful feeling. I greeted her warmly, but our conversation felt slightly awkward after being apart for what had seemed like an eternity. I was worried that she would be disappointed I hadn't managed to book a table for such an important meeting, but thankfully it didn't matter. When a place finally became available for afternoon tea, I grabbed the opportunity. We went into the lounge and things slowly became more relaxed between us while we chatted over our scones with jam. We both said that we had greatly missed one another, and I felt an enormous sense of relief when Yoshiko agreed to accompany me to the Royal Opera House that evening.

The break in our relationship had been an ordeal, but it was worth the wait. We spent that Christmas together in Malaysia . . . and we were married the following June in Japan.

★

My dispute with Simon over the family estate showed no sign of reaching a resolution, despite my best efforts to conclude things amicably. The advice that I now received from all sides, including friends, family and my legal team, was that we should just go to court and argue for 50 per cent of the estate. It was felt this was the minimum that I would be awarded, given the fact that Nita and I had been married for forty years.

I was still keen to explore the possibility of me taking over the cinemas and running the business in conjunction with David Rogers. However, the cinemas were by now running desperately short of cash, and in February 2012 a team of accountants from KPMG was appointed to advise on a way forward. This included the possibility of seeking new investors. I wasn't sure it was necessary, when we had a ready-made solution staring us in the face – it felt hurtful that the company couldn't seem to understand that the best lasting value for all of us would be created if David and I were allowed to take the reins. The business was losing money rapidly, but I was convinced we had the expertise to turn things around.

It later emerged that the company was on course to breach its overdraft facility and the banks were unwilling to lend it any more money. The financial strain was such that suppliers apparently faced a six-month wait for payment of outstanding bills. The board agreed to follow a recommendation by KPMG that Apollo should freeze its liabilities and make weekly payments to cover expected VAT and PAYE, so as not to accrue any further liabilities to HMRC. According to a report that was later published by the Office of Fair Trading, it was against this financial backdrop that the idea of selling the Apollo business came up. The family estate was apparently 'in no position to raise the significant monies required to fund the business in the long term', and the conclusion was that 'a buyer of the whole business had to be found'.

I was aghast when I heard the cinemas were being actively touted for sale. The third parties likely to bid for them included Cineworld and Vue. I wrote to Simon, reminding him that I had vast experience in the industry – and pointing out that no matter how difficult things had been between his mother and me, she had always sought my advice in a crisis. I truly believed that in no circumstances would Nita have considered selling the cinemas to any other operator. It seemed to me that the dispute between us was needlessly running up enormous bills for lawyers, accountants and various advisors when really, we should have been doing everything possible to avoid wasting family money.

After much discussion with David Rogers and Lionel Becker, I decided that I would offer to match the highest value that any bidder would place on the company. That could then be taken into account in any settlement that we might reach on my expected share of the estate.

Around this time, I learned from my brother David that Simon had just become the father of a baby boy. It was wonderful news, but I was sad that things had come to a point where I'd found out about the arrival of a grandchild through another family member. I still very much hoped that Simon and I would be able to resolve our differences one day and return to having a father-and-son relationship. I wrote again, this time to congratulate him, and said that I hoped his wife and baby were in good health.

Despite these efforts, the dispute continued to be acrimonious; it reached the stage where we were even debating the proposed sale of some paintings in one of the family homes. At the same time I was facing a tough situation within the Thomas Tucker popcorn business, which my brother David was now managing. We'd struggled to hold on to one of our major accounts, which put a lot of pressure on our bottom line. David was fighting to attract new business, but it looked increasingly likely that we would need to make at least two redundancies in order to balance the books.

Things came to a head in May, on the day I attended a lunch organised by the Cinema Exhibitors' Association (now known as the UK Cinema Association) to celebrate its 100th anniversary.

My brother David had been planning to attend, but something came up and he asked if I would like to go along instead with Jim Whittell. I was looking forward to seeing Jim and catching up with friends from the industry.

I arrived just before lunch was called. Jim and I were keeping an ear out for the latest gossip about any potential deal to sell the Apollo cinemas to Cineworld or Vue. When Jim bumped into an old colleague who was in the know, my worst fears were realised. Apparently a memo of understanding had been signed with Vue, and a formal deal was soon to be announced. My lunch was ruined, to say the least.

How could my own son do a deal with somebody else? I asked myself. Surely it would have been better for Simon to let me take the cinemas as part settlement, with him continuing to hold equity so that our family's legacy in the entertainment business could continue?

Of course, it was the executors of the estate who had made the formal decision to sell, but ultimately it was Simon I felt let down by. I believed that the proposal I had put forward with David and Lionel had made it clear we would match or pay a premium over the best offer, which would be funded from my share of the estate. I'm afraid I completely lost my head over lunch and fired off some emails to Simon that contained very strong language, which I now regret. I felt ashamed afterwards that I hadn't stopped to think before writing to him. It was a low point in our relationship.

The following day, the *Financial Times* published a report online that stated the purchase price was in the region of £20 million, although I believe that was somewhat higher than the actual sum. In truth, the value was not that important; what hurt the most was the lost opportunity to build a new leisure business using the knowledge that David Rogers, Jim Whittell and myself had acquired over the last fifty years.

My dispute with the family estate was eventually settled following a court hearing during which each side set out its case, leaving a judge to decide upon the outcome. I was awarded a substantial sum, although it was less than anybody had envisaged. My mind rewound to over a decade earlier, when we had sold the original Apollo Leisure Group to SFX. This family feud, along with a lot of poor financial planning, had now swallowed up the vast majority of the proceeds I had received at that time. I hadn't quite lost everything, but let's just say that I was left with a fraction of what I might otherwise have had.

This was very dark period, both professionally and financially, but at least the settlement was a form of closure. Besides, I now had other things in my life to concentrate upon, the most important of which was a new beginning with Yoshiko.

Unfortunately, there was one last shock in store. It happened when I was dropping off Yoshiko at her flat the night before we were due to fly to Japan for our wedding. We were talking in the car when two men opened the doors. One of them grabbed Yoshiko's handbag, but amazingly, she chased after him and snatched it back, before returning to rescue me. Thankfully, Yoshiko had trained in boxing and karate and neither of us was hurt!

Japan, India and Enlightenment

Yoshiko and I were married in a Shinto religious ceremony on the beautiful Japanese island of Hokkaido. The historic temple at which we exchanged our vows was a magnificent building that had previously been used as a summer home for the Emperor of Japan and his family. Today, it's an impressive shrine with lush gardens that transform into a sea of cherry blossom in spring. The temple is surrounded by dense woodland, which further adds to the peace and tranquillity of the location.

It was Yoshiko's wish that we should share a traditional Japanese wedding surrounded by a small group of her close family and friends. We agreed that we would also arrange a separate blessing later for friends in the UK, so in effect we were married twice. I was happy to respect her choice of ceremony in Hokkaido, but there was one aspect that presented me with a challenge: I would need to say my wedding vows in Japanese. Believe me when I say that this was no easy task for a Yorkshireman raised in Scarborough!

I had previously taken a few Japanese lessons in London, but I was by no means fluent – far from it – so I was grateful when

Yoshiko's father kindly offered to give me a crash course. This involved me listening quietly as he carefully pronounced the sacred vows, which I did my best to write down phonetically in order to create a guide. I then read aloud from the written sheet while Yoshiko's father listened patiently, gently coaching me where necessary. I also learned that during the marriage ceremony it would be necessary for me to take a number of sips from a sacred cup of Japanese sake, which is best taken in moderation. Sake is a formidable spirit and if you drink too much it can make your eyes water (in which case, I hoped everybody would think I was crying tears of joy). Thankfully there was plenty of opportunity to practise my language skills, along with a liberal intake of sake.

Prior to the wedding, Yoshiko and I stayed at her family's home in Asahikawa, which is the second-largest city on the island after Sapporo. It was a wonderful introduction to Japanese culture. I was made very welcome and Yoshiko was delighted to once again be reunited with her family. I slept in her brother's room on a futon, which took some getting used to but turned out to be quite comfortable.

One of the first things that Yoshiko and I did was go to select our Japanese wedding garments. These were traditional outfits consisting of elaborate kimonos made from the finest silk. We went to a huge store where Yoshiko's mother had previously worked many years earlier. It reminded me of Harrods, with large sections where men and women could try on various garments in privacy while being attended to by the expert matrimonial assistants. In Japan, most people hire their wedding outfits because they are too complex to buy. It seemed like there were a thousand choices of garments to rent, and it took the best part of three days to be measured and fitted with the correct attire. We had a lot of fun trying out different options. Japanese bridal outfits are particularly complex, with a magnificent headdress that takes several hours to fit. The groom's attire is less elaborate and to Western eyes bears some resemblance to a martial arts suit, or something a Samurai warrior might wear – minus the sword, of course! Various undergarments are worn beneath the groom's outer suit and these inner layers wrap around the waist, pulling in the tummy, which I hoped made me look a little like Sean Connery as James Bond in a karate suit (I'm not sure anybody else saw me that way, but then again, appearances can be deceptive).

On the day of our wedding, Yoshiko looked stunning in her white bridal outfit with a starkly contrasting black headdress that matched her beautiful hair. The wedding temple had special rooms set aside for the bride and groom to get changed into their outfits and ensure that everything was perfect. It typically takes a Japanese bride around four hours to prepare at the temple, and the groom at least one hour.

I was still nervous that I would make a hash of my vows, but thanks to the tuition from Yoshiko's father I made it through unscathed. A Russian friend of Yoshiko's, Oleg, took our wedding photos. He is a brilliant photographer with a great sense of humour. We held a bridal reception afterwards at a local hotel, where he entertained the guests and staff with his bubbly personality. Twenty of Yoshiko's guests joined us for a celebration dinner and the dining room was adorned with an amazing array of floral displays, which at the end of the evening were removed by guests to be enjoyed at home. This custom was new to me, but it's a good practice because none of the flowers are discarded after the wedding.

It was a wonderful start to our new life together. Japan is an incredible country and I enjoyed seeing a new side of it – the whole experience was very different from my first visit there, for the Michael Jackson tour. One favourite place that Yoshiko and I visited was Tokyo's chaotic Tsukiji market. This was the biggest fish market in the world at the time and it hosted an auction of giant tuna every day, just before dawn. The market was an amazing sight with its hundreds of stalls, each displaying a different kind of fish or crab in huge sizes, all recently landed from the sea and completely fresh. Restaurants and shops there opened early, so it was a good place to breakfast on fresh sushi while watching the sun come up in the 'land of the rising sun'. Today the main fish auction has moved elsewhere but the Tsukiji market is still a wonderful place to visit, with hundreds of stalls selling goods of all descriptions.

Yoshiko and I still enjoy travelling to interesting places around the globe. Before our wedding I had originally intended to formally propose six months earlier, during the Christmas break we spent together at the Genting Highlands resort near Kuala Lumpur in Malaysia. The Genting is a fantastic mountain retreat with numerous hotels, theme parks and casinos rivalling the best of anything Las Vegas can offer. Yoshiko's parents joined us there on that occasion, so it would have been an ideal opportunity to announce our engagement. However, she and her mother became unwell with heavy colds, so I abandoned my plan to propose. Instead we joined a VIP party on New Year's Eve and, when the celebratory fireworks were rained off, spent the evening inside listening to a live band. As midnight approached, Yoshiko's father delighted everybody by taking to the stage in order to lead the singing.

Following our stay in Malaysia, the two of us were due to travel to Vietnam (where I eventually did propose). There was a slight hitch en route when we tried to check in for our flight and I discovered that I would need a visa, which could only be obtained from the Vietnamese embassy in Kuala Lumpur. Three days later we flew to Ho Chi Minh City, where we were astonished by the sight of thousands of mopeds, cycles and taxis in huge lines of traffic. Some of the mopeds had up to four people crammed onto them, wobbling precariously as they snaked in and out of traffic. We stayed at the Park Hyatt Saigon, which is in a colossal white building that's beautifully illuminated by night. It was the perfect base for exploring the city. Yoshiko negotiated our taxi fares each day to ensure we got a fair price, but she also encouraged me to try other means of getting around.

'We don't need to take a taxi everywhere we go,' she told me. 'If you want to enjoy the city, we should also walk or take a bus.'

Being with Yoshiko gave me insights into the local culture that I might otherwise have missed. We ended up walking several miles each day as well as using public transport. It gave me a different perspective to the one I was used to, from the back seat of an air-conditioned limousine. The food markets were teeming with people, all going about the daily business of securing their basic needs. It was an amazing feeling to move on foot amid the bustle of the city. We also discovered the art of snacking in food stores, where you're invited to taste all kinds of products, from breads and cakes to meat, fruit and drinks. It's amazing how many different foods you can sample, to the extent that you feel quite full.

Later on, we were both moved by our visit to a local war museum where we witnessed some of the waste and horror that is the legacy of the Vietnam War. It was a humbling experience to read about what had happened and learn how the country had been devastated in so many different ways. Yet the people we encountered in Vietnam were universally kind and welcoming, despite the suffering many of them had endured over the years.

★

When we returned to the UK after the wedding, I began a new life that involved me trying many things for the first time. Together with Yoshiko, I visited art galleries and enrolled in dance classes. These were things that had never appealed to me before, but I began to realise that there was more to life than just going to a theatre or cinema (although I still love doing both of those things). For our UK wedding, Yoshiko wore a Western dress and we restated our vows at a church in Sloane Square, followed by a reception dinner at the Ritz for close family and friends. Among them were my brother David and my sister Christine, as well as my nephew Simon (David's son), with whom I'd stayed in touch over the years. One of the things Yoshiko has since encouraged me to do is spend more time with family.

JAPAN, INDIA AND ENLIGHTENMENT

When I settled my dispute with my son Simon it was an opportunity to pause and reflect upon the past, while also making plans for the future. The cinemas we'd once owned were gone forever, but I still had the Thomas Tucker popcorn business, which had good potential to grow. One of the people with whom I was still in contact was my old friend and business associate Leslie Rose. As I've previously said, he has a brilliant marketing brain (despite the fact that his choice of football team leaves a lot to be desired). When I purchased the Thomas Tucker business, Leslie joined the company's board of directors alongside Barbara, its founder. Together they charted the company towards a course of steady growth. As the business began to prosper, they felt we should appoint a new managing director to take things to the next level. They suggested that my brother David, who had some experience in the retail sector, would be an ideal candidate. From a personal perspective I felt my brother would benefit from this opportunity, as he was having some marriage problems at the time and was looking for a fresh start. He readily accepted and went about the role with great enthusiasm. Within twelve months he announced that we had secured a deal with the potential to further benefit the business.

'We've won a contract to supply Vue cinemas with their popcorn and other supporting products,' he told me proudly.

Thomas Tucker was able to prosper as a result and I was pleased to have a way of staying involved in the cinema industry, albeit from a different perspective. Until now a large part of the company's business had been supplying a niche market for premium popcorn, but the Vue deal enabled David to build a dedicated cinema division. We were eventually able to work our way up to supplying over 90 per cent of cinema operators in the UK, and we also made good profits on theatre sales. Whenever a Bond movie or a new Star Wars film was released, our production went into overtime to make sure no cinema ever ran out of popcorn. We would make daily deliveries to every Odeon, Vue or Cineworld location, as well as independent complexes throughout the UK. It was a very profitable arrangement for everybody, because the margins on popcorn at many cinemas were in the region of 90 per cent. Turnover was healthy and our profits were exceeding a million pounds a year.

Things took an unexpected direction for David when he announced that he and Barbara had fallen in love. The business continued to grow under their watch and also enjoyed considerable success supporting the Bourne Leisure Group with soft goods and toys for their holiday camp operations. We discovered that supplying supermarkets had the potential to be yet another area of growth, although the margins were tighter there than in cinemas. Our operation grew to the point where we were employing over a hundred people across two main sites, in Retford and Worksop.

A highlight for me was when my former Apollo colleague David Rogers joined the company in a financial capacity. Together we asked my brother and his team to submit a new five-year plan.

However, as is often the case when there are large profits to be made, other operators soon entered the market. In this instance we started to face competition from suppliers in Europe. You might think that with 90 per cent margins on high-quality popcorn, everybody would remain happy; but inevitably there

JAPAN, INDIA AND ENLIGHTENMENT

was a squeeze on prices, and we knew that we might face some difficult choices in the future.

I became involved with a number of other projects in the years that followed, with varying degrees of success. After we sold Apollo Leisure, my old friend Terry Smith contacted me with an interesting proposal. Terry had helped to brilliantly promote the Michael Jackson concert at Aintree via the Radio City station in Liverpool, and since then had gone on to broaden his interests in radio. He suggested that I should become a non-executive director of Kiss FM and Magic. I felt honoured and privileged to be invited to join the board of these two great radio stations. We would meet every three months to review trading and marketing plans; this included discussions about how to grow audiences and compete with other stations. It was a great time and I learned a great deal about the power of radio. Sadly, Terry passed away in 2022, but I continue to be indebted to him for the experience.

I also became involved with a number of projects in Saudi Arabia – some of which, unfortunately, led to me losing money. One memorable experience was when I helped to launch a tourist attraction in Riyadh based on the TV show *The Crystal Maze*. This involved the construction of a purpose-built venue and although we encountered some teething problems along the way, the attraction eventually opened to some very positive feedback.

Even though I continued to be active in business, I was learning how to strike a better balance between my work and my home life, which of course now involved spending quality time with Yoshiko. She was keen to learn about my childhood and we travelled to Scarborough together, where I introduced her to my Aunt Marjorie, still in fine form despite being over 100 years old. Yoshiko was fascinated to hear all about my early life from Marjorie, and I was pleased that they seemed to develop a mutual affection. When Marjorie eventually passed away at 104, she was buried in Malton in Yorkshire. My mother and father were buried in Scarborough's Woodlands Cemetery, which overlooks the open-air theatre that I helped to renovate. When Yoshiko and I visited their grave, she said that she believed my parents were looking down on us together with Marjorie, which was a comforting thought.

Being married to Yoshiko helped me to understand that many people from Japan and South East Asia have a different belief system to what we are used to in the West. I realised that most of my life had been spent in the pursuit of happiness through work, whereas in Eastern cultures there is a greater emphasis on seeking fulfilment through spiritual enlightenment. For example, Yoshiko is a great believer in the mental and physical value of Indian yoga, which aims to achieve wellbeing through the unification of mind, body and soul.

'Yoga is something that you will find of great benefit, but you must approach it with an open heart,' she told me.

It was a pleasure to learn about these diverse and interesting cultural experiences, although I admit that I was initially sceptical! I was in the final stages of settling my dispute over the family estate when Yoshiko suggested that we should take a break at a yoga retreat in India. Everybody assured me that India is an amazing place and that I would fall in love with the country. Even so, I am slightly embarrassed to admit that I had huge concerns about the local food and the fact that facilities would be very basic. Our destination was a modest hotel at Fort Cochin in Kerala on India's Malabar Coast. The itinerary involved waking at five thirty every morning for yoga lessons and a diet of simple food. Yoshiko suggested that I should prepare for the trip by attending a yoga centre in Hammersmith for some meditation sessions, which, despite my scepticism, did help me to relax.

When we arrived at Fort Cochin, we discovered that parts of our hotel were still under construction. It reminded me of the slightly dilapidated accommodation in the movie *The Best Exotic Marigold Hotel*, which I felt did not bode well. However, I needn't have worried. We spent the first two days visiting local spice markets before our yoga regime started on the following Monday. My first session went better than I had expected. It was quite relaxing but it did leave me with some aches and pains, no doubt due to the fact that I hadn't done any physical training in fifty years! However, the daily yoga sessions were very laid back and introduced me to a new form of exercise. I felt better for doing it, despite the physical challenges. By day three I was starting to get the hang of it and learning to breathe properly through my nose. Thankfully, our Yoga Master seemed willing to take things at a slow pace for my benefit. The food was indeed basic but very healthy, consisting of rice with some curry and other sauces plus Indian bread, and fruit for dessert.

Following our yoga sessions we were free to go out to explore, which generally involved a trip to the beach. Everywhere we went I was stopped by local youths who spotted that I was a Westerner, and they were inevitably keen to speak about football. There were four teams with which they were universally familiar: Manchester United, Liverpool, Barcelona and AC Milan – sadly, there was very little mention of Everton!

During the second week of our stay we travelled inland to stay in the town of Munnar, stopping off en route to see the breathtaking waterfalls at Athirappilly. The sheer natural beauty of the landscape was astonishing. We were later greeted with sprays of flowers by the staff at our new hotel, which was very comfortable. We ordered grilled fish with spices and ginger, which was served with egg fried rice and vegetables, together with a mixed salad of tomatoes, cucumber and onions. Everything tasted wonderful (so much for me being worried about the food!). During the day I even went for a ride on an elephant, during which I must have looked precarious sitting on top of the beautiful animal.

'Hold on tight! Don't fall!' shrieked Yoshiko as she waved me off.

When I returned she had bought five pineapples, which we fed to the elephant one by one. We watched in delight while the majestic beast ate each one of them whole after ripping off the spiky top! On our final evening we went on a night safari, where we spotted four bison grazing in the dusk before we returned to the hotel in order to relax in front of a blazing log fire.

★

Our trip to India was one of the best holidays I've enjoyed and an experience that I will never forget. It not only taught me to be open-minded about different cultures, but it also indirectly led to a long association that Yoshiko and I enjoyed with an

JAPAN, INDIA AND ENLIGHTENMENT

Indian spiritual guru called Sai Maa. We first heard about Sai Maa and her teachings through friends. Our memories of India were fresh in our minds, so when a couple we knew in Japan happened to mention that they were planning to attend a conference in Florida with a renowned spiritual guru, we decided to join them. Although we were not familiar with Sai Maa, our friends told us about her humanitarian initiatives and her route to personal transformation through spiritual enlightenment. In India she is known as Her Holiness Sai Maa and is the first woman to have been honoured as a Jagadguru spiritual master in the Vishnuswami lineage (which forms an important part of the Hindu tradition). Yoshiko and I were intrigued by her and felt it would be good for us to spend some time together at the conference in Florida, a part of the world I knew well.

When we arrived we discovered there would be eight hundred people attending from all over the globe, all there to take part in a three-day programme of meetings and presentations. The majority were dressed in white and although they were generally nice people, I sensed that many of them had something missing in their lives. Some had recently suffered bereavements or other traumas. At first I was quite wary, as it all seemed a little out of my comfort zone. However, Sai Maa was very impressive. She is an inspirational speaker with great charisma, and I found myself listening in fascination as she talked about how to seek an enlightened life. Her message reminded me of the holistic approach of yoga, with its emphasis on unifying mind, body and spirit. I was also impressed by her philanthropic aspirations to raise funds in order to help less fortunate people around the world.

One of her mantras was 'The soul cannot be happy unless the body is fed. If we all do just a little, it can achieve a lot.'

Yoshiko was particularly impressed. Prior to travelling to Florida, she had taken an introductory course that enabled her to understand the event far better than I did, but in my own way I found it interesting and relaxing. We were later introduced to Sai Maa in person. This was the start of a three-year association that would see us becoming friends with the guru. I later took an introductory course of my own and we also jointly signed up for a further course in the USA, designed specifically for couples. The event cost several thousand dollars to attend, but in fairness it was an excellent experience involving activities that were designed to help improve a relationship. I didn't always fully subscribe to all of Sai Maa's ideas, but I had learned by now not to be dismissive of unfamiliar things, and I found the practical side of her teachings very helpful.

I was later approached to help with raising funds for an ashram temple that Sai Maa was hoping to construct in the Indian city of Varanasi. The temple was located close to the banks of the Ganges river in northern India, at one of the most sacred sites within the Hindu religion. Varanasi is believed to be the oldest continually inhabited city in the world and it is visited by many millions of pilgrims every year. Many of them come to bathe in the holy waters, or to cremate their loved ones on funeral pyres before scattering their ashes into the river. The ashram temple would provide facilities to many of the pilgrims who flocked to the city. As well as being a spiritual centre, it would provide support for impoverished children.

The project had been under way for a period of time, but it was in need of urgent financial help in order to reach completion. Thanks to my experience of charitable work for the Variety Club and the Make-A-Wish Foundation, I was able to provide some advice. I suggested to Yoshiko that we should offer supporters of Sai Maa an opportunity to sponsor different parts of the ashram. This included everything from bedrooms and doors to individual paving stones. We produced a brochure complete with detailed plans for the building, which was circulated at a Christmas event in Florida. Yoshiko took charge of selling the sponsorship packages, which were very popular with the supporters of Sai Maa. In the space of just two days we raised over $1.75 million – a remarkable achievement.

We were obviously keen to ensure that funds went directly to the ashram as quickly as possible, but this proved to be a more complex task than I had anticipated. Sai Maa had appointed a right-hand man in Varanasi to oversee the construction project, but he had suffered a heart attack and was unable to continue. I wanted to reassure everybody who had donated money that the proceeds were being invested in the correct manner, so I offered to fly out to Varanasi myself to get a detailed progress report. There were two local trustees with whom I was keen to link up, one of whom was a local builder and the other a property developer.

When I arrived at Varanasi it was quite an eye-opener. The airport is approximately fifteen miles to the north-west of the city, so I made the final leg of the journey by car. It felt a little like I was entering the Wild West of India! There seemed to be cows everywhere, which of course are regarded as sacred animals. The streets were clogged with mopeds and crowds of people; the whole place was very vibrant, but it was also very chaotic.

The ashram was in a prime location on the main road that runs into the city above the Ganges, from where you can gaze down onto the dockside. As we approached, I glimpsed the majestic river below for the first time. It looked staggeringly huge, perhaps three or four times the width of the Thames in London. I could see groups of people carrying their deceased loved ones aloft as they made their way down to the water's edge in funeral processions. Some of the bodies had been covered in shrouds, but others were in open view. I learned that at any one time, there may be six or seven cremations taking place next to the river. At the waterside there were supplies of wooden logs ready to be used as funeral pyres. Clouds of smoke billowed slowly into the air, while people teemed around on the dockside. I got the impression that the people there came from many different walks of life, some wealthy and some of whom probably had very little money. Despite the slightly disorganised nature of the surroundings, I could sense that it was a special place worthy of great respect, with origins stretching back for many thousands of years. It was the first of several trips I would make to the area, but each time I arrived I would pause to take in the awesome scenery. The water level of the river rises and falls depending on the season, so during the wet periods it swells greatly and is very fast-flowing, whereas in the dry season people can paddle in the shallows at its edges.

My first impression of the ashram was initially less positive. Construction seemed to have ground to a halt, so it resembled little more than an empty shell. It was a circular white building consisting of several storeys, one of which was higher than the original plans had stipulated. Wild monkeys seemed to be running amok in and around the building and also on the streets nearby. While the monkeys looked cute, they were actually quite dangerous, more than ready to snatch food or deliver a nasty bite if they felt threatened. As for the temple, the trustees informed me that it might be necessary to 'compensate' certain local officials for the inconvenience that any further building work might cause (I think the word 'compensation' was a polite way of describing it, but in any event I declined). Overall, I wasn't happy with the existing set-up, which seemed to have previously allowed the construction work to drag on without any finishing date. In my opinion, all that achieved was to risk losing money by letting the bills continue to pile up, regardless of the outcome.

One of the things I did was to strongly recommend to Sai Maa that we should tighten the paperwork, which ensured her investors were better protected. We were then able to set a deadline for an opening ceremony for the ashram. The date we chose coincided with a huge religious festival called Kumbh Mela that was due to take place further upstream on the Ganges. This event is one of India's most important festivals and attracts many millions of pilgrims. Senior religious leaders, such as Sai Maa, traditionally erect huge marquee-style tents equipped with living quarters and meeting rooms. There are also thousands of lesser gurus in attendance, many of whom pack the streets in order to offer their services to passers-by in exchange for a fee. Some of the commercial aspects of the festival surprised me, but there was no doubt that the event gave many people enormous comfort and joy. The culmination of the festival is a huge trek down to the banks of the river, where the pilgrims proceed to bathe.

The festival was an ideal opportunity to invite Sai Maa's supporters to make a journey downriver to visit the new ashram. In the meantime, Yoshiko and I made five or six trips to Varanasi in order to ensure the work at the temple was now progressing. I was confident that we'd achieve the deadline, even if there would still be one or two parts of the building requiring further attention.

'We are in a good position now, despite everything, and the important thing is that we open our doors,' I reassured Sai Maa.

On the morning of the opening ceremony I was still laying grass on the floor of the temple to cover one or two bare spots, but overall the building was now a beautiful structure set within its own gardens. It was a very satisfying project that helped me to learn a great deal about India and how its people choose to celebrate life and death.

However, perhaps my favourite memory is of a 'Yagya' spiritual event that was hosted by Sai Maa in Japan, where attendees gathered in great numbers to make devotional offerings to purify the soul. On that occasion, Yoshiko and I made arrangements for sixty pilgrims to arrive from Varanasi to chant mantras. Sai Maa told us that if it rained at the end of the event, it would be a sign of a blessing for everyone. On the very last day, at four o'clock in the afternoon, the heavens opened and it poured with rain.

After all the domestic upheaval I had experienced during the past few years, I finally felt pleasantly at ease. I am not a deeply religious person, but I did indeed feel truly blessed to be enjoying life there, at that moment, with Yoshiko.

And finally …

It's now the summer of 2023 and it's been an eventful past couple of years, not just for me but for the nation as a whole. September of last year was a time of great sadness, when Queen Elizabeth II passed away at Balmoral Castle. Like almost everybody else in the country, I felt a great sense of loss. I reflected upon the many occasions when I'd had the privilege of meeting Her Majesty – there was the opening of *Starlight Express* at the Apollo Victoria Theatre, a show that ran for sixteen years and helped to transform the fortunes of the Apollo Leisure Group. Then there was the time the Queen visited the Lyceum twice in one day, first to meet the cast of *Oklahoma!* and then, later on, to see the show. There was also the time I presented Her Majesty with a teddy bear outside the Odeon in Leicester Square; plus, of course, the day she came to Scarborough Open Air Theatre, watched by my Auntie Marjorie in the audience. The Queen's passing also reminded me of the occasions on which I'd met Prince Charles – who I'm sure will now continue to be a great monarch as King Charles III.

Fond memories, all of them.

And what does the future now hold for me personally? Sadly, the Thomas Tucker business is no more after going into administration, a victim of the pandemic and ever-squeezed profit margins. But I have come to learn that such setbacks are part of the regular ebb and flow of life. As one door closes, another opens, and there are some exciting new opportunities on the horizon. At the time of writing, I've recently brought a fantastic new show to London called *Tony n' Tina's Wedding*. It's an immersive theatrical experience, during which the audience themselves are guests at a chaotic Italian–American wedding. The idea is that you roll up dressed to the nines, see the bride and groom get hitched and then sit back and enjoy a three-course meal while the fun and chaos of a raucous family wedding unfolds all around you. *Tony n' Tina's Wedding* has already been a huge hit off-Broadway in the USA and elsewhere around the globe. Yet for some reason it's never been brought to London, so when I heard that the UK production rights were available I jumped at the chance to acquire them. The production is like a party and a show combined into one. There's never a dull moment. The mother of the bride is a stern traditionalist, the father of the groom owns a strip club and the priest gets drunk at the reception. I'll leave the rest to your imagination. I was convinced that audiences in London would love it. What's more, I had the perfect venue in mind.

What could possibly go wrong?

Well, you're probably aware from reading this book that nothing in show business is ever that simple! *Tony n' Tina's Wedding* turned out to be a great success with London audiences and the press also loved it, but the production later became plagued by difficulties. The location that I had in mind was the Queen Elizabeth Olympic Park in Stratford, where I'd recently launched a joint venture with a colleague called Kern, whom I met through mutual contacts. Together, we had acquired a temporary lease to operate the ArcelorMittal Orbit attraction in the Olympic Park. The venue consists of the UK's tallest steel sculpture at 375 feet high, combined with the world's longest tunnel slide. Within the same complex there are bar and catering facilities. It was ideal for the new show because patrons could watch Tony and Tina get married at the top of the ArcelorMittal Orbit (where there is a viewing platform with breathtaking 360-degree views of London) before being seated downstairs in the restaurant to enjoy the rest of the show.

The Queen Elizabeth Olympic Park is one of London's cultural landmarks due to the legacy of the 2012 Games, but I've always felt that it has untapped potential. The BBC, Sadler's Wells, the London College of Fashion and the V&A Museum are in the process of opening facilities on East Bank of the site. Plus, of course, West Ham United play nearby at the London Stadium. Hence, the first thing that we did upon taking over at the Orbit was to change the opening times to seven days a week (as opposed to a partial shutdown at certain times of the year). The result was that we increased the cash flow by £80,000 per week during the first eight weeks, compared with the previous year. We enjoyed a great relationship with the West Ham fans, who on match days would drink at The Last Drop bar within the complex. We also hosted VIP dining on match days at the top of the ArcelorMittal Orbit.

Unfortunately, it wasn't all plain sailing. In October, builders arrived to replace the surface outside the venue. This effectively closed down access to the cafe and the Last Drop due to roadworks. This was doubly frustrating because we'd just arranged to transform the tunnel slide into an *Alice in Wonderland* attraction. Two months later in December, another disaster struck when the lifts broke down. I soon discovered that attempting to run a venue that's 375 feet in the sky without working elevators is a major challenge. Engineers informed us in January that it would be impossible to fix the lifts until March at the earliest. I watched painfully as bookings were cancelled while we were powerless to do anything about it. It wasn't until Easter that we eventually had one of the elevators working again.

It was following that rather bumpy start at the Olympic Park that I took the plunge and decided to open there with *Tony n' Tina's Wedding*. I could feel that familiar tingle of excitement at the prospect of once again being involved in a live show. Of course, there were still many weeks of preparation ahead. The show's original director Larry Pellegrini agreed to come to the UK to help get to things off the ground. We had over two and half thousand applications from young people who were anxious to break into show business and wanted to attend the auditions. We assembled a great cast and the first preview show was pencilled in for a Saturday matinee in April. The preparations were extremely complex, because in addition to organising the show itself we had the major logistical task of planning a wedding dinner for the audience. It was a terrible rush to get everything ready in time, but as I rode the lift to the top of the Orbit when the big day arrived I was pleased to see that it was a sunny afternoon.

JAPAN, INDIA AND ENLIGHTENMENT

A good omen, I hoped.

The first few moments as 'Tony' and 'Tina' prepared to say their vows felt slightly subdued, but I knew that it was normal to expect that at an opening preview (besides, who *isn't* nervous on their wedding day!). The real show would start downstairs, when the 'reception' began. I'm happy to say that it turned out to be a very memorable afternoon. The bride and groom were soon in full flow (as was the wine that we served). The audience quickly grasped the fact that the main point of the show is to have fun. Many of the guests chose to join the cast on the dance floor. By the end of the show, I was busy working the room in order to ask people what they thought. About half of the audience were invited guests, but the paying customers were the ones who I listened to the most. The general consensus was that they'd had a great time. They told me that they felt was as if they'd been wined, dined and entertained at a real wedding!

A few weeks later we held our official press night, where the invited journalists included a theatre critic from *The Times*. There's always a bit of risk involved in any press night. I was confident that we had a great show on our hands, but I also remembered how dearly a few dreadful reviews had cost us all those years ago for Richard Harris in *Camelot*. So it was with some apprehension a few days later that I read the review for *Tony n' Tina* in *The Times*. I needn't have worried: the newspaper gave the show the top spot on its theatre page, with a headline that urged readers go along to drink, dance and 'scoff the lasagne'. The critic had the good grace that say that even though it wasn't his type of show, it was great fun for those who were prepared to get into the spirit of things. The majority of the other reviews that we received were also positive.

We also received a huge amount of attention when Transport for London banned a poster for the show because it featured a picture of a wedding cake. Apparently, this contravened the advertising guidelines on the London Underground, because it was feared it might encourage people to eat unhealthily. This seemed preposterous to me, but we had to redesign the posters. The row that followed was covered by all the main newspapers and broadcasters, as well being reported overseas!

Sadly, despite enjoying such a great start, the production eventually ran into problems. We encountered difficulties behind the scenes due to various issues connected to the scale of the logistics involved the show, which led to one or two personality clashes. I was also aware that our lease at the ArcelorMittal Orbit was due to expire at the end of the year, so I began to look for an alternative venue. The show has now ended its short but successful run at the Olympic Park, but I very much hope to find another home for it in the future.

My adventure at the Olympic Park and with *Tony n' Tina's Wedding* has reminded me of so many other highs and lows that I've experienced in the entertainment industry. When I watched people enjoying the show, I couldn't help but think how lucky I am to have been involved in things that have brought joy to people. Today, *The Lion King* continues to play to audiences of around 16,000 people a week at the Lyceum, which means it been seen by around 19 million people since it first launched there. If you include all the other great shows over the years at the grand theatres that were saved from dereliction by the

JAPAN, INDIA AND ENLIGHTENMENT

Apollo Leisure Group, then it must add up to in the region of 100 million people. It makes me feel very happy to know that I've played a part in that, while being greatly supported by others.

I've recently rekindled some of my working relationships with old friends and colleagues. Among them is Michael Barrymore, who currently has over two million fans who regularly watch his videos on TikTok. I hope to work with Michael on a possible new stage tour. Meanwhile, I have plans to open an events brand called Coliseum at venues at Bluewater in Essex and in Limerick.

I also received a wonderful surprise recently when I opened an email from the current chairman of Variety, the Children's Charity (formerly the Variety Club of Great Britain), which read in part as follows:

> *Dear Paul . . . The current Trustees recognise your immense contribution over the years, for which we are deeply grateful, and feel honoured to now be custodians of. It is important that Variety of which you have been such a key part of the journey allows you the opportunity to remain involved with a position of note. So, for all previous Chief Barkers / Chair of Trustees we wish to bestow the honorary life title of 'Chair Emeritus – Variety, the Children's Charity'.*

I'll close this book now by saying that writing my story has in some ways been a cathartic experience. It has helped me to reflect upon the good times I've been privileged to enjoy, as well as some of the events in my life that were painful. One wonderful piece of news is that, with Yoshiko's help, I have been reunited with Robert, one of my sons born to my first wife, Jetta, all those years ago in Scarborough. Robert and I later spent a wonderful Christmas together – I hope that we will share many more to come. He has turned out to be a fine young man, despite the setbacks he experienced in earlier life. Robert is now a father himself, so I also had the pleasure of meeting an additional grandchild.

Thankfully, I also remain blessed that Yoshiko and I continue to enjoy life together. We still love travelling very much, having spent time at various points over the last two years in Japan, France and Ibiza, to name but a few of the places that we've recently revisited together. Continuing to travel the world with my own Japanese princess seems a good way to end this story, so I'll leave it there.

WITH SPECIAL THANKS TO THE FOLLOWING

I am grateful for my wonderful life and also to so many wonderful people who have made things truly special. There are far too many to list here, but my special thanks go to the following . . .

Family and loved ones: To my beautiful princess Yoshiko (and SHIRO, our beautiful puppy). My ex-wives Nita Gregg and Jetta Gregg, and our children Simon, Debbie, Robert and David and their families and children.

The Apollo Fab Four: To my best friend David Rogers who helped to manage Apollo Leisure Group. To Sam Shrouder, who helped me find the best entertainment in the world. To Steve Lavelle who enabled us to rebuild many great theatres. Together, we were the Apollo Fab Four.

Other friends and colleagues: To all who played a part in this story including Mike Adamson, Colin Berlin, Danny Betesh, Keith Bishop and team, Nicky Carter, Barry and Linda Clayman, Annalisa Dobson, Harold Davidson, Andrew De

BACKSTAGE WITHOUT A PASS

Rosa, Barry Dickens, Elizabeth Edwards, Graham Gilmore, Harvey Goldsmith, David Ian, John Jarvis, Jerry Katzman, Paul Latham, Stuart Littlewood, Cameron Mackintosh, Nicky Monk, Stephen Murtagh, Jimmy Nederlander, David Pearson, Leslie Rose, Gary Thompson, Nick Scandavies, Terry Smith, Lucy Sturton, Andrew Lloyd Webber and Michael White. Harvey Goldsmith, Derek Block, Phil Bowdrey, Sharon Bailey Harry Crosbie Danny Betesh, Paul Betesh, Caroline Monk Philip Solomon, John Jarvis Robert Dewynter and his team at Dewynters. Alan Cavill, Raymond Gubbay, Jeffrey Archer, Patrick McKenna, Michael Rose, Matt Goss, Roger Stevenson and Miles Stevenson, Nick Grace, Nick Thomas, Laurie Mansfield, Rachel Hague. To all at the Variety Club of Great Britain, plus of course my special friend since my days at the ABC in Sheffield, Jim Whittell and his wonderful wife, Jenny.

Paul Gregg

Winter 2023

Endnotes

Chapter 1

1. Charles Dickens, Jr., *Dickens's Dictionary of London*, 1879, quoted at http://www.arthurlloyd.co.uk/LyceumTheatre.htm.

Chapter 8

2. *The Stage*, 11 December 1980, p. 7, quoted at http://www.arthurlloyd.co.uk/ApolloVictoria.htm.
3. *The Times*, 24 November 1982, p. 31.

Chapter 9

4. 'Looking back at when Michael Jackson brought his world tours to Cardiff', *Wales Online*, https://www.walesonline.co.uk/news/wales-news/looking-back-michael-jackson-brought-1824418.
5. 'Michael Jackson at Aintree Racecourse, 1988', Hidden Liverpool, *YouTube*, https://www.youtube.com/watch?v=YvdCFUX2bDQ.

Chapter 11

6. *The Times*, 31 July 1996, n.p.
7. 'Royal Opera House's troubled past', BBC News, 20 September 2001, http://news.bbc.co.uk/1/hi/entertainment/1400569.stm.
8. *Apollo Today*, Lyceum Special Edition, 31 October 1996, p. 10.
9. *Apollo Today*, Lyceum Special Edition, 31 October 1996, p. 11.
10. *Apollo Today*, Lyceum Special Edition, 31 October 1996, pp. 8 and 9.
11. *Apollo Today*, Lyceum Special Edition, 31 October 1996, p. 2.
12. 'The Lyceum is saved . . . for rock musical fans', *Independent*, 16 October 1996, https://www.independent.co.uk/news/business/the-lyceum-is-saved-for-rock-musical-fans-people-business-1358808.html

Chapter 13

13. 'Kenwright clinches Smith deal', *Liverpool Echo*, 27 December 1999, p. 43.
14. 'There was always something about Everton', *Liverpool Echo*, 16 March 2022, https://www.liverpoolecho.co.uk/sport/football/football-news/david-moyes-everton-peoples-club-23396659.

Chapter 14

15. 'Kenwright breaks Barmby silence', *BBC Sport*, 6 July 2000, http://news.bbc.co.uk/sport1/hi/football/teams/e/everton/821602.stm.
16. *The Evertonian*, June 2000, p. 16.

17. 'Chairman's Statement', *Everton FC Annual Report and Accounts*, 2001, p. 5.
18. 'Turning a dream into reality', *Liverpool Echo*, 10 July 2001, https://www.liverpoolecho.co.uk/sport/football/football-news/turning-a-dream-into-reality-3562532.

Chapter 15

19. 'Smith: We can win the Cup', *Daily Post*, 9 March 2002, n.p., https://www.bluecorrespondent.co.uk/March%202002.htm.
20. 'Smith on a knife-edge', *Liverpool Echo*, 11 March 2002, https://www.bluecorrespondent.co.uk/March%202002.htm.
21. 'Blues make their move', *Liverpool Echo*, 13 March 2002, https://www.bluecorrespondent.co.uk/March%202002.htm.
22. 'Blues closing in on Moyes', *Daily Post*, 14 March 2002, n.p., https://www.bluecorrespondent.co.uk/March%202002.htm.
23. *Everton FC Annual Report and Accounts*, 2002, p. 20.
24. *Rooney* (documentary), dir. Matt Smith, Amazon Original, 2022.
25. 'We won't overplay Wayne', *Liverpool Echo*, 3 August 2002, https://www.bluecorrespondent.co.uk/August%202002.htm.
26. 'Premier League clubs spent £272 MILLION on agents' fees in the last year', *Mail Online*, 31 March 2022, https://www.dailymail.co.uk/sport/football/article-10672961/Premier-League-clubs-spent-272MILLION-agents-fees-2021-22.html.
27. 'New Stadium: Kings Dock', *ToffeeWeb*, https://www.toffeeweb.com/club/kings-dock/new-stadium.asp.

28. *Daily Post*, 30 August 2002, n.p., https://www.bluecorrespondent.co.uk/August%202002.htm.
29. 'Kings Dock "move is on"', *Liverpool Echo*, 25 October 2002, https://www.bluecorrespondent.co.uk/October%202002.htm.
30. 'Everton fail in King's Dock bid', *BBC Sport*, 11 April 2003, http://news.bbc.co.uk/sport1/hi/football/teams/e/everton/2940481.stm.

Chapter 16

31. 'Rooney admits prostitute visits', *BBC Sport*, 22 August 2004, http://news.bbc.co.uk/1/hi/england/merseyside/3588112.stm.

Chapter 17

32. 'Fortress "will not launch takeover"', *Daily Post*, 8 December 2004, https://bluecorrespondent.co.uk/December%202004.htm.
33. 'Merseyside groundshare deal falls through', *Guardian*, 11 January 2005, https://www.theguardian.com/society/2005/jan/11/communities.football.

Chapter 19

34. 'Queen opens Scarborough open air theatre', 20 May 2010, *BBC News*, http://news.bbc.co.uk/1/mobile/england/north_yorkshire/8694256.stm.

★ For more about Apollo see Sam Shrouder's book *Play It Again … Sam*. For the history of theatres, go to the excellent arthurlloyd.co.uk. See also Wikipedia.

Index

PG indicates Paul Gregg.

ABBA 91
ABC cinemas
    Hull 27–8
    Scunthorpe 46
    Sheffield 33–4, 41–6, 47–8, 49, 68
    Wakefield 46–7, 49, 93
ABC Group 48, 49, 58
Abercromby, Arthur 202–3, 241, 264, 266
Adelphi Theatre, London 150
advance bookings/ticket sales
    Apollo Group and 93
    Bristol Hippodrome and 129
    Camelot and 108, 109, 111
    Cats and 147
    Cliff Richard and 116
    Fiddler on the Roof and 112
    Jesus Christ Superstar and 176
    Lyceum and 164, 176
    PG realises importance of 83–4
    Starlight Express and 118, 170
    theatre industry and 48
    The Sound of Music and 102
Aintree Racecourse 133–4, 136–9, 141, 323
Albert Dock, Liverpool 211, 214
Alexandersson, Niclas 219
Allerton, Terry 94
Allman, Greg 83
Amsterdam Arena Ltd 226
Apollo Cinemas
    Apollo Cinema, Manchester 79–81
    EMI and 79–81
    Nita Gregg's will and 297
    PG and family buy back from Clear Channel 293–4
    PG explores possibility of taking over from Simon Gregg 301–2, 309, 310–14
    Simon Gregg chief executive of 301–2, 309, 310–14, 321
    Vue, sold to 312–14, 321
Apollo Coventry 95
Apollo Leisure Group 1, 5–11
    Apollo Cinemas *see* Apollo Cinemas
    fault lines develop within 179
    financial troubles 111–13
    formation of 80–5
    high point of 11, 179
    HQ, New Theatre 92
    leadership group 1, 343
    Make-A-Wish Foundation and 156
    Nita Gregg becomes more involved in 184–5
    Nita Gregg's growing dissatisfaction with life at 187, 291
    ownership structure 186–8
    sale of 11, 180–93, 195, 218, 245, 288, 299–300, 314, 323
    Sangster becomes chairman 112–13
    stock market flotation, possibility of 188

theatre acquisitions *see individual theatre name*
theatre productions/live shows *see individual production/show name*
Variety Club and 153
venues *see individual venue name*
Apollo Theatres Ltd 80–5
Apollo Victoria Theatre 96–121, 189
  Camelot at 6, 106–13, 180, 339
  Cliff Richard at 100–1, 115–16
  Dean Martin at 114–17
  Fiddler on the Roof at 112, 113, 114
  New Victoria Theatre acquisition 96–8
  opening night 98–100
  restoration 96–8
  Sound of Music at 101–3, 105, 107, 151
  Starlight Express at 117–21, 335
ArcelorMittal Orbit attraction, Olympic Park 337–41
Archer, Lord Jeffrey 154
Arsenal FC 200, 204, 214, 224, 237, 284
Arts Council 87–9, 130, 162, 175
Arts Lottery 166, 169
Astaire, Jarvis 153, 187
Aston Villa 209, 231, 274, 278
Astoria cinema, Hull 26–7
Athirappilly, India 326
Aznavour, Charles 78

Bacharach, Burt 65–6
Bad tour 123–8, 132–9, 141, 318, 323
BAFTA 305
Bangkok Mandarin Oriental 254
Bank of Scotland 166
Barber, Harold 62
Barmby, Nick 218–19
Barron Knights, The 58–61, 62
Barry, John 27
Barrymore, Michael 131, 146
Basie, Count Bill 67
Bassey, Shirley 5, 40, 65, 85, 98–100
Bates, Alan 45
BBC TV 51, 64, 69, 156, 219, 250

BCC (Barry Clayman Concerts) 124, 190
Beatles, The 27–8, 58, 211, 230
Beauty and the Beast 176
Beazley, Samuel 7, 163
Becker, Lionel 74, 81, 82, 90, 94, 112–13, 128, 312, 313
Bee Gees 116
Beever and Struthers 74
Benjamin, Louis 101, 129
Berlin, Colin 81, 82, 90
Birch, Trevor 263–6, 274
Birmingham Hippodrome 88, 95
Black, Cilla 154
Blackpool Opera House 145, 146
Blair, Tony 277, 279
Blood Brothers 198
Blue Hawaii 44
Bolshoi Ballet 64, 149
Boomtown Rats, The 83
Bourne Leisure Group 322
Bovis Lend Lease 226, 243
Bowie, David 28, 83
Branson, Richard 141–5
Brent Walker 9, 159–60
Brightman, Sarah 119
Bristol Hippodrome 88, 90, 128, 129
British Leyland 22, 55
Broadway 106, 166, 181, 183, 336
Brolly, Brian 116, 147
Bruno, Frank 153
Brynner, Yul 101
Bullseye! 156

Caborn, Richard 276, 277
Caine, Michael 156
Cambridge Theatre, Covent Garden 106
Camelot 6, 106–13, 180, 339
Cannon and Ball 69, 75, 131, 146, 151
Cardiff Arms Park, Wales 132
Carter, Sir Philip 131, 201, 205, 216, 221, 237, 247, 263
Carter, Lady Rita 205–6
Cats 117, 145–9, 157

INDEX

Champions League 280
Chang Beer 253–7
Charles, Prince of Wales (later, King Charles III) 152, 335
   Bad tour, attends with Princess Diana 136
   Lyceum Theatre reopening, attends (1996) 10, 174–6, 179–80
   Royal Variety Charity patron 152
   Royal Variety Performance, Dominion Theatre, attends with Princess Diana (1992) 157–8
Chelsea, London, Gregg home in 288–9, 290
Chelsea FC 260, 263
Cher 83
Cheslyn-Curtis, Barbara 192
Children in Need 156
Chrysalis Group 124
Cinema Exhibitors' Association 312–13
Cineworld 311, 313, 322
Clark, Petula 102, 103
Clash, The 83
Clayman, Arnold 78
Clayman, Barry 5, 63, 77–8, 112, 124, 132, 190
Clayman, Linda 78, 142
Clear Channel 226, 290–3
Cliff Richard and the Shadows 45–6
Cohen, Oscar 98–9
Collins, John 220
Columbia Pictures 43
Come Dancing 51
Como, Perry 63, 67
Connolly, Billy 91
Coventry Theatre 95
Cranbrooke Mansions 129
Craven, Edgar 50
Crestas, The 28
Crew, Bertie 163
Cromie, Robert 151
Crosbie, Harry 141–2, 145–6, 148–50, 187
Crosbie, Rita 141–2, 143, 145

Crosby, Bing 65
Crowe & Nicholas 171
Crowe, Mike 171
Crystal Maze, The 323
Cummings, Peter 81

Daily Mail 182
Dash 113
Davidson, Harold 63
Davidson, Jim 131
Davis, Tony 73–4
Dawson, Les 69, 131, 146
Delfont, Lord 80–1
Denver, John 5, 79–80, 98
De Wynter, Robert 151
Dewynters 102
Diamond, Neil 5, 65, 78, 131
Diana, Princess of Wales 136, 157–8
Dickens, Charles Jr 7
Dietrich, Marlene 65–7, 69, 70, 98–9
Disney 43, 176, 180–3, 186
Dodd, Ken 69
Doherty, Moya 149
Dominion Theatre, London 89, 130, 141, 150–3, 157, 166, 185–6, 187, 189
Downtown Manhattan nightclub, New Theatre 94–5
Dracula 163
Dr Strangelove 43, 46–7
Dr Zhivago 33, 43
Dunford, Michael 220, 263

Earl, Robert 282
Eckart, Derek 49, 50
Eckart, Rodney 49, 50
Egan, Vince 181
Eisner, Michael 183
Elizabeth II, Queen 109, 119, 120, 121, 131, 152, 156, 163, 182, 306, 335
EMI 79, 80, 95
Emirates Stadium 284
English Heritage 163
English National Opera 87

351

English Partnerships 217, 225–6, 228, 229
Equity 87, 88
Estefan, Gloria 157
European Championships
   (1996) 213
   (2004) 257, 260, 261
European Capital of Culture 212–13, 222, 248
European Cup 200, 263
European Cup Winners' Cup 200
European Union
   European Regional Development Fund 229
   Objective 1 programme 214
Eurovision Song Contest 149
Everton Football Club 1, 11, 131, 195–285, 278, 290, 291, 325
   Barmby sale and 218–19
   Bramley-Moore Dock stadium 283–4
   Chang Beer sponsorship 253–7
   Dunford chief executive of 220, 263
   Goodison Park and *see* Goodison Park
   Kenwright and *see* Kenwright, Bill
   King's Dock redevelopment plan and 211, 214–18, 221, 222–30, 231–4, 237–8, 241, 243, 245–6, 247–51, 263, 264, 283–4
   Moyes and 204, 234–7, 240, 259, 261, 263, 264–5, 273
   PG first becomes involved with 195–206
   PG sells Everton shares 281–5
   PG's public profile at 232
   Rooney and 236–7, 241, 253–4, 256–65, 268, 269, 273
   Stanley Park shared stadium proposal and 266, 275–80
   True Blue Holdings and 202–3, 218, 237, 241–2, 245, 251, 264–71, 273, 280
   Walter Smith and 201, 206–8, 218–21, 231–5, 236, 241, 244, 263
Everton Shareholders' Association (ESA) 202, 203, 267–8, 270, 273

Evertonian, The 220
Evita 116

FA Cup
   (1965–6) 275
   (1983–4) 199
   (1984–5) 200
   (2000–1) 209
   (2001–2) 232–3
FC Schalke 223, 227
Ferguson, Duncan 201, 207, 219–20
Ferguson, Maynard 63
Fiddler on the Roof 112, 113, 114
Financial Times 313–14
Fitzgerald, Ella 67
Fletcher, Amanda 170
Floral Hall, Southport 61–70, 71
football agents 218, 219, 242–3, 260, 261, 262, 265
Football Association (FA) 187, 242
Fort Cochin, Kerala 325
Fortress Sports Fund 270, 271, 273–6, 278
Franklin & Andrews 226
Fullerton, Fiona 108, 111

Gascoigne, Paul 220
Gaumont, Sheffield 42–6
Gaumont-British 97, 151
Gaumont Palace 151
Genting Highlands resort, Malaysia 318
Gibb, Andy 116
Ginola, David 231
Glasgow Apollo 90–1
Gledhow Valley, Leeds 50
Goldman Sachs 282
Goldsmith, Harvey 131–2
Goodison Park 234, 236, 237, 253
   construction of 200
   Everton matches at 197, 199, 209, 269
   'Goodison for Everton' 216
   redevelopment of 200, 205, 213–18, 225, 245, 279
Gowrie, Lord 175

INDEX

Gravesen, Thomas 219
Grease 152
Great Ormond Street Hospital 155
Green, Hughie 28
Green, Sir Philip 202, 246–7, 262, 271, 281–2
Gregg, Christine (sister of Paul Gregg) 25, 36, 38, 39, 40, 320
Gregg, David (brother of Paul Gregg) 25, 36, 38, 39, 40, 309, 312–13, 320, 321–2
Gregg, Gertrude (aunt of Paul Gregg) 16, 26
Gregg, Joan (mother of Paul Gregg) 14, 16–17, 18, 20, 22, 25, 26, 29, 30–2, 35, 36–40, 41
Gregg, Marjorie (aunt of Paul Gregg) 16, 18, 36–7, 306, 324, 335
Gregg, Kenneth (father of Paul Gregg) 13–16, 17, 22–3, 25, 27, 29, 32, 36, 37, 38, 39, 41, 53, 61
Gregg, Nanny (grandmother of Paul Gregg) 16, 17, 18–20, 22, 23
Gregg, Jetta (ex-wife of Paul Gregg) 34–5, 41, 52–3, 341, 343
   Anthony (son) 41, 52–4
   Robert (son) 41, 52, 53–4, 341, 343
Gregg, Anita 'Nita' (ex-wife of Paul Gregg)
   Apollo Leisure Group, ownership of 51 per cent of shares 187–8, 288
   Apollo Leisure Group sale and 187–91, 288–90
   Bad tour and 123–4, 125, 126, 127, 138
   birth of son 75
   Boars Hill home 94, 96
   Camelot and 106–7
   David (son) 53, 56, 71, 91–2, 184, 186, 288, 343
   Dean Martin, meets 115
   Debbie (daughter) 53, 56, 71, 91–2, 184, 343
   death 295–7, 299, 300, 301, 303
   Everton FC shareholder 196, 280–3
   fiftieth birthday on Necker Island 141–5
   Lyceum Theatre acquisition, reaction to 5–6
   marriage to PG breaks up 174, 179–80, 182, 183–8, 287–97, 301
   marries PG 61–2
   Melling Road house and 71–3
   PG first meets 52–4
   positivity and willingness to seize an opportunity 56–7
   Prince Philip, meets 156–7
   Queen, meets 120–1
   Simon (son) *see* Gregg, Simon (son of Paul Gregg)
   Starlight Express opening and 119–21
   The Lion King and 182
   will 296–7, 301, 310
Gregg, Paul
   Apollo Cinemas and *see* Apollo Cinemas
   Apollo Leisure Group *see* Apollo Leisure Group
   Apollo Theatres Ltd and 80–5
   childhood 11, 12–31
   children *see individual child name*
   Clear Channel role 226, 290–3
   Ellerman Lines midshipman 31
   family and *see individual family member name*
   family estate 296–7, 301–3, 309, 310, 311, 313, 321
   future 335–6
   homes *see individual place name*
   Hull Nautical College 29–30
   live performance, on best witnessed 84
   marriage, first *see* Gregg, Jetta
   marriage, second *see* Gregg, Anita
   marriage, third *see* Gregg, Yoshiko
   musical acts and *see individual musical act name*
   private jet rental company 193
   producing, first attempt at 107–13

promoter, first outing as 73–4
SFX group European chairman 189, 190, 195, 223, 226, 290
theatres acquired *see individual theatre name*
theatrical productions and *see individual theatrical production name*
Thomas Tucker popcorn brand and 192, 297, 302, 312, 321–2, 335–6
travel *see individual nation name*
Gregg, Simon (son of Paul Gregg)
  Apollo Cinemas chief executive 301–3, 309, 310, 311, 313, 321
  Apollo Group sale and 190, 191, 288, 291
  Apollo Group shareholder 186
  birth 75
  child, first 312
  childhood 91–2, 93, 106, 184
  death of mother and 295, 296, 297
  will of mother and 297
Gregg, Wendy (daughter of Paul Gregg) 52
Gregg, Yoshiko (wife of Paul Gregg) 1, 314
  close friendship with PG develops 305–10
  first meets PG 300–3
  future with PG 342
  India trip with PG 324–8
  Jun-Ai screening and 305
  Malaysia trip with PG 318–19
  marries PG in Japan 310, 315–20
  PG's reunion with son and 341
  Sai Maa and 326–33
  Scarborough, travels with PG to 323–4
  UK wedding 320
  Vietnam trip with PG 319–20
  yoga and 324–5
Guinness Book of Theatre 102
Gulf War (1990–1) 155

Hammersmith
  Apollo 141, 151–2, 189
  Odeon 151–2
Hampton, Lionel 63
Harris, Richard 6, 106, 107–8, 110, 111, 339
Hatton, Derek 130
Heinz 47
Helley, Reg 41–6, 49, 58
Henry, Thierry 237
Henshaw, David 221–2, 225, 248, 277–8
Heston, Charlton 34, 130
Hideaway, The, Marco Island, Florida 184
Highbury Stadium 200
Hilton, Ronnie 28
Hochhauser, Victor 64
Hogg, Colin 59, 62, 73
HOK Sport Venue Event 226, 284
Hokkaido 315
Holohan Associates 170
Houllier, Gerard 219
Houston Securities 218, 229
Howard & Wyndham 88, 90
HSBC 73, 166, 201–2
Hull 4, 25–30, 32, 74
Humperdinck, Engelbert 78
Hutchison, Don 220

Iggy Pop 83
India 1, 306, 324–32
IRA 109
Irving, Sir Henry 163, 172, 175, 176
Isaacs, Sir Jeremy 167
It's a Knockout 18, 69

Jack and the Beanstalk 90
Jackson, Michael 5, 123–7, 132–9, 141, 318, 323
James Bond films 27, 43, 44, 317, 322
James, Henry 67
Japan 1, 27, 327, 332, 342
  Bad tour in 123–8
  PG's wife and 300, 304, 305, 307–8, 324

INDEX

PG marries in 310, 315–18
Jarrett, Eddie 68, 98
Jarvis Hotels 153, 188
Jarvis, John 153, 174, 188, 190
Jesus Christ Superstar 10, 116, 168, 170, 175, 176
Jethro Tull 83
JLL Property Valuation 226
Johan Cruyff Arena 226
Johnson, Peter 196, 200–1, 203, 207, 216, 217
Jones, Jack 67, 73
Jones, Tom 5, 77–8, 154
Jun-Ai 305

Keane, Roy 214
Keegan, Kevin 263
Kejian 237–9, 255, 256, 283
Kendall, Howard 199, 201
Kenwright, Bill
  Barmby sale and 218–19
  buys Everton FC 196–206, 214
  Dunford and 220
  King's Dock redevelopment plan and 214, 216–18, 223–4, 227, 243, 245, 246–51
  Moyes and 235–6, 240, 265
  PG demands resignation of 267–8
  PG public falling out with 251, 253, 257, 259, 260–5, 267–71, 280–3
  PG's sale of Everton shares and 281–3
  public profile at Everton 232
  Rooney and 253, 259, 260–3, 265
  shared stadium, Stanley Park proposal and 275–80
  True Blue Holdings and 202–3, 218, 237, 241–2, 245, 251, 264–71, 273, 280
  Walter Smith and 206–8, 218, 220, 232–4, 241
Kern 337
Kim Promotions 74
King and I, The 101–2
King, Ron 68

King's Dock, Liverpool 211, 214–18, 221, 222–30, 231–4, 237–8, 241, 243, 245–6, 247–51, 263, 264, 283–4
Kiss FM 323
KPMG 244, 310, 311

Labatt's Apollo Hammersmith 141, 151–2, 189
Land, David 129
Las Vegas 65, 114, 115, 207, 278–9, 318
Las Vegas Sands Corporation 278–9
Last Drop bar 337–8
Last, James 63, 67, 73
Latham, Paul 134–5, 164
Lavelle, Steve 1
  Apollo Cinemas and 293
  Houston Securities and 218
  King's Dock development and 215, 218, 223, 225–6, 227
  Liverpool Empire and 198
  Lyceum and 6, 8, 164, 165, 169, 170, 173, 175, 343
  SFX role 190, 226, 290
  working rapport within Apollo Group and 179, 188
League Cup 199
Leggett, Adrian 164
Lerner and Loewe 107
Les Misérables 212
Leslau, Nick 186–7
Lewis, Ernest Wamsley 97
Lion Awards 44, 46
Lion King, The 11, 176–7, 180–3, 186, 307, 340
Li Tie 237, 239–40
Little and Large 69, 75, 131, 146
Littlewoods family 212
Live Aid (1985) 132–3
Liverpool 66
  Bad tour and 130–1, 133, 134, 138
  European City of Culture 211–13, 222, 248
  regeneration plans 212–18, 221–30, 231–2, 237–51, 276–85, 323

Liverpool City Council 130, 162, 211, 227, 228, 229, 248
Liverpool Echo 201, 206, 222, 267
Liverpool Empire 63, 66, 67, 88, 90, 128, 130, 150, 162, 198, 205, 212, 238
Liverpool Empire Theatre Trust 130, 205, 238
Liverpool FC
    Barmby and 218, 219
    Champions League final (2005) 280
    First Division (1984-5) 199
    First Division (1985-6) 200
    international support base 204, 237, 328
    League Cup Final (1984) 199
    NTL and 220
    Robinson and 131, 208
    Shinawatra and 255–6
    stadium, search for new 224, 225
    Stanley Park shared stadium proposal 276–8, 279–80
Liverpool Vision 217, 225, 228, 250
Li Weifeng 240
London College of Fashion 337
London Evening Standard 151, 191
London Palladium 101, 162
London Stadium 337
London Trocadero 186–7
Longman, Peter 165, 173–4
Lulu 131
Lyceum Theatre 3–11, 159–77, 179–80, 181, 182–3, 189, 215, 307, 343
    Apollo Group buys 3–11, 160–1
    history of 159–60, 162–3
    Jesus Christ Superstar at 10–11, 116, 168, 170, 175, 176
    Oklahoma! at 182, 335
    opening of restored 10–11, 174–6, 179
    renovation 163–74, 179–80
    Theatres Trust and 159, 160–2, 163, 164, 173, 174
    The Lion King at 11, 176–7, 181–3, 307, 340–1

Mackintosh, Cameron 113, 147, 161, 162, 182
MacLaine, Shirley 67, 78, 154
Magic FM 323
Major, John 158
Make-A-Wish Foundation 156, 329
Malaysia 310, 318–19
MAM (Management, Agency and Music) 63, 77–8, 82–3, 90, 99, 124
Manchester Apollo 4, 5, 79–85, 87, 89, 91, 92, 98, 134, 148, 188
    Apollo Theatres Ltd buys 79–85
    Cats at 148
    Glasgow Apollo and 91
    Queen play at 84–5
    renovation 82–3
Manchester Arena 223–4
Manchester City 256
Manchester United 199, 200, 204, 214, 225, 231, 237, 257, 260, 261, 262, 326
Manilow, Barry 157
Marco Island, Florida 184, 289, 291, 292, 294, 295
Margaret, HRH Princess 109, 110
Martin, Dean 5, 40, 114–15
Martin, Sir George 124
Mathis, Johnny 67
Maylon, Ron 171
McCann, Brian 171
McCartney, Paul 116
Meadmore, Robert 108, 111
Mecca Leisure 49, 50–2
Megson, Gary 234
Mercury, Freddie 84–5
Mercury Press 131
Merseyside Development Corporation 216
Metro-Goldwyn-Mayer (MGM) 43–4
Midland Bank 73
Milburn, Thomas 89, 130, 150
Milburn, William 89, 130, 150
Milton Keynes Bowl 132, 136

INDEX

Minnelli, Liza 5, 63, 98
Miss World 51, 153
Moody Blues, The 78
Moonman, Eric 233
Moore, Roger 156
Moores, David 279
Moores, Sir John 269
Morecambe and Wise 64–5, 69–70
Morley, Eric 51, 153
Mouskouri, Nana 65
Moyes, David 204, 234–7, 240, 259, 261, 263, 264–5, 273
MPL 116
Munnar, India 326
Muppet Show, The 181
Murphy, John 170
My Fair Lady 43, 107, 108

National Lottery 166, 169
Necker Island 141–5, 149, 156
Nederlander, Jimmy 150–1, 166, 187, 189, 300
Neptune 226
New Amsterdam Theatre, New York 181–2
Newcastle City Hall 74
Newcastle United 201, 220, 261, 262
New Theatre, Oxford
    Apollo Group acquire 88–90, 91, 112
    Apollo Group HQ in 92
    Cliff Richard in 98
    design of 89, 130, 150
    Downtown Manhattan in 94–5
    refurbishment 89–90
New Victoria Theatre, London 96–103
Nolan Sisters 131
North West Development Agency 217, 226, 228, 229, 276
Nothing But the Best 45, 267
NTL 220–1
Nyarko, Alex 219

Obertelli, Ricci 156
Odeon Cinema, Sheffield 32–3, 43, 44–5
Odeon Group 150, 151–2, 153, 293, 322
Odeon, Hammersmith 151–2
Odeon Leicester Square 156, 335
O'Donovan, Danny 96–7
Oklahoma! 182, 335
Olympic Stadium, Munich 226
One Mo' Time 107, 108, 180
O'Neill, Martin 264–5
Opera House, Manchester 88
O'Regan, Denis 85
O'Sullivan, Gilbert 78

Pacino, Al 130
Palace Theatre, Manchester 88
pantomime 90, 129, 153, 163, 258
Parry, Rick 224, 277
Paterson, Robert 64–6, 98–9
Paul, Ken 113
Pepsi 138
Phantom of the Opera 147, 148
Philip, Duke of Edinburgh, HRH Prince 156, 287
Phoenix, Charing Cross Road 106
Pistone, Alessandro 219
Playhouse, Edinburgh 128
Plaza Theatre, Haymarket 293
Point Theatre, Dublin 141, 148–50
Premier League 193, 198, 204, 206, 214, 220, 234–5, 237, 239, 242–3, 274, 281
Prendergast, Jack 27
Presley, Elvis 44
Prestcold 22, 32
Pressed Steel Company 22
Pressed Steel Fisher 53, 55, 57
Preston North End 234–5
Prince Concert Promotions 79
Prince of Wales Group 78–81, 92
Prince of Wales Hotel, Southport 78
Prince Theatres 79
Prince's Trust 153, 174, 175
Princess Anne Theatre, BAFTA, Piccadilly 305
Proactive 262–3

Procol Harum 83
punk 83, 87

Queen 84–5
Queen Elizabeth Olympic Park, Stratford 336–41
Quill, Jimmy 156
Quinlan, Tim 9–10

Radio City (radio station) 131, 133, 134, 323
Rank Organisation 42, 43, 49
Real Sociedad 269–70
Really Useful Theatre Company 116, 147, 170
Reiki 300
Rice, Sir Tim 10, 116, 180, 181
Rich, Buddy 63
Richard, Cliff 5, 45–6, 68–9, 79, 98, 100, 115–16, 154
Riverdance 149–50
Robinson, Peter 131, 208
Rodgers and Hammerstein 101, 102
Rogers, David 1, 343
   Apollo Cinemas and 301, 302, 310–11, 312, 313, 314
   Apollo Group, joins 92–3, 95
   Camelot and 108, 111–12
   Clear Channel and 293
   Lyceum and 6, 8, 9, 160, 164, 166, 175
   Necker Island holiday with PG 142
   Nita Gregg and 187–8
   SFX deal and 188–91, 290
   Starlight Express and 118
   The Lion King and 181
   Thomas Tucker and 322
   working rapport within Apollo Group and 179
Rolling Stones 28, 58
Ronson, Mick 28
Rooney, Coleen 257, 258
Rooney, Wayne 236–7, 241, 253–4, 256–65, 268, 269, 273

Rose, Leslie 156, 253, 321
Rossiter, Leonard 128–9
Roundhay Park, Leeds 132
Royal Bank of Scotland 166
Royal Court, Liverpool 86
Royal Fine Art Commission Trust 163
Royal National Theatre 182
Royal Naval College, Greenwich 156–7
Royal Opera 7, 167, 168–9
Royal Opera House 7, 167, 169, 309, 310
Royal Variety Charity 152
Royal Variety Club of Great Britain 114, 152–3
Royal Variety Performance 152, 157–8
Royle, Joe 234

Sadler's Wells 337
Sai Maa 327–33
Samuelson, Christopher 270, 274–6, 278
Sangster, Robert 112–13
Saudi Arabia 323
Scarborough 146, 315
   Open Air Theatre 303, 306, 335
   PG childhood in 4, 16–23, 25, 40, 142, 323–4, 335, 341
Schneider, Peter 108, 180
Scrooge: The Musical 152
Second World War (1939–45) 3, 14–16, 22, 25, 28, 31
Sesame Street 181
Sex Pistols, The 87, 95
SFX 188–93, 195–6, 218, 223, 226, 288, 290–2, 314
Sheffield
   ABC cinema 33–4, 41–6, 47–8, 49, 58, 68
   City Hall 72, 74, 111
   Gaumont cinema 42–6
   Odeon Cinema 32–3, 43, 44–5
   PG's family move to 32
   PG marries in 35
   PG marries for second time in 61
Shepherd, Freddy 261–2
Shinawatra, Thaksin 255–6

INDEX

Shrouder, Ben 142, 144
Shrouder, Freda 96
Shrouder, Sam 1, 95–6, 343
   Apollo Group, joins 95–6
   Camelot and 110, 112
   Clear Channel severance package 292
   Lyceum and 163, 164
   Necker Island holiday with PG 142, 144
   Nita Gregg's growing dissatisfaction with life at Apollo and 187
   SFX hire 190, 290
   working rapport within Apollo Group and 179
Sillerman, Robert F.X. 188, 190, 192
Simpson, Fallas 46, 47, 93
Sinatra, Frank 63, 114
Sky TV 209, 302
Sleep, Wayne 113
Smith, Terry 131, 133, 323
Smith, Walter 201, 206–8, 218–21, 231–5, 236, 241, 244, 263
Society of West End Theatres 130
Sound of Music, The (film) 43, 45
Sound of Music, The (musical theatre) 101–3, 105, 107, 151
Southport
   Council 53–4, 61–77
   Floral Hall 61–70, 71
   PG properties in 71–3
   Prince of Wales Group, PG works for in 78–81
   Simon Gregg born in 75
   Southport Theatre 66–70
Special Branch 109
Spinners, The 62, 73–4, 75–7, 79, 81
Stage, The 105
Stanley Park, Liverpool 204, 276, 279
Star Cinemas 49–51
Starlight Express 117–21, 124, 170, 335
Starr, Freddie 131, 146
Status Quo 83
Stewart, Rod 91
Stigwood, Robert 116, 129

St Joseph's Hospice Extension Appeal 108–9
Stoll Moss 88, 101, 120
Storey, Mike 222, 227
Stranglers, The 83
Streisand, Barbra 5, 100, 131–2
Sugar, Alan 192–3
super-casinos 279

Taylor, Ross 100–3, 107, 113
Thailand 253–7, 261
Thatcher, Margaret 130, 155, 211
Theatre Royal, Brighton 129
Theatre Royal, Drury Lane 107
Theatre Royal, Haymarket 128
Theatres Trust 159–60, 162, 163–4, 173–4
Thomas Tucker popcorn brand 192, 297, 302, 312, 321–2, 335–6
Thorburn Colquhoun 171
Three Degrees, The 68, 95
The Times 88, 111, 161, 339
Tokyo, Japan 123–7, 318
Tony n' Tina's Wedding 336–40
Topol, Chaim 112
Tottenham Hotspur 199, 204, 219, 236, 254, 255, 284
touring theatres 87
Transport for London 340
Trent, William Edward 97
Triumph Theatre Productions 128
True Blue Holdings 202–3, 218, 237, 241–2, 245, 251, 264–71, 273, 280
Turner, Tina 65
20th Century Fox 43

UEFA Cup 280
Unicorn Leisure 91
United Artists 43

V&A Museum 337
Varanasi, India 328–33
Variety, the Children's Charity 154, 341
Vietnam 319–20

Villarreal CF 280
Vue 311, 313, 321–2

Walker, George 9
Walt Disney Company 43, 183
Warner Brothers 43
Waterfront Stadium and Arena (WSA) 227–8, 229
Watson, Steve 219
Webber, Andrew Lloyd 183
   Cats and 145, 147
   Jesus Christ Superstar and 10, 168, 170
   Lyceum and 161, 162
   Really Useful Theatre Company 116, 147, 170
   Starlight Express and 116, 118, 119, 120
Weldon, Duncan 128–30
Wembley Stadium 117, 128
   Astaire and 153
   Bad tour at 132–6, 138
   HOK and 284
   League Cup Final (1984) 199

West Ham United 265, 337
Westminster Council 163, 165
White Elephant Club, Curzon Street 100
Whitfield, David 28
Whittell, Jim 43, 152, 153, 191, 293, 295, 301, 313, 314
Willmott Dixon 171
Woods, Jon 202–3, 241, 264, 266, 267, 268, 269, 271
World Cup
   (1966) 213
   (1974) 226
   (1990) 220
   stadiums 284
Wray, Nigel 186–7
Wyness, Keith 274, 276, 277, 282

'Yagya' spiritual event, Japan 332–3
yoga 324–7
Yorkshire Evening Post 50

Zingarevich, Boris 270–1